PREDICTION AND PROPHECY

PREDICTION AND PROPHECY

Keith Ellis

Distributed in the United States by
CRANE, RUSSAK & COMPANY, INC.
52 Vanderbilt Avenue
New York, New York 10017

SBN 85340 233 7

Copyright © 1973 by Keith Ellis
First published in 1973 by
Wayland (Publishers) Limited
101 Grays Inn Road London WC1
Made and printed in Great Britain by
The Garden City Press Limited
Letchworth Hertfordshire SG6 1JS

CONTENTS

ACKNOWLEDGEMENTS

The author and publishers thank the following for permission to reproduce illustrations in this book: The Mansell Collection, plates 1, 3, 4, 5, 6, 7, 9, 13, 14; Mary Evans Picture Library, plate 2; Fox Photos Ltd., plate 8; Mr Cutten, plate 10; Popperfoto, plates 11, 12; Keystone Press Ltd., plate 15.

LIST OF ILLUSTRATIONS

1   Science or Superstition?

We all need to predict the future. We do so many times a day. How long will it take me to walk to the station? What time does my train leave? When can I expect my colleague for lunch? How long will meat keep in the deep freeze? What "O" levels do the children need to qualify them for university? What pension shall I collect when I retire? Unless we know such things, we cannot make intelligent plans.

If our methods of prediction are verifiable, repeatable and consistent with existing knowledge, we all accept them. We know that water boils when heated and that the light goes out when we press the switch. Arriving at a fork in the road, we rely on a map to tell us whether we need to branch left or right to reach our destination. Astronomers can forecast the exact positions of the stars and planets a hundred years from now and physicists can say with certainty that some 5,600 years hence, a given sample of radiocarbon will have shrunk to half its size, the rest having changed into nitrogen. We call such predictions scientific. Without them, civilization would be impossible. Life would indeed be "solitary, poor, nasty, brutish and short."

Most of us feel however that there is another type of prediction which is completely *un*scientific. It is unreliable and can only rarely be pinned down in laboratory experiments. Even then it is usually unrepeatable. It cannot be explained in any known terms of cause and effect. Yet almost all of us have experienced it at some time or another.

I have a barrister friend with a highly matter-of-fact mind and an encyclopaedic knowledge of road traffic law. He is not given to making wild claims. "But there is one thing I have never been able to explain," he told me. "When I was at school during the Second World War, I decided that it would have to end on a particular date, just as the First World War ended on November 11th, 1918. I used to amuse myself guessing what that date would be. I thought of numerous possibilities and gradually discarded all but two. However hard I tried, I could not choose between them. In 1943, I gave up and jotted them both down in my diary. One was May 8th, 1945, the other was August 15th, 1945."

To his astonishment, both were right. The Second World War ended on two separate days, May 8th, 1945, when the Allies celebrated victory in Europe (V.E.-Day), and August 15th, 1945, when the British (not the Americans) celebrated the Allied victory over Japan (V.J.-Day). The odds against him hitting on one of these dates by chance are big enough. The odds against him hitting on both are incalculable. Yet there is no way of explaining the incident by any principle known to science, and we are left with the assumption that some other, as yet unexplained influence, was at work.

He himself has not had a comparable experience before or since, but a few people seem to catch repeated glimpses of the future. In *The Story of Fulfilled Prophecy* (Cassell, U.K. 1969), the late Justine Glass mentions "an amateur psychic" called Cyril Macklin who during the Second World War had many premonitions of disaster. While working in a south-west London aircraft factory, he had a vision while sitting in the canteen. "He heard what he describes as 'a sound like an X-ray machine starting up.' He saw the canteen disintegrate —chairs and tables smashed; blood and broken bodies. Mr. Macklin gave in his notice, leaving the factory just before a direct hit demolished the canteen, the machine shops and an oil-tank." He left his next job in an Acton factory after once again correctly predicting a direct hit. During a spell on night shift in a Wimbledon factory, he heard a voice warning him, "Don't go tonight." He obeyed, and next morning found that his department had been bombed. Once more he changed jobs, and on his very first day with his new employer predicted that three bombs would fall in a lane outside the factory—two more on the coke dump and one, which would fail to explode, near the canteen. The foreman threatened him with internment for spreading alarm and despondency but, once again, Mr. Macklin was proved right.

Experiences of this kind can rarely be proved or disproved, because they happen unexpectedly to individuals. Yet we hear of them so often from people whom we know to be trustworthy that they cannot be ignored. Particularly common is the type of premonition by which someone "knows" from hearing a voice, seeing a vision or simply feeling uneasy and restless that news will shortly arrive of the death or serious illness of a member of the family living many miles away. Do we all have this power? Or just a favoured few? If we don't have it, can we find out about the future by consulting those who do? Are there systems of prediction that work for everyone?

Collectively, we spend millions in our attempts to delve into the future. Prediction has become an industry. There is at least one mail order firm offering everything from crystal balls to divining pendulums, from aluminium trumpets for *séances* to aura goggles that help the wearer to see mystic auras more clearly. Lucky numbers, spells and charms are advertised in magazines. One firm offers a variety of talismans that promise to enhance our chances of overcoming our enemies, winning at cards, passing examinations, recovering from illness or gaining a loved one's favour. *The Aquarian Guide to Occult, Mystical, Religious, Magical London and Around* (ed. Francoise Strachan, The Aquarian Press, U.K., 1970) lists scores of societies and individuals offering insight into the future. Esoteric groups seek knowledge in everything from Yoga to the Grail, from the Pyramids to the Kabbala. Professionals include astrologers, palmists, numerologists, tarot consultants, clairvoyants, psychometrists, trance mediums, sand diviners, card readers, a pyromantic, a rainmaker and a firm which manufactures "tranquillizer touchstones."

All these are doubtless sincere in their claims and presumably attract clients who feel they benefit from the services offered. If some of their methods seem far-fetched, we should remember that many distinguished scientists now believe that there is at least a *prima facie* case for thinking that our dreams may sometimes crash the barrier between present and future. Others have shown that some people seem to have the faculty of precognition, even when tested under laboratory conditions. Practical men too have faith in these powers. In many country districts, farmers have relied for years on the local water diviner before choosing the site for a well. Many business firms use handwriting and colour preference tests to predict the future performance of job applicants. Some even retain astrologers. Are they just the victims of superstition?

As Gustav Jahoda shows in *The Psychology of Superstition* (Penguin, U.K. and U.S.A., 1969), it is almost impossible to define "superstition" objectively. Dictionaries do not help. "An irrational or unfounded belief" (*Shorter Oxford English Dictionary*) sums up most of them. But who decides whether a belief is "irrational or unfounded"? Atheists would unhesitatingly say that the Resurrection, the Virgin Birth and the Miracles were superstitions, but most Christians would be deeply offended at the suggestion. Eye-witnesses do not help because they are notoriously unreliable. There are innumerable eye-witness accounts of flying saucer sightings, but how much weight do they carry with scientists? On the other hand, it could be argued that flying saucers have no objective existence but are projections of unconscious elements of the observer's mind. Such a view could be taken of other psychic phenomena. Would it mean that their existence was any less "real" than if they were measurable by orthodox scientific methods? If not, is it meaningful to call a belief in them "superstition"? Moreover, the views of scientists themselves change. Many of the beliefs now labelled "superstitions" were once accepted without question. Five hundred years ago, astrology, alchemy, witches and magic were part of the orthodox world picture. While banishing them to outer darkness, scientists have repeatedly shown that they can do things thought impossible only a few generations ago. They can now transplant hearts, land men on the moon, create life in dead matter.

Jahoda concludes, "There is no objective means of distinguishing 'superstition' from other types of belief and action. . . . Hereafter, the word 'superstition' will be used in the sense of the kind of belief and action a reasonable man in present-day Western society would regard as being 'superstitious'."

This definition raises more problems than it solves. Is there such a person as "the reasonable man"? Or is he simply an abstract idea? If he exists, can we expect him to be reasonable at all times? Or is he totally unreasonable in his attitude to prediction?

Almost all of us take notice of prophetic claims, even when we know from experience that they are unreliable. A National Opinion Poll survey reported in the *Daily Mail* in January, 1971, found that nine people out of ten knew their sign of the Zodiac and eight out of ten regularly read their horoscope. Yet only one in five confessed to believing in it. A half said horoscopes were "not at all accurate." Does this mean we read them "just for fun"?

I do not think so. Our urge to divine the future is so strong that most of us are ready to use almost *any* system of forecasting. Meteorology is one example. In some countries, it is possible to give precise weather forecasts with an accuracy of almost 100 per cent. In Britain, we know that this is usually out of the question because of our geographical position. Forecasts are often wrong. Even when they are right, they are often so vague as to be useless. "Cloudy, with bright intervals, possibility of rain, temperatures around the seasonal norm" is a typical summary which could apply to 300 days a year. Even so, we spend millions of pounds working out these forecasts with the most elaborate equipment known to science. There is a twenty-four hour telephone service giving forecasts for every part of the country. Radio and television channels transmit them dozens of times a day.

Or take our obsession with party politics. In the weeks before a general election, newspapers devote almost as much space to the forecasts of commentators as they do to the election issues. The commentators are not particularly reliable as prophets. They contradict each other wildly. Yet many people read their speculations more and more avidly as the campaign goes on, working themselves up for the climactic frenzy of election night. The polls have closed and in a matter of hours, the result will be clear. Any sensible person would go to bed and wait for the morning papers. Yet millions of citizens glue themselves to the television screen, watching goggle-eyed while the computer clatters out new extrapolations as each individual result comes in. Meanwhile, some of our most brilliant political scientists try to disprove the computer results with their slide-rules, discussing whether a particular seat can be regarded as typical and if not, whether the computer has made sufficient allowance.

Both weather forecasting and political speculation are taken "seriously" because the one claims to be scientific and the other cloaks itself in reason. Yet they have an odd affinity with astrology. Millions read them every day, while remaining totally sceptical. The same is true of financial pundits, racing tipsters and gossip columnists who claim to be "in the know." Judging by results, and there may be exceptions, can we say that they are any more reliable than palmists or crystal-gazers? If they are taken seriously, even though unreliable, is it unreasonable at least to examine the claims of other forms of prediction?

It is no answer to say that these other forms of prediction are irrational. They do not claim to be rational. They work, if at all, on a completely different level. They do not pinpoint future events precisely. They indicate trends. They give access to a world of feeling and intuition from which we are so often excluded by the conventions of modern life. How many of us can look at the signs of the Zodiac or turn over a pack of tarot cards without feeling, however remotely, the existence of mental categories unknown to the computer? For most of us, they are far more real than nano-seconds, binary numbers and such esoteric languages as COBAL and FORTRAN. Their magic sets up vibrations in unsuspected depths of the mind. It draws us; it sharpens our intuition, revealing truths about ourselves and

13

about the outside world which we should never have discovered by logic.

Dreams are the most potent of all. We often wake with the feeling that we have been in contact with a world that is at once more terrible and more beautiful, more frustrating and more deeply satisfying than anything we find in everyday life. We can dismiss the experience as "only a dream" or we can try to understand what it has to tell us. As we shall see in Chapter 6, there is good evidence that dreams can sometimes give us a preview of what is about to happen in our waking life. Taken symbolically, they can be even more prophetic.

One of the most famous dreams in history is that of John Chapman, a tinker of Swaffham, Norfolk, who suddenly became so rich that he was able to pay for the north aisle of the village's magnificent fifteenth-century church. While still poor, he three times had a dream telling him he would find a fortune in London. He put on his best clothes, went up to London and walked aimlessly up and down. He had almost given up hope when a merchant approached him and asked him why he was wasting his time. Naively, Chapman told the story of his dream. The merchant burst out laughing. "Fancy taking a dream seriously," he scoffed. "Only the other night, I heard a voice telling me to go to Swaffham and dig in the garden of a tinker called John Chapman. The voice promised I should find a crock of gold under a tree." Chapman said nothing, but hurried home and dug under the tree in his garden. A few feet down, he found a pot of gold coins. It carried a message, "Dig on. Beneath me lies one bigger than I." He did so and found a second pot, twice as big as the first, also filled with gold coins. Chapman's dream had make him a rich man.

Should we take the story literally? We have the solid evidence of his church building. On the other hand, it has a much deeper meaning symbolically: we shall find true wealth not by rushing up to London (or New York or Los Angeles) but by digging in our own back garden. Old but true, and exactly the sort of advice so often dispensed by diviners of every kind.

Intellectual attitudes to divination have changed surprisingly little over the centuries. At one extreme are the credulous, who are ready to believe anything. At the other are the total sceptics. It was the same in Roman times. The credulous Pliny (23–79) wrote:

Nature has bestowed on many animals the faculty of observing the heavens and of presaging the winds, rains and tempests, each in its own peculiar way. They warn us of danger not only by their fibres and entrails but by other kinds of warnings as well. When a building is about to fall down, all the mice desert it beforehand and the spiders with their webs are the first to drop. In Thrace, when all parts are covered with ice, the foxes are consulted. It has been observed that this animal applies its ear to the ice for the purpose or testing its thickness. Hence it is that the inhabitants will never cross frozen rivers and lakes until the foxes have passed over them and returned. . . . A woodpecker came and lighted upon the head of Aelius Tubero, the city praetor, when he was sitting on his tribunal dispensing justice in the Forum. It showed such tameness as to allow itself to be taken with the hand. Thereupon the augur declared that if it was let go, the state would be menaced with danger, but if killed, disaster would befall the praetor. In an instant, he tore the bird to pieces and before long, the omen was fulfilled . . .[seventeen members of the praetor's family were killed at the battle of Cannae.] . . . Julia Augusta, when pregnant by Nero, was particularly desirous that her offspring should be a son and accordingly employed the following mode of divination, which was then much in use among young women. She carried an egg in her bosom, taking care, whenever she was obliged to put it down, to give it to her nurse to warm in her own [bosom]. In this way, there was no interruption of the heat. The result promised by this mode of augury was not falsified. [The resulting chicken was a cock—and Julia gave birth to a son, Tiberius.]

Cicero was as sceptical as Pliny was gullible. He poured scorn on every type of divination. The astrologers' claim that they could predict a child's "genius, disposition, temper, constitution, behaviour, fortune and destiny throughout life" by calculating the influence of the planets at the moment of birth was "incredible insanity." Augurs claimed that they could predict the future by examining the entrails of sacrifical animals. The accumulated experience of centuries, they said, guaranteed a high degree of accuracy. Cicero wrote:

Can you persuade any man in his senses that those events which are said to be signified by the entrails are known by the augurs in consequence of a long series of observations? How long, I wonder? For what period of time can such observations have been continued? What conferences must the augurs hold among themselves to determine which part of the victim's entrails represents the enemy and which the people; what sort of cleft in the liver means danger and what sort presages advantage? Have the augurs of the Etrurians, the Eleans, the Egyptians and the Carthaginians arranged these matters with one another? But that, besides being quite impossible, cannot be imagined. For we see that some inter-pret the auspices in one way and some in another, and no common rule of discipline is acknowledged among the professors of the art.

Cicero was equally scathing in his attack on the idea that dreams can foretell the future. Different "experts" found different meanings in the same dream. In any case, how could they possibly work out a "science" of dream interpretation?

Can dreams be experimented on? If so, how? For the varieties of them are innumerable. Nothing can be imagined so preposterous, so incredible or so monstrous as to be beyond the power of dreaming. By what method can this infinite variety be either fixed in memory or analysed by reason? What order or variety can be discerned in dreams?... The same dreams are followed by different results to different people and indeed are not always attended by the same events in the case of the same person.

It was not enough to argue that dreams *sometimes* came true.

What person who aims at a mark all day long will not sometimes hit it? We sleep every night. And there are very few on which we do not dream. Can we wonder then that what we dream sometimes comes to pass?... Let us reject, therefore, this divination by dreams, as well other kinds. For to speak truly, superstition has extended itself through all nations and has oppressed the intellectual energies of almost all men and has betrayed them into endless imbecilities.

Yet need we be as dogmatic as either Pliny or Cicero? Between their white and black are infinite shades of grey. Both they and the people who today hold similarly extreme views overlook one simple fact.

There is little point in examining astrology, the tarot and other methods of prediction as if they were exact sciences. They belong to a different category of knowledge. They cannot be proved by logic or by repeated experiment. Believers claim only that they work. But do they, and if so how, and on what level? Are they a relic of a more primitive level of civilization which we should long ago have out-grown? Or are they indicative of powers we have allowed to atrophy and which we should be well advised to revive and develop?

Certainly our ancestors believed in them. Some have been practised continuously for ten thousand years.

2   Prophets, Oracles and Latter-Day Saints

In the ancient world, generals and politicians consulted oracles and soothsayers as readily as our own leaders call in technical experts. Ordinary people turned to priests, temple officials, astrologers, wizards and spirit mediums. Some of these seers had genuine insight. Others were charlatans. Probably the majority were something in between. But everyone, from the king to the meanest beggar, had access to some form of advice and many took advantage of it. We can see this clearly in the Old Testament, and though the various books cover a period of some fifteen hundred years, three main patterns emerge. First and best known are the prophets, whose reputed sayings are recorded in the so-called prophetic books. They frequently made predictions, usually pessimistic. Jeremiah's warning that Jerusalem was to be turned into a valley of slaughter was typical: "And I will make void the counsel of Judah and Jerusalem in this place; and I will cause them to fall by the sword before their enemies, and by the hands of them that seek their lives: and their carcases will I give to be meat for the fowls of the heaven and for the beasts of the earth. And I will make the city desolate . . ." (Jeremiah xix:6–8).

The Old Testament prophets were not, of course, primarily concerned with prediction. They were men who believed that God had spoken to them personally and that their mission in life was to preach, or reveal, God's will. They came from many different backgrounds— Amos was a shepherd, Ezekiel a member of the priestly caste—and they prophesied as individuals, often in an ecstasy. They held forth on public affairs, denouncing sin and wrongdoing with a passion that often made them unpopular with kings and priests.

Secondly, the priests and other temple officials counted it a part of their function to find out the will of God and to predict future events. We shall see later (Chapter 3) how they used the *urim* and *thummim* to do this. They also interpreted dreams and had, especially

17

in the older tradition, elaborate rituals for discovering the truth when it was in doubt. A man suspecting his wife of adultery was supposed to take her to the temple with a gift of barley meal. The priest mixed dust from the floor of the tabernacle with holy water to make "bitter water". The woman sat with her head uncovered and held the barley meal in her hands, while the priest spoke a solemn "oath of cursing." He then burned a handful of the meal on the altar and the woman drank the bitter water. "It shall come to pass, that, if she be defiled, and have done trespass against her husband, that . . . her belly shall swell, and her thigh shall rot : and the woman shall be a curse among her people. And if the woman be not defiled, but be clean; then she shall be free, and shall conceive seed." (Numbers v : 11–28). If the procedure was ever carried out, the effect of suggestion on a guilty wife must have been powerful.

The third kind of prophecy is rarely reported in the Bible. It clearly offended the priests, scholars and religious zealots who handed down the oral tradition and later compiled the written text, and we hear of it only when they condemn it. Even then, they do not go into any great detail. They merely record that magicians, wizards, sooth-sayers and spirit mediums were denounced by the orthodox and sometimes driven out or even killed. The injunction "thou shalt not suffer a witch to live" (Exodus xxii : 18) typifies the official attitude.

The story of the Witch of Endor gives us a rare glimpse into this forbidden form of prediction and also illustrates the ambiguous attitude of the authorities who condemned it. In fact, the Witch of Endor had none of the unpleasant associations we usually associate with the word "witch" and in the Authorized Version is not even called one. She seems to have been a kind old woman who lived around 1100 B.C., possibly in a cave that can still be seen in the rocky landscape east of Nazareth in the shadow of Mount Tabor. She was clever enough to escape Saul's purge of magicians and spirit mediums, and to recognize him when he visited her by night and in disguise. He was desperate for reassurance about his coming battle with the Philistines. She called up the spirit of Samuel who predicted, correctly, that he would lose the battle and that he and his sons would die. When Saul collapsed, she prepared him a meal of roast calf and unleavened bread.

No other nation has ever had prophets like those of the Old Testament, but in Egypt and Rome we find priests, temple assistants and state augurs acting as seers when required. Of many Greek oracles, the most famous was that at Delphi, north of the Gulf of Corinth. It was built on a series of curved terraces forming a natural amphitheatre round a gloomy chasm. The face of Mount Parnassus towered over it. According to legend, it had been established by Apollo himself on the site of an ancient temple dedicated to the Great Earth Mother and guarded by the dragon Python, which Apollo slew. The priestess of Apollo's temple was always known as Pythia. After elaborate rites of purification, she took her seat on a tripod which straddled a cleft in the rock. The suppliant, who made his way to the shrine up a steep and difficult path, had to present a cake and sacrifice a sheep or goat before being allowed to put his question. Pythia's answer was an ecstatic and incomprehensible scream. Attendant priests explained the god's meaning, usually in badly constructed hexameters.

Delphi was an all-purpose oracle to which squabbling city states brought their queries and problems. Its word was accepted as final on religious matters. It gave judgement on legal and moral questions and according to some traditions had passed down Sparta's entire code of law. Rich and powerful suppliants wishing to propitiate the god whom they were consulting brought lavish gifts. Delphi's treasuries were stuffed with plate, ornaments and even ingots of solid gold.

The priests of the oracle often hedged their bets by giving obscure and even deliberately ambiguous answers. When King Croesus, who ruled Lydia in Asia Minor from 560–546 B.C., asked if he should attack the Persians, the oracle told him that he would destroy a mighty empire if he did so. Overjoyed, he gave every Delphian a present of two gold staters and in return was granted numerous privileges, including first call on the oracle's services and exemption from all fees. "How long shall my kingdom last?" was his next question. The oracle replied, "Until a mule is monarch of Media." It seemed impossible that Media should ever be ruled by a mule, so again he was pleased. The answer to his third question was less reassuring. He asked whether anything could be done for his deaf-and-dumb son. The oracle told him that it would be a bad day for Croesus when he first heard his son speak.

Despite this personal disappointment, Croesus pressed on with his plans. He mounted an expedition against the Persian usurper, Cyrus the Great, and crossed the river Halys into Cappadocia. He quickly subdued the inhabitants but was then stopped by the Persians in a hard-fought but inconclusive battle at Pteria. He withdrew to his own capital, Sardis, and disbanded his army, intending to renew his campaign the following year. He never had the chance. Cyrus had followed him with the entire Persian army. Croesus scrambled together what forces he could and went out to meet him. The result was inevitable. Croesus was driven back into Sardis, which fell after a short siege.

The meaning of the Delphic oracle's prophecies now became clear. A Persian soldier attacked Croesus, not realizing who he was. Croesus, completely demoralized, neither resisted nor told him. His deaf-and-dumb son looked on in horror. "Man," he burst out, "do not kill Croesus." The shock of seeing his father in danger had carried him through some psychological barrier and he retained the power of speech for the rest of his life.

Croesus was taken prisoner. After narrowly escaping death by burning, he became friendly with Cyrus, who gave him permission to ask the Delphic oracle for an explanation of its disastrously misleading prophecies. The oracle's answer was dusty. Croesus had been punished for the crime of a remote ancestor who had seized the Lydian throne by fraud. But the prediction that his expedition would lead to the fall of a mighty empire had come true. Croesus's own mighty empire had fallen. It was his own fault that he had not asked which empire was meant. The answer about the mule was easily explained. It simply meant Cyrus, who had been born of mixed parentage. His father was a Persian, his mother a Median princess.

Ambiguities of this kind did much to destroy the oracle's credibility. It became a pawn in Greek politics. It was burnt down, rebuilt, looted. Like the less important Greek oracles at Dodona, Trophonius and elsewhere, it was reduced to answering personal and even trivial questions. One man wanted to know whether he would have any more children. Another enquired whether his coverlets and pillows had been lost or stolen. Even so, the oracle was still sometimes asked about more important matters and as late as the fourth century A.D., we read that the Emperor Julian consulted it before his expedition to Persia. After that, it passes from history.

Rome too had its official prophets, usually the public augurs and court astronomers whose activities are studied in a later chapter. It had innumerable oracles and also unattached sects and magicians of whom the best known today is Spurinna—the soothsayer who warned Julius Caesar of his approaching death on the Ides of March. Some of these fortune-tellers were known throughout the Roman Empire.

Apollonius of Tyana was one of these. Born in Cappadocia in Asia Minor around 4 B.C., he is reputed to have worked miracles and set up talismans that drove scorpions away and stopped rivers flooding. Since his biography was not written until well over a hundred years later by one of the writers who share the name Philostratus, we cannot be sure how true this was. Philostratus was a conscientious researcher, visiting many of the places frequented by Apollonius, but his aim was to write an entertaining romance rather than a strictly factual biography. There is little doubt, however, that Apollonius was a Pythagorean mystic who wandered the length and breadth of the Roman Empire, as familiar a figure in India or the Sudan as in Spain, Babylon or Rome itself. He was intelligent, eloquent and witty, but also generous and humane, with an intuitive understanding of his fellow men. He was a vegetarian and an ascetic who gave away his considerable patrimony and lived a life of poverty. He was, too, a trained healer. He seems to have spent his life wandering from temple to temple, preaching, giving advice and attending to the sick. He was tolerant of most religions and was consulted alike by emperors, priests and common people. "O Gods," he prayed, "grant that I may have little and want nothing."

Numerous stories were told of his prophetic powers. On one of his visits to Greece, he travelled on a Syracusan ship. When it put in at Leucas, he advised his friends to leave it. They continued their journey in another ship and found later that the one they had left had gone down with all hands. He was also said to have predicted the exact way in which the emperors Galba, Otho, Vitellius and Domitian were to meet their deaths.

Unlike the wise and honest Apollonius, Alexander of Abonuteichus was a charlatan who prophesied for money and fame. In the second century A.D., thousands flocked to the oracle he set up in his native city in Paphlagonia, Asia Minor. Even the Emperor Marcus Aurelius consulted him. We know of him from a work of the writer Lucian, a bitter enemy who on one occasion literally bit him. It is just possible that he was not quite so much a rogue as Lucian suggests, as Rupert Gleadow points out in his *Magic and Divination*. (Faber, U.K., 1941.)

It seems that Alexander started life as a sorcerer's apprentice, touring Asia Minor with his master while learning the arts of magic and quack medicine. He next teamed up with Cocconas, a Greek song-writer, and together they extorted large sums of money from a rich and foolish Macedonian woman. They now had the means to set up their own oracle and went about it with the combination of mystification and razzamatazz that has characterized showmen throughout the ages.

They chose Alexander's native city as the site. They knew that the local peasants were more likely than cosmopolitan city dwellers to swallow their performance, especially in the crucial early stages. Cocconas arranged the advance publicity. He planted bronze tablets in the temple of Apollo in Chalcedon, Bithynia, prophesying that

Prediction and Prophecy

Aesculapius, the god of healing, would soon appear in Abonuteichos. The news spread quickly. The credulous peasants were persuaded to start work on a sanctuary. Psychologically, they were well prepared for the unexpected return of Alexander, now a strikingly handsome figure in his mid-thirties, who carried documents "proving" he was the son of Apollo and related to Perseus, the hero who beheaded Medusa. He swaggered round the city in brilliantly coloured clothes, swinging his scimitar and occasionally passing into the ventriloquial, mouth-foaming trances then expected of prophets.

When he had stirred up enough interest, he gave a frenzied speech from the altar of the new temple, plunged into a nearby pool and scooped out an egg. In full view of the wondering spectators, he cracked it open. Out slithered a tiny snake. Nobody guessed that the egg was a blown goose egg into which he had slipped the baby snake before hiding it. They knew only that the snake was a symbol of Aesculapius. His performance was so convincing that they were only too ready to believe that it was an incarnation of the god himself. Alexander called it Glycon, which is Greek for "sweet one."

Alexander did not wait for the completion of the temple. Nor did the death of his partner Cocconas upset his plans. He opened up for business while interest in Glycon was still strong. The citizens of Abonuteichus queued to file through the small room which he had set aside for the oracle. They saw Alexander swathed in priestly robes with Glycon draped round his neck. In a few days, the tiny snake had grown to full size. Apparently it had also developed a human head and the gift of speech.

In the next thirty years, the oracle became famous throughout the Roman Empire. It employed a large staff of priests and helpers to cope with the crowds of suppliants who came to be healed or to have their questions answered. Alexander's agents ranged all over Europe and the Near East. He was especially attractive to women and put on mystic pantomimes for their edification.

His fees were small. His considerable income came from his huge turnover and, according to Lucian, from a profitable sideline in blackmail based on the incriminating information included in some of the questions put to him. He was consulted by the cream of the Roman aristocracy, and even by the Emperor Marcus Aurelius.

How did he get away with it? We must remember that the Roman Empire as a whole, and Asia Minor in particular, was a hotbed of self-appointed gods, mystics and heretics of every description. Alexander guarded against sceptics, rigorously excluding from his oracle Christians, Epicureans and atheists. In a world in which miracles, magic and astrology were intellectually respectable, it was not difficult for a clever and persuasive charlatan to gull the superstitious and the uncommitted of every race and class. When they handed in their sealed questions and received appropriate answers written on the outside of the scroll with the seal still unbroken, it never occurred to them that the seals had been tampered with and skilfully reaffixed. Nor did they guess that Glycon's real head was hidden in the folds of Alexander's robe, while his "human" head was a contrivance of canvas and paint, manipulated by horse hairs and linked by a speaking tube to an accomplice behind the scenes. Whenever a spoken oracle was required, it came through loud and clear.

During the next five hundred years, the ancient world was transformed. Rome fell to the barbarians and Christianity became the official religion of most of Europe. Patterns of prophecy changed too. The Church condemned wizards, magicians, oracles and spirit mediums, but it could not destroy them altogether. Some of the old practices survived in the teaching of the gnostics and various heretical sects. Intellectuals of every calibre discreetly studied writers and systems that were officially rejected. Ideas infiltrating from the Arabic schools of Spain stimulated a new interest in the ancient arts of alchemy and astrology. On the fringes of civilization, pagan practices continued to flourish and the common people everywhere still turned to local soothsayers, in spite of the Church's disapproval. Christianity itself brought a new type of prediction, which has persisted to the present day. For two thousand years, self-appointed prophets have foretold the Second Coming of Christ, leading to the Millennium, literally a period of a thousand years in which Christ himself will reign. They have usually linked it with a resurrection of the dead, with a day of judgement and sometimes too with the end of the world.

The prophets of the Old Testament had, of course, foretold the coming of a Messiah who would lead the Jews from catastrophe and judgement into a new golden age. In the teaching of Jesus himself, the idea of a spiritual kingdom of God is sometimes confused (perhaps by the compilers of the Gospels) with worldly power. The mighty vision of Revelations xxi promised "a new heaven and a new earth."

Many, perhaps most, of the early Christians took these prophecies literally. In a worldly sense, Jesus had ended his life in defeat. Inevitably he must return and conquer. In Phrygia, not very far from the oracle of Alexander at Abonuteichus, the Christian Montanus claimed in A.D. 156 that he was the Holy Ghost incarnate. Within twenty-five years, he had a large following of ascetics throughout the Roman

23

Empire, all living in daily expectation of the Second Coming. Montanism was outlawed as a heresy, but in those early days churchmen and theologians of impeccable orthodoxy believed in an earthly Millennium. The doctrine was not officially discredited until St. Augustine of Hippo (354–430) asserted in his *City of God* that the Millennium had already arrived with the establishment on earth of the Church.

Yet the idea of a Second Coming had an irresistible appeal. It was fed by the so-called Sybilline Oracles, (not to be confused with the Sybilline Books of ancient Rome), which were prophecies compiled as late as the seventh century A.D. They told of an "Emperor of the Last Days" who would fall victim to Antichrist in Jerusalem itself. After a short reign, Antichrist would be killed by the returning Christ and the Last Judgement would take place.

Numerous "Christs" appeared, some of them with a "Virgin Mary" in tow. A few were little better than gangsters, terrorizing the countryside with their bands. Others thought themselves so "holy" that they handed out their hair-clippings, nail-parings and even bath-water as talismans. Aldebert, who first appeared in the eighth century near Soissons, France, had his own churches and was thought to be a serious threat to Rome. A synod consisting of Pope Zachary and twenty-four bishops eventually decided he was mad and allowed him to die in obscurity.

In *The Pursuit of the Millennium* (Temple Smith, U.K. 1970; Oxford, U.S.A., 1970), Norman Cohn discusses at length the numerous apocalyptic movements that struck like tornadoes at times of social unrest. Some identified a particular ruler—for instance, Charlemagne —as the "Emperor of the Last Days." After his death, some even awaited his resurrection.

A wandering French beggar called Bertrand of Ray claimed that he was the Count of Flanders, who had been installed as Baldwin IX, Emperor of Byzantium in 1204, and had been killed shortly afterwards. Bertrand was acknowledged throughout Flanders and Hainault, and installed as Count and Emperor. Churchmen paid homage. The common people regarded him as the Messiah. He was unmasked during a state visit to Louis VIII, King of France. Louis questioned him about other European royalty whom the real Emperor was known to have met. Bertrand failed the test. After a reign of seven months he was hanged.

However bizarre his ideas, a plausible prophet could rely on the support of the poor and starving. The Pope was cursed as Antichrist, Rome as Babylon. Yet another resurrection took place, this time of

Frederick II, the Holy Roman Emperor, who had been regarded by some as the "Emperor of the Last Days" while he was still alive. Other Messiahs inflamed feeling against the rich or the clergy. They led massacres of the Jews. During the Crusades, they organized armies of peasants and even of children to march on Jerusalem. Most of their followers died on the journey.

Perhaps the most remarkable of all the apocalyptic movements that swept Europe in the late Middle Ages was the reign of Jan Bockelson (John of Leyden) as King of the New Jerusalem in Münster, North Germany. Among the many consequences of Martin Luther's challenge to the authority of the Roman Catholic Church was the rise of loosely organized groups of zealots called by their opponents Anabaptists. They turned directly to the Bible for guidance. They rejected the authority of both state and Church. They were exclusive, elgalitarian and sometimes even communistic. They appealed strongly to the poor and the suffering. They included militant preachers who believed that the Millennium was at hand and it was a group of these, mainly Dutch, who arrived in Münster between 1532 and 1534. At that time, Münster was an independent state nominally ruled by its absentee bishop who had, however, been forced to recognize it as Lutheran.

The Anabaptists were extraordinarily successful. In a single week they made 1,400 converts. In February, 1534, a religious frenzy gripped the town. Fits and visions became commonplace. Fearful for their safety, wealthy Lutheran merchants packed their belongings and fled. The Anabaptists prophesied world doom by Easter, with Münster the sole surviving town. Thousands of believers, most of them armed, poured in. They won control of the town council. They drove Catholics and Lutherans into the freezing countryside, without food, money or possessions. They spared neither women nor children, old nor sick.

Belatedly, the bishop moved up mercenaries to besiege the town. While highly efficient defences were organized, the Anabaptist leader, a former Haarlem baker called Jan Matthys, preached the abolition of private property. First money, then food and homes were requisitioned on pain of death. The proceeds were distributed among poor immigrants or used to hire mercenaries. All books except the Bible were ordered to be burned. In the churches, sculptures were smashed, paintings defaced. By the time Matthys was killed leading a sortie, Münster was living under a reign of terror.

Jan Bockelson, a former Leyden tailor who succeeded Matthys, proved himself even more remarkable. Young and handsome, he had a flair for amateur dramatics as well as a genuine religious sense. He turned the screw even tighter, ordering universal conscription and making every crime, from lying to murder, punishable by death.

Women outnumbered men by three to one. After a vision in which God ordered the Anabaptists to "increase and multiply," Bockelson instituted polygamy. He executed fifty objectors and himself set a good example by taking on fifteen extra wives. Next came a law requiring all unattached women to marry, even though they had husbands outside Münster. Because of the shortage of men, many had to join a harem. Those who refused were put to death.

Bockelson now took the final step to realizing the Millennium. It was revealed to Dusentschur, a goldsmith, that Bockelson was King of the New Jerusalem, destined to reign over the whole world. Even his loyal supporters found this hard to swallow. Such were his powers of persuasion, however, that he was proclaimed Messiah. Streets, holidays and days of the week were all renamed to celebrate the arrival of the Millennium. Coins were inscribed "The Word has become Flesh and dwells in us."

Life in Münster now took on the quality of a nightmare. Bockelson and his favourite wife ruled as king and queen over a court consisting mainly of foreigners, all living in sybaritic luxury and protected by guards mounted on the only riding horses in town. Meanwhile, the ordinary people had their bedding and surplus clothing confiscated for the benefit of poor immigrants. Prophecy followed prophecy, each more preposterous than the last. The inhabitants of Münster were the Children of God. At three blasts of the Lord's trumpet, they must be ready to set out for the Promised Land.

Outside the gates, the bishop was mustering his forces. At last he had enough men and equipment to make the siege of Münster effective. As before, men and women alike defended its walls with fanatical efficiency. But the bishop did not attack. He realized that his most effective weapon was starvation.

Bockelson and his courtiers continued to live richly on their vast stocks of food, much of it confiscated from the ordinary people, who were driven to eat dogs, cats and rats. Before long, corpses littered the streets. These too were eaten. Only a new reign of terror prevented mass desertion or betrayal.

The end was inevitable. Two starving citizens managed to slip out and show the besiegers how they could breach the defences. The inhabitants were mostly massacred. Bockelson and two of his henchmen were tortured to death with red-hot irons. It was remarkable that he had been able to defend a town of 10,000 people with a militia of only 1,500 for a whole year. Such was the strength of the fervour he inspired.

In his book, *The Pursuit of the Millennium* (*op. cit.*), on which I have drawn for much of the foregoing, Norman Cohn points out that "revolutionary millenarianism" flourished only when social conditions favoured it. In a stable society, people

> were not, on the whole, prone to follow some inspired *propheta* in a hectic pursuit of the Millennium. These *prophetae* found their following, rather where there existed an unorganized atomized population, rural, or urban or both. . . . Revolutionary millenarianism drew its strength from a population living on the margin of society—peasants without land or with too little land even for subsistence; journeymen and unskilled workers living under the continuous threat of unemployment; beggars and vagabonds—in fact from the amorphous mass of people who were not simply poor but who could find no assured and recognized place in society at all.

Cohn points out that revolutionary millenarianism also appeared in seventeenth-century England, especially in such sects as the Diggers and the Ranters:

> Ecstacies were everyday occurrences, prophecies were uttered on all hands, millennial hopes were rife throughout the population. Cromwell himself, especially before he came to power, was moved by such hopes; and thousands of soldiers in the New Model Army and thousands of artisans in London and other towns lived in daily expectation that through the violence of civil war the Kingdom of the Saints would be established on English soil and that Christ would descend to reign over it. (*op. cit.*)

From the Age of Enlightenment, however, revolutionary politics and prophetic religion tended to part company. The Puritans of Massachusetts Bay and the Quakers of Pennsylvania, not to mention the Christian Socialists of nineteenth-century England, did not expect the Millennium. They wished only to establish the conditions for a Christian life on earth.

The last of the old-type prophets was Joseph Smith (1805–44), head of a hierarchy ruling the Church of Latter-day Saints and their community at Nauvoo, Illinois. His promise of heaven on earth brought a flood of eager converts from the Northern States and even from England. Nauvoo might have been another Chicago but

27

squabbles over polygamy led to Smith's death and the expulsion of the community by the state legislature.

Their new prophet, Brigham Young, chose the basin of the Great Salt Lake as the site for their new settlement. It was then in Mexican territory. In 1846, he led several thousands of his followers across the continent on a largely new trail, which they had to forge *en route*. On arrival, they started to lay out Salt Lake City, dig irrigation canals and establish small farms. Successive bands of immigrants brought thousands of cattle, sheep, chickens, hogs and horses to stock them.

The Prophet ruled as an autocrat, looking only to God for guidance. Polygamy continued. Heresy was stamped on. Spiritually and materially, the settlement thrived. But when the area became part of America in 1848, the Latter-day Saints could not hope to maintain their theocratic enclave. After its incorporation into the territory of Utah, they fought a series of delaying actions, chasing out Federal judges and beating off Federal troops, but the end was inevitable. Polygamy was proscribed by the Church itself in 1890. Utah was admitted as a democratic state in 1896. Even so, Salt Lake City will always remain a monument to perhaps the sanest, most courageous and most constructive attempt to achieve the Promised Land.

Since the nineteenth century, revolutionary movements have been strictly secular, though some historians have seen echoes of Biblical prophecy in Marxism. It is tempting to equate the proletariat with the Chosen People, who are led in revolt against the Antichrist, capitalism, by an Emperor of the Last Days. The Millennium will be ushered in when the state "withers away." In practice, of course, communism has followed somewhat different paths. The murder of six million Jews by the German Nazis also had parallels in the anti-semitic massacres organized by earlier prophets.

Meanwhile, religious milleniarism has become the preserve of small groups who boldly predict that the world will end on a particular day. Sometimes they climb a mountain the previous night, presumably so that they will be a little nearer heaven at the appointed time. Next morning, they struggle down again—shamefaced, disappointed and cold. As recently as January, 1971, the True Light Church of North and South Carolina, U.S.A., expressed "shock and surprise that the world did not end in 1970."

Apart from public prophecy, there have always been individuals who have made their own private predictions, either spoken or written. Often, these have been highly obscure. Later generations of scholars have tried to make sense of them by relating them to subsequent events. St. Malachy O'More is a case in point. His real name was Maelmhaedhoc Ua Morgair and he was born in Armagh, Ireland in 1095. We know quite a lot about him because his biography was written by his famous contemporary, St. Bernard of Clairvaux. Malachy's father was a leading scholar, his mother the daughter of a wealthy family from Bangor, County Down. When Malachy was eight, his father died and Imhar O'Hagan, a monk later appointed Abbot of Armagh, became his tutor. "Meek," "obedient" and "diligent" are the adjectives used to describe Malachy. His vocation was never in doubt. He was ordained by St. Celsus, an Irish Benedictine of Glastonbury, who was then archbishop of Armagh. Promotion was rapid. He became vicar-general to Celsus, abbot of Bangor and bishop of Connor. When Celsus lay dying, he sent his pastoral staff to Malachy who succeeded to the archbishopric in 1132.

For six years he was known as a firm disciplinarian. He then resigned and went on pilgrimage to Rome. On the way he visited St. Bernard at the great French abbey of Clairvaux, and was so attracted to him that he asked to remain as an ordinary monk. The Pope, Innocent II, would not allow him to do so. He wanted Malachy to be primate of the combined see of Armagh and Tuam. This plan never materialized. We hear of Malachy travelling in England, Scotland and Ireland, and of undertaking a second pilgrimage to Rome. On his way back to Ireland he died at Clairvaux.

Even during his lifetime, Malachy won a reputation for prophecy. After sprinkling King David of Scotland's critically ill son with holy water, he said rightly that the boy would survive. He foretold the early death of a trouble-maker who tried to stop the building of an oratory. He predicted the date, place and manner of his own end. We have, of course, only St. Bernard's account of these stories and his evidence was largely hearsay. We have no other confirmation.

Malachy's papal prophecies are a different matter. They consist of a long series of Latin mottoes relating to future popes. The line starts with Celestine II (1143–44) and continues through Paul VI, the present pontiff, to four popes yet to be elected. In some cases, the mottoes are astonishingly apt, the first three being (a) *Ex Castro Tiberis* ("from a castle on the Tiber"), (b) *Inimicus Expulsus* ("the enemy driven out") and (c) *Ex Magnitudine Montis* ("from the great mountain").

The three popes to which they referred (a) came from Tuscany where the Tiber rises and had the family name of Castello; (b) had the family name of Caccianemici, which is a combination of the

Prediction and Prophecy

Italian "cacciare" ("to drive out") and "nemici" ("enemies"); and (c) was born in Montemagno ("the great mountain").

Are the prophecies really by Malachy? Or are they sixteenth-century forgeries? Scholars are still unsure. In either case, they score some fair hits, as Peter Bander shows in *The Prophecies of St. Malachy* (Colin Smythe, Gerrards Cross, U.K., 1969). *De Bona Religione* ("of a good religious background") seems exactly right for Innocent XIII (1721–24) whose family, the Conti, has provided so many popes. *Aquila Rapax* ("a rapacious eagle") could refer to Napoleon's eagle emblem which undoubtedly blighted the pontificate of the pope to which it refers—Pius VII (1800–23). As for Benedict XV (1914–22), it would be hard to find a more appropriate motto for his times than *Religio Depopulata* ("religion laid waste"). The present Pope and his predecessor have also been well served. Paul IV (1963–) has three fleur-de-lys on his armorial bearings, which fits in well with *Flos Florum* ("flower of flowers"). John XXIII (1958–63) had *Pastor et Nauta* ("shepherd and mariner"). Happily he was patriarch, and, therefore, "shepherd" of the great port of Venice, Italy, immediately before his election as pope.

In a witty footnote to *Pastor et Nauta,* Mr. Bander writes, "During the conclave (in which Pope John was elected) the rumour circulated in Rome that Cardinal Spellman of New York, who was known to be very interested in the Prophecies of Malachy, had hired a boat, filled it with sheep and sailed up and down the River Tiber." This is clearly the spirit in which the prophecies are best interpreted. The question of their genuineness must remain open. But as Archbishop H. E. Cardinale, apostolic nuncio to Belgium and Luxembourg, commented, "Se non è vero, è ben trovato" (If they are not true, they are well found). Spotters of future popes may be interested to learn that the mottoes for the next four are *De Medietate Lunae* ("of the half moon"), *De Labore Solis* ("from the toil—or eclipse—of the sun"), *Gloria Olivae* ("the glory of the olive") and *Petrus Romanus* ("Peter, the Roman"). After that, says Malachy, Rome will be destroyed and the Day of Judgement will arrive.

Joan of Arc, who undoubtedly had "visions," is also credited with worldly predictions: the imminent death of a knight, the fall of Tourelles, her wounding by an arrow, the date of her capture and the final expulsion of the English from France. Robert Nixon, a fifteenth-century ploughboy of Over, Cheshire, was invited to the court of Henry VII on the strength of a local reputation for prophesying the birth of a three-thumbed boy, the draining of a pool and the demolition of a mill. He is said to have foreseen the entire course of English history, from the Civil Wars of the seventeenth century to the industrial revolution. He is also said to have predicted his own death by starvation. It seems an unlikely end for a court favourite, but he was ugly and uncouth and was disliked by the royal servants. When Henry VII was away, they locked him up. On the King's return, he was found to have died from lack of food.

The history of England's ancient families is rich in dooms and curses, some of them pronounced by ancestors, others by wandering minstrels or seers. A few are conditional, like that of the Tichbornes, who own a property of the same name in Hampshire, England. Eight hundred years ago, the title was held by Sir Roger de Tichborne, who was both fierce and mean. He was married to Lady Mabell, a chronic invalid well known for her charity. When she was about to die, she begged her husband to endow a fund for providing the poor with bread each Lady Day in perpetuity. The story goes that he contemptuously promised her the income from as much ground as she could walk over. She dragged herself from her sickbed, dressed with the help of her maid and crawled round twenty-three acres. Before dying, she placed a curse on the Tichborne family : if her husband or any of his successors failed to give out the bread, the line would come to an end. Warning of this would be given by the birth of seven sons in one generation followed by the birth of seven daughters in the next.

For more than six hundred years, the terms of the charity were carried out to the letter but by the end of the eighteenth century it had become so famous that the village was besieged each Lady Day by hordes of marauding tramps and beggars. The magistrates warned Sir Henry Tichborne, the reigning baronet, that the dole had become a public nuisance. Sensibly, he stopped handing out bread to all and sundry, and instead gave money to the local poor. It may have been in the spirit of the charity but it was against the letter. Lady Mabell's curse quickly came into effect. Sir Henry himself was the father of seven sons, the eldest of whom had seven daughters, just as she had prophesied. In a sense, too, the line of Tichbornes came to an end. Sir Henry's third son had no reason to expect that he would succeed to the baronetcy and when he inherited the property of a Miss Doughty in Lincolnshire he changed his own name to Doughty.

In Scotland, Kenneth Mackenzie had a similar reputation. He was known as the Warlock of the Glen and also as the Seer of Brahan. He looked into the future through a stone with a hole in the middle. He is said to have foreseen the Battle of Culloden, the depopulation of the Highlands and the building of the Caledonian Canal. He is best known, however, for the pronunciation of the Doom of the Seaforths.

31

Prediction and Prophecy

Soon after the Restoration of 1660, the Earl of Seaforth journeyed to Paris, leaving his wife Isabella in Brahan Castle in the Highlands. She was ugly, violent and uncultivated and when he delayed his return home, she began to suspect that he had found more congenial company.

One evening, when her hall was thronged with guests, she called in the Warlock and asked if he could see her husband through his stone. He raised it to his eye and burst out laughing. He refused to say what he had seen. Isabella insisted. After refusing several times more he finally told her that the Earl was comfortably engaged in Paris with one girl on his knee and another stroking his hair. Isabella's anger was uncontrollable. Apart from jealousy and rage at her husband's treachery, she had been humiliated in front of her guests. Like many a seer who has brought unwelcome news, the Warlock of the Glen suffered the full force of her fury. Some accounts say that she had him hanged on the premises, others that he was handed over to the authorities, condemned as a magician and executed by having his head forced into a barrel of boiling pitch.

All agree, however, that he predicted the Doom of the Seaforths before he died. In his *Curses, Lucks and Talismans* (Bles, U.K., 1938; Saunders, U.S.A., 1939), J. G. Lockhart quotes the version of the doom given in Mackenzie's *The Prophecies of the Brahan Seer*.

I see into the future and I read the doom of the race of my oppressor. The long-descended line of Seaforth will, ere many generations have passed, end in extinction and in sorrow. I see a chief, the last of his house, both deaf and dumb. He will be the father of four fair sons, all of whom he will follow to the tomb. He will live careworn and die mourning, knowing that the honours of his line are to be extinguished for ever, and that no future chief of the Mackenzies shall bear rule at Brahan or in Kintail. After lamenting over the last and most promising of his sons, he himself will sink into the grave, and the remnant of his possessions shall be inherited by a white-coiffed lassie from the East, and she is to kill her sister. And as a sign by which it may be known that these things are coming to pass, there shall be four great lairds in the days of the last deaf and dumb Seaforth—Gairloch, Chisholm, Grant and Rassay—of whom one shall be buck-toothed, another hare-lipped, another half-witted, and the fourth a stammerer. Chiefs distinguished by these personal marks shall be the allies and neighbours of the last Seaforth; and when he looks around him and sees them, he may know that his sons are doomed to death, that his broad lands shall pass away to the stranger, and that his race shall come to an end.

The Doom was pronounced in 1663. It did not come to pass immediately. Like many Scottish families, the Seaforths backed James II in the Revolution of 1688 and his exiled son, James ("the Old Pretender"), in the rising of 1715, but their loyalty to the monarch in 1745 helped bring them back into favour. By 1771, their lands and title were restored. Twenty-six years later, the title was inherited by Francis Humberston Mackenzie.

The Warlock's curse was now all but forgotten. The new Lord Seaforth had three sons, as well as six daughters, so there seemed little chance of the line coming to an end. True, a childhood attack of scarlet fever had left him deaf and dumb, but he later recovered the power of speech and carved out a successful career in the army. It could only be an unhappy coincidence that the lairdships mentioned in the Doom should be held at the time by men suffering from the handicaps listed. Mackenzie of Gairloch was buck-toothed, Chisholm of Chisholm was hare-lipped, Grant of Grant was half-witted and Macleod of Rassay stammered.

One of Seaforth's sons died, then another. The third, and last, was in poor health. Now seriously worried, his father sent him to the south of England for medical treatment. Daily bulletins brought news of his progress, usually bad. When a more hopeful letter arrived, a friend mentioned it to the family piper. "He'll never recover," said the old retainer. "It's decreed that Seaforth maun outlive *all* his three sons."

Shortly afterwards, the boy died. When Seaforth himself "sank into his grave" in 1815, the title lapsed and the first part of the Doom was fulfilled. The only error in the prophecy made by the Warlock a century and a half before was in the number of Seaforth's sons. The Warlock had predicted four. In fact there were only three. The rest of the Doom was to be fulfilled to the letter.

Seaforth's daughter, Mary Frederica Elizabeth, inherited his estates. She had married Admiral Sir Samuel Hood, who served under Nelson at the battle of the Nile. He finally became commander-in-chief of the East Indies and died at Madras, India shortly before his father-in-law. Lady Hood returned home wearing the traditional white cap of the widow. The Seaforth lands did indeed pass to the Warlock's 'white-coiffed lassie from the East." They had already shrunk considerably through mismanagement, extravagance and an earlier government fine imposed for the family's support of the

Jacobites. Further sales now became necessary, among them the Isle of Lewis. Tenants recalled the Warlock's prophecy, "his broad lands shall pass away to the stranger."

The final tragedy came some years later. Lady Hood had married again, her new husband being a grandson of the Earl of Galloway who agreed to take the name of Mackenzie. The couple lived at Brahan and one day, Mrs. Mackenzie took her young sister Caroline for a drive through the woods in a pony carriage. Suddenly the ponies bolted and the carriage overturned. Mrs. Mackenzie escaped with cuts and bruises, but Caroline's injuries were fatal. "The lassie from the East" had killed her sister. The Doom of the Seaforths was fulfilled to the last detail. Whether it really *was* pronounced before the event prophesied is impossible to say.

English folklore too has its seers, the best-known of whom are probably Joanna Southcott and Mother Shipton. Joanna's inspiration was religious, Mother Shipton's worldly. A domestic servant and shop assistant of Gittisham, Devon, Joanna (1750–1814) was a Methodist who came to see herself as the "great wonder" referred to in Revelations XII : 1. She was "a woman clothed with the sun, and the moon under her feet, and upon her head a crown of twelve stars : and she being with child cried, travailing in birth, and pained to be delivered. . . . And she brought forth a man child, who was to rule all nations with a rod of iron. . . ."

She attracted so many followers (one estimate is 144,000) that they opened a special chapel in London. Even at the age of sixty-four she was still sure of her destiny. She was convinced that the man child she was to bring forth was none other than the saviour of Genesis XLIX : 10 : "The sceptre shall not depart from Judah nor a lawgiver from between his feet, until Shiloh come; and unto him shall the gathering of people be." She made elaborate preparations for the birth, which was due to take place on October 19th, 1814. It never happened. Shortly afterwards, Joanna died of dropsy and was buried in the churchyard of St. John's Wood Chapel, London.

That was not the end of the story. She left behind a sealed wooden box containing her prophecies. It was to be opened only at a time of national crisis in the presence of the English bishops. Not surprisingly, their graces were unwilling to be associated with Joanna's writings and attempts to assemble a quorum first in the Crimean War and then in the First World War came to nothing. Eventually, one single bishop agreed to be present at the opening of the box in 1927. As many people expected, it contained only the kind of odds and ends likely to be left by any eccentric old woman. The most interesting item was a lottery ticket. But was it the right box? The Panacea Society of Bedford, England, say that they have Joanna's original and that it has never been opened.

Mother Shipton has rather more to show for her life's work. A 2,000 word leaflet of 1641 sets out her "Prophesie . . . foretelling the death of Cardinal Wolsey, the Lord Percy and others, as also what should happen in insuing times." An illegitimate child of Agatha Southell, she is said to have been born in a cave at Knaresborough, Yorkshire, in July, 1488. At twenty-four, she married Toby Shipton and set up as a village soothsayer. Unwisely, she started to dabble in politics and let it be known that Cardinal Wolsey would "never come to York." Wolsey had fallen from favour through refusing to sanction Henry VIII's marriage to Anne Boleyn and had been stripped of all his numerous offices, with the single exception of the archbishopric of York. Alarmed at the suggestion that this too might be taken from him, he sent the Duke of Suffolk, Lord Percy and Lord Darcy to find out what the old woman had to say. Naturally, they went in disguise.

They arranged for a local man, Master Besley, to take them to her house near York. She sat them down in front of a large fire and sent for some cakes and ale. "They drunk and were very merry," says the "Prophecy." They were surprised that she knew their names and went on to ask what she predicted for Cardinal Wolsey. "I said he might see York," she replied, "but never come at it."

The Duke told her that Wolsey intended to burn her as a witch. " 'We shall see about that,' said she, and plucking her handkerchief off her head, she threw it into the fire, and it would not burn. Then she put it on again. 'Now,' said the Duke, 'what mean you by this?' 'If this had burned,' said she, 'I might have burned'."

The prophecy clearly impressed the three lords, especially as it came true. Wolsey set out for York and at Cawood, eight miles away, saw the city from the top of a tower. But he was destined never to enter it. Before he could go any further, he was arrested on a charge of high treason and escorted back to London. He died at Leicester Abbey on the way. As Mother Shipton had foretold, he had seen York but "never come at it."

In the rest of the "Prophecy" and a number of riddling couplets, various interpreters have found reference to almost every event in history from the Marian persecution to the invention of the electric telegraph. A typical passage of the "Prophecy" reads ". . . a ship come sailing up the Thames till it come against London, and the Master of the ship shall weep, and the Mariners shall ask him why he weepeth, being he hath made so good a voyage, and he shall say; Ah what a goodly City this was, none in the world comparable to it, and now there is scarce left any house that can let us have drink for our money." Some have seen here a prediction of the Great Fire of London but it could equally well refer to the blitz of the Second World War, or to the city's destruction in some future holocaust. Mother Shipton's prophecies are at best the maunderings of a crazy old woman. They may well be forgeries, though why anyone should bother to make up such nonsense is hard to imagine. It has been suggested that she never even existed.

While Mother Shipton has always been something of a joke, except perhaps in her native Yorkshire, Nostradamus has appealed to scholarly minds all over Europe. The son of a notary, Michel de Nostredame was born in 1503 in St. Rémy, France. He went on to study arts at Avignon and philosophy and the theory of medicine at the ancient university of Montpellier. After a period of general practice, he returned to Montpellier and took his doctorate. There followed a spell at Agen on the Garonne where he married but his wife died and he moved on to Aix-en-Provence, which was then stricken by the plague. The city fathers paid him a salary and were so pleased with his work that they granted him a pension for several years afterwards. From now on, accounts vary, but he seems to have settled in Salon de Craux and to have married again.

In the middle of the 1550s, his life abruptly changed course. He suddenly felt himself compelled to write prophecies. Some accounts say that he had already studied astrology as an aid to medicine and that he had published potted predictions in almanacs. None of these have come down to us. All we know is that he published his first seven *Centuries* of quatrains in 1555 and shortly afterwards he became a court favourite of King Henry ii. Back in Salon, he wrote another three *Centuries* of quatrains. *Sixains* (verses of six lines each) followed and then *Présages* (*Prophecies*).

He was now a rosy-cheeked old man who worked hard, suffered from gout and took only four or five hours' sleep a night. There seemed nothing unusual about him. Yet during the last few years of his life, he was visited by almost every man of learning in Europe. When Charles ix, who had succeeded Henry ii, visited Provence in 1564, he made Nostradamus his Physician in Ordinary and honoured him with the title of Counsellor. Eighteen months later, Nostradamus died of dropsy.

The mountain of material he left behind has been quarried by generations of scholars. Nostradamus himself said that his prophecies covered the years from 1555 to 3797, so the game of "hunt the reference" is likely to go on for many centuries. It is complicated not only by his use of metaphors, allegories and allusions. He also mixes Latin words with his obscure and highly elliptical French. Moreover, the interpreters claim to have discovered such anagrams as Rapis for Paris, Herne for Reine (queen), Ergaste for Estrange (the foreigner—*i.e.* the Austrian Marie Antoinette) and Lonole for Old Noll or Cromwell. In the last three cases it will be seen that the "rules" allow the interpreter to add or change one or two letters in each anagram.

It is not surprising that many scholarly interpretations seem far-fetched to the uninitiated, nor that scholars disagree among themselves. But a fair number of his quatrains seem to foretell future events with a precision which cannot be ignored. Here are just a few of them in Charles A. Ward's version (*The Oracles of Nostradamus.* Simpkin, Marshall, U.K., 1891.)

> The rejected one shall at last reach the throne,
> her enemies found to have been traitors.
> More than ever shall her period be triumphant.
> At seventy, she shall go assuredly to her death,
> in the third year of the century.
>
> (Century VI—Quatrain 74)

It is hard to resist the suggestion the "the rejected one" is Elizabeth 1 of England who died in 1603 at the age of seventy. After her struggle to reach the throne, her enemies were indeed regarded as traitors and her reign was one of the most triumphant in British history.

Many quatrains are thought to be allusions to the English Civil Wars, and of these, one that foretells the fall of Charles 1 seems highly apposite :

> He who had the right to reign in England shall be
> driven from the throne, his counsellor abandoned
> to the fury of the populace. His adherents will
> follow so low a track that the usurper will come to
> be Protector (or half king).
>
> (Century III—Quatrian 80)

Here we have not only the defeat of the king and the installation of Cromwell, but also the sacrifice of Strafford, the King's adviser, in the face of popular anger.

The searing events of 1665–67 can easily be read into these three successive quatrains :

37

Prediction and Prophecy

> The blood of the just shall be required of London,
> burnt by fireballs in thrice twenty and six; the old
> Cathedral shall fall from its high place, and many
> (edifices) of the same sort shall be destroyed.
>
> Through many nights the earth shall tremble: in the
> spring two shocks follow each other; Corinth and
> Ephesus shall swim in the two seas, war arising
> between two combatants strong in battle.
>
> The great Plague of the maritime city shall not
> diminish till death is sated for the just blood,
> basely sold and condemned for no fault, the great
> Cathedral outraged by feigning (saints).
>
> (Century II—Quatrains 51, 52, 53)

The first can clearly be taken as a reference to the Fire of London in 1666, seen as a judgement on the City for the execution of "the just", i.e. Charles I. "Thrice twenty and six" gives the year, if not the century, and the fall of the Old Cathedral and similar (edifices) refers to the destruction of old St. Paul's and many other City churches. The second quatrain is a fair stab at the Anglo-Dutch maritime war of 1665–67, with Corinth standing for England and Ephesus for Holland. The third sees the Great Plague as a further judgement on the regicides and their offences against the Church. Apart from putting the Fire before the Plague and not after it, these quatrains too are surprisingly apt.

Numerous references to the French Revolution and to Napoleon have been discovered. One runs as follows:

> By night shall come through the forest of Reines
> Two parts, face about, the Queen a white stone,
> The black monk in gray within Varennes.
> Chosen Cap. causes tempest, fire, blood, slice.
>
> (Century IX—Quatrain 200)

Varennes is clearly the key word. It is, of course, a small town near Verdun where Louis XVI and his queen were intercepted on their attempted flight from France in 1791. Given this, much falls into place. The "two parts" are man and wife. We know that the queen was dressed in white and the king in grey and that they would have to pass through the forest of Reines to reach Varennes where they were compelled to "face about". Louis XVI was recognized as a Capet at his trial and this could reasonably be linked with "tempest, fire, blood, slice (the blade of the guillotine)."

Numerous quatrains have been associated with Napoleon. One at least hits off neatly the royalist point of view :

> An emperor shall be born near Italy,
> Bought by the Empire at a bankrupt rate :
> You'd say the herd he gathers to himself,
> Denote him butcher rather than a prince.
>
> (Century i—Quatrain 60)

Another seems to prophesy his escape from Elba in 1814 and his defeat at Waterloo in 1815 :

> The captive prince, conquered, is sent to Elba;
> He will sail across the Gulf of Genoa to Marseilles;
> By a great effort of the foreign forces he is overcome,
> Though he escapes the fire, his bees yield blood by the barrel.
>
> (Century x—Quatrain 24)

Nostradamus is one of the most difficult prophets to assess. Many of his quatrains are so obscure that they can mean anything or nothing. The interpretations placed on them by some commentators can only be described as outlandish. We can also dismiss as nonsensical the stories that have gathered round his memory—for instance, that when his body was dug up 150 years after his death, a medal was found hanging round his neck, inscribed with the exact date of his disinterment. Yet allowing for the obscurities and absurdities, we cannot dismiss him altogether. How on earth did he hit on the date of the Great Fire of London, on the exact place of Louis xvi's arrest, on the "emperor born near Italy" who was later to escape from Elba?

But can anyone truly see into the future? Or is prediction an impossibility? If so, how can we explain the apparent success of so many practitioners both past and present? These are the questions we shall be examining at length in the rest of this book, as we consider individually the various techniques used in prophecy.

3   Coins, Livers and Shoulder Blades

"The object of divination," wrote Sir E. A. Wallis Budge, former keeper of Egyptian and Assyrian antiquities at the British Museum, "is to find out what is the Will of God and what the course of future events is going to be, whether they concern an individual or a people." Men of almost every age and civilization, including our own, have regularly practised divination. Their methods have varied widely. Often they have been odd, even bizarre. The only thing they have in common is their empiricism. They do not rely on a cause-and-effect relationship between present observation and future event. They are outside the framework of accepted science. Those who believe in them claim only that they work.

As early as the third millennium B.C., the Sumerians, who dwelt in the triangle of land between the Tigris and Euphrates in what is now Iraq, developed numerous methods of divination which are recorded in cuneiform texts. In his book *Amulets and Superstitions* (Oxford University Press, U.K. and U.S.A., 1930), Sir E. A. Wallis Budge writes:

> The priests derived omens from dreams, whether dreamed by the priest or a private individual, from the planets and stars, from eclipses, from the movements of animals, from the flight of birds, from the appearance of snakes at certain places, from locusts, lions, the actions of dogs, the direction of the winds, the state of the rivers, from peculiarities in newly-born children and animals, from the birth of twins, from accidents that may happen to men, from deformities in children, from the birth of monstrosities, from the symptoms which occur in diseases etc. According to the Sumerians and Babylonians everything that happened to the king, and to men and animals and birds and reptiles, portended something, and the priest was expected to tell the enquirer what that something was.

Priests even tried to make divination scientific by keeping a record of subsequent events and repeatedly modified their techniques in attempts to make them more reliable.

Other practices which have found favour at various times include :

Axinomancy. For finding hidden treasure. A round stone was balanced on the edge of a red-hot axe. If it stayed in place, there was no treasure. If it rolled off, the enquirer should dig where it came to rest. If it landed on a different spot each time, he should try somewhere else.

Capnomancy. Divination by the smoke from burning poppy seeds.

Hippomancy. Divination by the neighing of sacred horses. Alternatively, by noting whether the horse left the temple right hoof first (lucky) or left hoof first (unlucky).

Hydromancy. Divination by the noise or eddies of a river pouring over falls or rapids.

Ichthyomancy. Divination by examining the entrails of a fish.

Kephalomancy. Divination by the crackling of a donkey's head when burnt.

Lithomancy. Divination by the sound made when two stones were struck together.

Margaritomancy. Divination by a pearl. It had to be placed in a in a glass of water near a fire. The name of a person suspected of a crime was then spoken aloud. If the pearl exploded, the suspect was guilty.

Myomancy. Divination by mice or rats, for instance, rats leaving a sinking ship.

Onychomancy. Divination by reflections from the oiled finger-nails of "an unpolluted boy or a young virgin."

Sycomancy. Divination by putting questions to a fig tree whose leaves either kept their freshness (answer—Yes) or withered (answer—No).

The practice of divination is not restricted to primitive peoples. In *The Golden Bough* (St. Martin's Press, U.S.A., 1952; Macmillan, U.K., 1954), Sir James Frazer mentions that in Sweden, old people watch the smoke of the traditional May bonfire. If it blows north, spring will be cold and late; if south, mild and early. In North Wales, it was the custom at Hallowe'en for each member of the family to write his name on a white stone and throw it in the embers of the bonfire. If he was unable to find it next morning, he would die within a year. In Alabama, U.S.A., young girls were advised to retire to a little-used room on Hallowe'en with a mirror, a candle, an apple and a clock. At a quarter to twelve, they were to eat the apple by candlelight, finishing exactly at midnight. If they looked in the mirror, they would then see the face of their future husbands. In the north of England it is still possible to find people who believe that a single magpie brings bad luck and that if a child picks hedge parsley, his mother will die. In some parts, hedge parsley is even called "mother-die." Other ideas are more widespread. Four-leaved clovers, horse-shoes and St. Christophers are all thought to bring good luck. Every year, millions of diaries note July 15th as St. Swithin's Day. It would hardly be worth mentioning this obscure ninth-century bishop of Winchester unless many buyers of the diaries still believed, against all the statistics, that rain on St. Swithin's Day meant rain on every one of the forty days following.

The odd thing about divination is this. According to our generally held views of cause and effect, it cannot possibly work. Yet it has been practised for thousands of years and is still in vogue today. So we are forced to ask ourselves, "Does it work after all? If so, how? If not, why do people continue to believe in it? How did it start in the first place?"

There are no easy answers to these questions. Often, we simply do not know. Sometimes, we can discover a great deal from the findings of historians, psychologists, anthropologists and mathematicians. Even so, the subject is highly controversial and there may be experts of equal standing who take opposite views. Also, methods of divination are quite different from each other. Inspection of entrails, for instance, has little in common with coin-tossing, or either of them with card-reading. All these raise different issues and need to be looked at separately.

Let us start with methods which seek to find a meaning in apparently chance events completely outside the control of the observer. Usually, these were interpreted not by the diviner's individual insight but by set rules laid down by tradition.

In *amniomancy,* the ancient Greeks inspected the caul at birth. If it was pinkish, the baby would be lucky; if bluish, unlucky. In *Oomancy*, a pregnant woman wishing to foretell the sex of her unborn child incubated a hen's egg between her breasts. If the chick was male, she would have a boy baby; if female, a girl. *Pyromancy* was divination by fire. If powdered resin thrown on the flames gave a clear blaze, all would be well, but smoke meant disaster. Eggs, flour or incense could also predict the future, according to the way they burned. If an invalid stood in front of a fire in a dark room, a straight shadow indicated a speedy recovery but an oblique shadow was an omen of death. Candle flames flickering from side to side indicated migration but if they alternately flared and faded, the future was uncertain. A curling spiral of flame meant that secret enemies were plotting destruction.

The Sumerians and Babylonians were probably the first to consult sheep's livers. "For the king of Babylon stood at the parting of the way, at the head of the two ways, to use divination . . . he looked in the liver" (Ezekiel xxi : 21), and clay models of livers used for training novices have been found inscribed in both Babylonian and Hittite. One in the British Museum has the various parts clearly indicated. The surface is divided into some fifty squares, each showing the significance of a mark found in that position. Bronze Age Chinese of the second millennium B.C. studied the cracks that formed in heated ox bones and tortoise shells.

Both the Greeks and the Romans consulted the entrails of sacrificial animals, the Romans calling in Etruscan soothsayers as the recognized experts. The Greeks also took note of thunder and lightning, the flight and song of birds, a sneeze or a chance meeting. The Romans too were impressed by verbal coincidences and armies on the march carried sacred chickens. If they gobbled their food, the omens were favourable. State officials, called augurs, were consulted both privately and on public occasions. After saying a prayer, they sat facing southwards in a square marked out on the ground. There were permanent squares on the Capitoline hill and it was forbidden to obscure the view from them by building. The augur would pronounce on any signs that came to hand, especially thunder, lightning and the movements of birds and animals. If they appeared on the left, they were lucky; if on the right unlucky. Monstrous births, freak weather and unusual animal behaviour were all regarded as portents of disaster.

It is easy to understand why this type of divination was held in such high regard. Primitive peoples believed they were surrounded by unseen gods and spirits, or even by *mana,* a supernatural power flowing in men, in objects and sometimes in events as well. A magnetic personality, a frightening cavern, a lucky charm or a moving ritual could be charged with *mana.* Given a belief in these unseen powers, it was natural to seek for signs of their tendencies or intentions. We do so even today. Our intellect tells us that masses of berries on holly or hawthorn relate only to the past, when soil and climate favoured the production of berries. Yet in some dark recess of our mind, we have a feeling that there is a benevolent spirit who keeps a watch over the birds and when he foresees bad weather ahead, ensures they will have an abundant supply of food. So we draw a lesson for the *future*. "It's going to be a hard winter," we say if the trees are well berried or "Winter will be mild this year," if the branches are bare.

Similarly, the ancients believed that thunder, lightning, fire and other natural phenomena carried messages for those capable of reading them. The liver was especially significant because it was thought to be the seat of the emotions. The argument by analogy seemed irrefutable. If a pregnant woman hatched a male chick between her breasts, who could deny there was some male principle at work in her, a principle which was bound to ensure that her baby too would be male?

These beliefs were not just a matter for the individual. They were the cement of society. They were part of a system of belief, largely magical, that helped impose order on the surrounding chaos. How and why these took the form they did varied from culture to culture and anthropologists themselves do not always agree. Konrad Lorenz, the Austrian behavioural scientist, describes the importance of magical rituals in his book *On Aggression* (Methuen, U.K., 1966; Harcourt Brace, U.S.A., 1966):

> In a mild form, the same phenomena can be observed in many children. I remember clearly that, as a child, I had persuaded myself that something terrible would happen if I stepped on one of the lines, instead of into the squares of the paving-stones in front of Vienna Town Hall. A. A. Milne gives an excellent impression of this same fancy of a child in his poem Lines and Squares.
>
> All these phenomena are interrelated. They have a common root in a behaviour mechanism whose species-preserving function is obvious: for a living being lacking insight into the relation between causes and effects it must be extremely useful to cling to a behaviour pattern which has once or many times proved to achieve its aim, and to have done so without danger. If one does not know which details of the whole performance are essential for its success as well as for its safety, it is best to cling to them all with slavish exactitude. The principle, "You never know what will happen if you don't" is fully expressed in such superstitions.

The enquirer, then, did not wish to contradict the soothsayer. All the psychological pressures were on the side of belief. Every successful prophecy reinforced faith in the system. Mistakes could be blamed on a failure to carry out some detail of the complicated ritual laid down. In any case, many predictions were so vague, riddling or remote that they could later be held to mean almost anything. Suppose, to take a modern example, that a soothsayer had pronounced favourably on Hitler's plan to invade Russia in 1941. The invasion paved the way to Germany's defeat and in 1945, we might have said the soothsayer was wrong. Yet citizens of the free, stable and prosperous Germany of today might reasonably take a different view. Any event that helped bring about the ultimate defeat of Hitler and the Nazis might be thought of as favourable. From this standpoint, the soothsayer would have been right. In other words, history is a continuum and by choosing different points of vantage, we can interpret almost any happening in almost any light we find convenient.

Even so, the soothsayers must have had some degree of identifiable success; otherwise it would have been difficult to sustain the basic minimum of faith over such long periods even with the support of magic and ritual. There is reason for thinking they may have been more often right than our present-day science-orientated outlook would care to admit.

First, and least important, is the anecdotal evidence. In 217 B.C. the Consul C. Flaminius scorned suggestions that he should not join battle with the Carthaginians because the omens were unpropitious. At the ensuing battle of Lake Trasimene, he was killed and his army shattered. On the other hand, the Consul Aemilius Paullus was said to be delighted when his daughter announced the death of their dog, Persa, in 168 B.C. He was about to lead the Roman army in the war against Macedon which had so far been going badly. The Macedonian king was called Perseus and Aemilius believed, rightly as it turned out, that the death of Persa was an ill omen for Perseus. At Pydna, the Macedonian army was also wiped out.

Such stories mean little themselves but there is reason to suppose that soothsayers and omens would *tend* to be accurate by the very nature of the problems put to them. A general who was wondering whether to join battle would assess the relative strengths of his own army and that of the enemy. If he decided, "I am sure to lose," he would probably stand still or even retreat without bothering to call in a soothsayer. If he decided, "I am sure to win," the only reason for consulting the omens would be to choose between alternative plans and as he was already in a favourable position, either would probably be successful. The soothsayer was on "a winner to nothing." The general would, of course, seek advice when the outcome was uncertain. Here, on the basis of chance alone, the odds of the soothsayer being right were no worse than evens. Taking an average of his probable chances of success on the two types of situation in which he was likely to be consulted, we can see he could reasonably expect to be right something like three times out of four.

The same applies to most of the problems likely to be posed. A young man contemplating marriage would not ask for help in choosing between two equally poor, ugly, bad-tempered girls. He would reject them both. He would seek advice only if his choice lay between two equally rich, beautiful and sweet-tempered brides, or if both girls, though broadly acceptable, had possible drawbacks. Again, taking both situations together, the soothsayer would have an average success rate of 75 per cent.

It was possibly higher still. All prophecies have a tendency to be self-fulfilling. A general who led his army into battle, confidently believing in the victory promised by the omens, had a clear psychological advantage. So did the young man whose marriage was approved by the soothsayer. Numerous cases of illness and even death have been reported among primitive people following spells placed upon them by practitioners of voodoo and other forms of magic. They are still occurring, even in the "advanced" countries of the West. A letter in the *British Medical Journal* (August 7th, 1965), told of a 43-year-old Canadian woman who went into hospital for a minor gynaecological operation. She collapsed an hour after regaining consciousness and died the next day from a rare type of haemorrhage unconnected with the operation. Her doctors were puzzled but relatives and nurses remembered her saying that she would never leave hospital alive. Thirty-eight years before, when she was five, a fortune-teller had predicted that she would die at forty-three and she had believed it ever since. One could, of course, explain her death by coincidence but her doctors were prepared to take into account the effect of the prophecy. "We wonder if the severe emotional tensions of this patient, superimposed on the physiological stress of surgery, had any bearing on her death," they wrote.

Apart from these general reasons for thinking that divination may have worked, or at least *seem* to have worked, modern research has shown how some individual methods may have been successful.

If we leave aside inheritance and family influence, there seems no reason to believe that one name should give a child a better, or worse, chance in life than any other name. Yet belief in onomancy, or divination by name, has persisted for thousands of years. The derivation of a man's name, the number of vowels it contained or even the number of letters have been held to determine his future. Any of these methods could conceivably work through the principle of self-fulfilment. There is another possible way. In any society, some names are held in higher esteem than others. While the broad mass of names are regarded as "normal," a few are thought to be odd, pretentious or distinguished. These attitudes must clearly have some influence on the bearers and among both Harvard students and Ashanti children in Ghana, it has been found that names affect personality. Harvard students with unusual names were found more likely to be drop-outs than the rest of their contemporaries. Ashanti children tended to grow into the type of personality with which their names were generally associated. In a survey of girls at two comprehensive schools and one private school in England, Dr. Joseph Weber of Bristol University noted the associations: Doris—"gossipy, fat and dim;" Jane and Susan—likeable; Amanda—attractive and "upper-class;" Elizabeth and Rachel—likeable, intelligent and attractive. Girls with unusual names were happier during their later years at school because they found these a focus for emerging individuality.

Christopher Bagley and Louise Evan-Wong of Sussex University, England, wondered just how far a name could affect the attitude of friends and so, the owner's self-image. After establishing a list of nineteen "odd" surnames such as Stutter, Squelch, Pansey and Mucky from a list of mentally disturbed children, they paired them off with ordinary names and asked a group of children to "guess" which of each pair was always in trouble. The set with odd surnames were nearly always assumed to be the troublemakers. But how far had this affected their mental health? Bagley and Evan-Wong chose at ran-dom sixty-four mentally disturbed children with "normal" names and compared their clinical histories with those of the nineteen with odd names. They were especially interested in the number of psychological crises, such as early separation from the mother, which the children in each group had undergone. They found that the sixty-four with "normal" names averaged twice the number of crises. So it seemed as though the stress arising from social attitudes to an "odd" name might bring a child to the breaking-point much sooner than the more tolerant social attitudes to a "normal" name. In other words, some names seem to be more propitious than others. So there is some evidence at least that onomancy may not be so fanciful as it sounds.

Perhaps the most surprising indication of ancient methods of divination came from recent research in Canada. It seems to validate practices that have so far been thought absurd. Omar Khayyam Moore, an assistant professor of sociology at Yale University, sug-gested a reason for thinking that scapulomancy, or divination by shoulder-blade, may have provided at least "some approximate

47

solutions for recurring problems" (*American Anthropologist*, February, 1957). The method has been reported from both Europe and Asia and is similar to the ox-bone and tortoise-shell oracles used by the Chinese in the middle of the second millennium B.C.

Moore started out as a sceptic. While studying the varying methods by which groups solved their problems in a project sponsored by the U.S. Office of Naval Research, he thought it would help to study methods that seemed not to work. One of these was the ritual followed by the Mantagnais-Naskapi tribe of Indians in Labrador. These Indians live by hunting and when they have no reports of game, they take the cleaned and dried shoulder-blade of a caribou, heat it gently over a fire and line it up with the landscape as though it were a map. The cracks and other marks brought out by the heat are then used to indicate the direction in which they should hunt. How could such a method possibly be effective?

Moore tried to imagine what would happen if the Naskapi had no shoulder-blade oracle. "It seems likely," he concluded, "their selections of hunting routes would be patterned in a way related to recent successes and failures." Time and again, they would be drawn to areas where they had previously been lucky, not realizing that they had already creamed off the pick of the game and taught the surviving birds and animals to be wary of man. So they would be "victimized by their own habits."

Divination by shoulder-blade prevents such habits forming. The cracks and marks vary according to the individual bone, the way it is held, the heat of the fire and so on. They are interpreted according to traditional rules. There is little scope for the diviner to impose his own ideas, consciously or unconsciously. True, every shoulder blade is basically similar so that some patterns are more likely to appear than others but the Naskapi are constantly on the move and even identical patterns would point to different hunting grounds on different days. What the oracle does, if only imperfectly, is to ensure that the Naskapi hunt *at random*. This sounds elementary but experiments have shown that humans find it extremely difficult, if not impossible, genuinely to randomize their activities unless they rely on a special instrument or a table of random numbers.

Moore points out that many oracles "involve the use of impersonal, chancelike devices in arriving at decisions." As with the shoulder blade, it is difficult to show how far such methods are in fact successful. "Nevertheless, it is possible that through a long process of creative trial and error, some societies have arrived at some approximate solutions for recurring problems." So there is at least scope for further investigation. He concludes, "It seems safe to assume that human beings require a functional equivalent to a table of random numbers if they are to avoid unwitting regularities in their behaviour which can be utilized by adversaries. Only an extremely thorough study of the detailed structure of problems will enable scientists to determine to what degree some very ancient devices are effective."

To sum up, then, we can assume that soothsayers and oracles were often correct because of the nature of the questions put to them, because many of their prophecies were self-fulfilling, because they took account of social pressures we have tended to ignore, and because they sometimes acted as a method of randomizing choice when precisely that was needed.

The methods of divination so far discussed all draw on observations which were outside the control of the soothsayer, who made his predictions according to strict, traditional rules. Leaving aside fraud, which undoubtedly occurred on occasion but is irrelevant to our purpose, it is hard to see how the soothsayer himself could have modified the interpretations, either consciously or otherwise. The Roman augur sitting in his square in the prescribed south (or sometimes east) facing position, could not *will* the appearance of a bird or a flash of lightning. Nor could he influence the direction from which it appeared. Any Roman augur, whatever his personal feelings, would have to say it was unfavourable if it came from the left, favourable if it came from the right.

Now let us take a different group of methods: those in which selection has to be made, usually by the soothsayer. One of the oldest known ways of ascertaining God's will was by the *urim* and *thummim,* described in Exodus xxviii:30 as being carried in the high priest's breastplate. They were probably two small stones or pieces of wood or bone. Questions had to be capable of only two answers: "Shall we do this or that?" or "Is it a good time to fight—yes or no?" The *urim* and *thummim* were then marked with the alternative answers and the priest chose one of them in some way that we do not know. This answer was regarded as the will of God.

There were many variants of the same idea. In Babylon, the priest kept a case of two arrows, one marked with a sign meaning "yes," the other with a sign meaning "no". These were shuffled and a blind selection made. Sometimes, a third arrow was added with the meaning "don't know" or "do as you please." Occasionally too, a whole flight of arrows was marked up, shuffled and a blind choice made. Dice have been thrown since early times, for instance in the Temple of Heracles near Bura, in Achais, Greece, and the score interpreted by a simple odds-evens choice or by a more complicated system of adding up the numbers. Coin-tossing can also be traced to ancient times.

Here we should mention the present-day custom of tossing a coin to decide choice of play in cricket, hockey, football and other games. We persuade ourselves this is a "fair" way of deciding between the two sides. But is it? We know from experience that a given team may lose the toss far oftener than its rivals, even over many seasons. If we really wanted to be fair, we could arrange for every team playing in a competition to have choice of play as often as every other team; or we could make a rule, as in baseball, that the visiting side should always have first play. We could even, as in billiards, have a preliminary test of skill. Instead of ensuring the fairness we claim to cherish, we *un*fairly toss. We are rejecting our scientific principles. Like the ancients, we prefer an appeal to the will of God, fate or chance.

Two further points are worth noticing. First, God, fate or chance *seems* to favour some people more than others. Many psychologists believe that some people really are luckier than others. Mr. D. J. van Lennop, Director of the Netherlands Foundation for Industrial Psychology, wrote in the journal *Progress* (1962): "There are clear indications that some people have a certain flair for attracting good fortune. . . . They seem to have been 'born under a lucky star', if this archaic expression is permissible, whereas others seem to have a continuous rush of bad luck. Some people seem to attract good fortune, others never rise to the occasion and cannot but fail. . . . Perhaps we are confronted here with the deepest and most fundamental relation between man and his environment." (Quoted by Gustav Jahoda, *op. cit.*).

The second point to notice is the difference in attitude between the ancient king who consulted the *urim* and *thummim* and similar devices, and the captain of a modern sports team who tosses a coin. The ancient king wished only to find out the will of God so that he could act accordingly. In theory at least, he did not care whether the answer was "yes" or "no." Provided he obeyed, he could be assured of divine approval whatever the result. The modern sportsman does care. He calls "heads" or "tails" while the coin is still spinning in the air and if he wins, he is entitled to choice of play which may well give him a considerable advantage over his opponent. He therefore has a strong motive for predicting the result and calling accordingly. If we assume a fair coin and a fair toss, success could be the result of chance and doubtless often is, but there are at least two other possibilities. One is that the caller *foresees* whether the coin will fall "heads" or "tails." This faculty, if it exists, is known as pre-recognition and we shall discuss the evidence for it in Chapter 7. The other possibility is that the caller does not foresee "heads" or "tails" but while the coin is still in the air, *wills* it to fall in the way he has called. Mental influence of this kind is called psychokinesis or P.K. But can its existence be proved?

The power of "mind over matter" has long been accepted in medicine. It is generally agreed that peptic ulcers, disorders of the colon, psoriasis, eczema, asthma and many other physical ailments may be caused at least partly by the state of the patient's mind. Most of us acknowledge the power of suggestion, whether or not the subject is hypnotized, and even the most confirmed sceptic would find it hard to deny that there are at least some genuine examples of healing by faith. The appearance of stigmata, marks corresponding to the wounds of Christ, has been authenticated in a number of religious enthusiasts. Some people can raise blisters under hypnotism and there are well attested reports of spontaneous dermographia, or skin-writing, in which the subject can develop red marks forming letters or objects just by taking thought.

Examples of a mind directly influencing outside objects are more controversial but poltergeists and other puzzling phenomena have been explained in this way and, coming back full circle, so has the fact that some people seem to be luckier than others when tossing a coin or guessing cards. Not surprisingly, it was the belief of "a young member of the gambling profession" that the fall of dice could be similarly explained that led to the most comprehensive survey of P.K. yet undertaken: the experiments, under Dr. J. B. Rhine, Professor of Psychology at Duke University, North Carolina, U.S.A., which lasted from 1934 to 1942. He tells the story in *The Reach of the Mind* (Sloane, U.S.A., 1947, Faber, U.K., 1948).

Before embarking on such an ambitious programme, Rhine decided to find out whether there was in fact a *prima facie* case for P.K. He and his wife, Dr. Louise E. Rhine, and later a group of friends, systematically threw a pair of dice which they willed to fall "high", *i.e.* the pips on the uppermost faces should total eight or more. The results were encouraging. But had the thrower developed a knack of picking up the dice or tossing them in such a way that favoured high scores? Modifications were introduced to eliminate manual skills, first a cup in which the dice were vigorously shaken, then a cup with roughened sides, finally a number of gadgets which rolled the dice mechanically. One of the first consisted of an inclined plane with a number of corrugations; another was a rotating wire cage. Originally, the dice had been tossed on to any convenient surface, a floor perhaps or a polished table top. Now, a padded surface was used consistently. The form of the experiments was also standardized with the subject throwing and the controller calling out the results and recording them on a test sheet. Various targets were set, including high, low (six and under), sevens and doubles with two dice; and individual numbers, either continuing throughout the experiment or regularly changed, with one die. It was important that the results of each experiment should be comparable with those of others, so a standard run of twenty-four dice was adopted. Sometimes they were thrown singly, at other times in pairs, three, fours, sixes, twelves or even in a single throw of twenty-four.

The results continued to be significant. If two dice are thrown, we could expect by pure chance five highs, five lows and two sevens in a standard run of twenty-four faces. In 900 runs in which highs were willed, however, an average of 5.5 highs was scored. This result could admittedly have come about by chance but, according to Rhine, "it would take a number of about twenty digits to state the odds against getting it." Equally interesting results were obtained by other experimenters aiming at both combinations and singles. But one doubt had to be cleared up : how could they be sure the results were due to P.K. and not just to biassed dice?

Rhine decided early on not to seek scientifically perfect dice because "even if we got the same results, we would suspect their perfection and be right back where we were." Instead, the experiments were designed to offset any possible bias. Targets were switched from high to low, single dice were thrown an equal number of times for each face and there were other precautions, too. But it was "the decline effect" which finally disproved the possibility of bias. It was discovered only towards the end of the research when in 1942 Dr. Rhine and Dr. Betty M. Humphrey, also of Duke University, surveyed the results of the early work.

They noticed that in sets of two or three runs, the number of hits was nearly always higher in the first run and fell off sharply in the second and/or third runs. In 123 sets aiming at highs, for instance, they found a total of 134 hits above chance expectation in 123 first runs, compared with 19 in 123 second runs and 4 in 75 third runs. Chance expectation of such a big difference between first and second runs is something like one in 100,000. It also ruled out the possibility of bias in the dice because any bias would have shown up equally in all three runs. Nor could it be said that a subject, being fresh, might have unconsciously exploited a hidden bias by unwittingly throwing the dice more vigorously in the first run. Otherwise, why should results with mechanically released dice show a similar decline? Moreover, when records of later and longer series were examined, an even more interesting effect was noticed. As before, the number of hits declined *horizontally,* that is when the early runs were compared with later runs, but there was also a *vertical* decline. In most runs, the number of hits above chance scored in the top half of the score sheet was greater than that scored in the bottom half. Taken together, the vertical and horizontal declines produced a *diagonal* decline. The record pages were quartered and the top left, consisting of early throws in early runs, regularly showed a far greater number of hits than the bottom right, consisting of late throws on late runs. The bottom left (late throws on early runs) and the top right (early throws on late runs) usually came somewhere in between. Odds against this happening by chance were reckoned at a million to one.

More recent experiments with both dice and coins, for instance those of Dr. Robert E. Thouless, Professor of Psychology at Cambridge University, have produced both positive and negative results. Attempting to pinpoint the factors that made for success, Professor Thouless confessed that he "was very far from having solved the problem." Unfavourable psychological conditions and continued experimentation seemed to work against P.K. and so did mental tension of any kind. The most favourable attitude of mind was apparently one of "effortless intention to succeed . . . that expressed by the words 'I want to succeed but I don't really care whether I do or not.'" (Proceedings of the Society for Psychical Research, vol. 49, page 123.)

Rhine himself went on to show that distance did not affect P.K. scoring, nor did the shape of the dice, but heavier metal dice worked better than wooden dice and, significantly, throwers preferred their "feel." If subjects were assured they would do well in particular circumstances, they often did so. Finally, Rhine pointed out a striking aspect of the experiments involving two dice. A single act of will had to influence each of them at the same time and in such a way that they *jointly* produced the combination required. From all these observations, he concluded that P.K. was not a physical force but a "purposively orientated operation." He went on, "The process of P.K. is not a brain-to-object reaction. It is not the brain as a physical process, but the mind as a non-physical force, that influences the rolling dice. We have no idea how such psycho-physical action takes place. . . ."

Prediction and Prophecy

Some scientists are sceptical of Rhine's results. Many of their objections are discussed by C.E.M. Hansel, Professor of Psychology at the University College of Swansea, University of Wales, in his book *E.S.P.—A Scientific Evaluation* (MacGibbon and Kee, U.K., 1966; Scribner, U.S.A., 1966). Other scientists, equally distinguished, believe that Rhine has at least established the need for further research.

If P.K. did exist, it would clearly be relevant to our second broad category of divination, those methods where coins, dice, arrows, *urim* and *thummim,* and various kinds of lots are manipulated by a priest, soothsayer or team captain to give a yes/no or either/or answer. In the first place, Rhine's discovery that not everyone has the faculty of P.K. would explain why some people seem to be luckier than others in winning the toss or choosing a lot that favours them. The finding that even those who have it cannot exercise it unless conditions are right fits in well with the essential unreliability of the method. It would explain why a cricket captain wins the toss four times but fails to win it on the fifth. We are dealing with *average* results, not particular ones.

Secondly, P.K. could help explain why an apparently blind choice of lots might reveal which of two possibilities was indeed the more favourable. Few of us would deny the value of a second opinion when we are in doubt. Should we take the new job offered? We talk it over with a friend. Would the patient best respond to treatment A, B, or C? The doctors calls in a consultant. Has the plaintiff really a case worth taking to court? The solicitor asks for counsel's opinion. In many situations, we do not need an expert, just someone with detachment and commonsense, someone who will see the issues clearly and will not be swayed by emotion or wishful thinking. We would expect professional priests and soothsayers to have this capacity, otherwise they would not be in these callings. If the king was not sure whether to join battle and wished the *urim* and *thummim* to be consulted, the high priest might be expected to weigh up the facts of the military situation and add to them his knowledge of the king's character and current state of mind and health. The priest would note too the morale of the soldiers and perhaps, if it was known, that of the enemy. Everything considered, he would have a shrewd idea whether or not it was a good idea for the king to fight. If we assume the existence of P.K., the priest's view of the situation would presumably influence his manipulation of the *urim* and *thummim,* consciously or unconsciously, and so produce the answer his insight favoured.

Clearly, this hypothesis is speculative and does not pretend to be otherwise, but the more we look at techniques of divination, the more we realize that they involve powers and influences that are often oblique in their operation and sometimes barely within the scope of our present understanding. Unless we are prepared to dismiss them as nonsense or explain them *only* as survival mechanisms, we must break out of our rigid patterns of thinking and be prepared to consider possibilities largely ignored by orthodox science. We shall now consider some of these possibilities in relation to some other methods of prediction that were first used thousands of years ago and are still being used today.

4 Intuition—Tarot and the *I Ching*

Every Christmas, millions of families pull crackers containing funny hats, toys and mottoes even feebler than the bangs: "Fools rush in where angels fear to tread," "A stitch in time saves nine," "Don't spoil the ship for a ha'porth of tar." We scorn them, yet few of us fail to read them and if mottoes were suddenly left out of crackers, there would be letters to *The Times* and perhaps even questions in Parliament. In the U.S.A., guests at fêtes buy rice cookies. They too have mottoes baked inside which are scanned with the same mixture of scorn and genuine interest. Neither cracker-pullers nor cookie-munchers realize they are practising modern versions of aleuromancy, an ancient method of divination in which the soothsayer wrote brief words of advice on scraps of parchment, screwed them up and mixed them in a bowl of flour. The flour was divided and after the suppliants had stated their questions, they each chose a share and took their answer from the scrap of parchment it happened to contain.

The presence of the soothsayer and the formality of the ritual made the ancient believers in aleuromancy treat the answers much more seriously than we moderns treat our mottoes. But we have the same basic hope. Like them, we are eager to know our destiny and if possible, how we can influence it. However sceptical we may be, we are unable to shed the feeling at some level of our consciousness that someone or something can tell us, if only we can make contact. Yet how can a few words of advice, unexceptionable in themselves, cast light on problems that are linked to them only, apparently, by chance? Leaving aside the possible explanations we discussed in the previous chapter, are there any reasons for thinking they could give us useful knowledge or guidance?

The time has now come for us to examine those forms of divination which rely heavily on a factor almost completely absent in coin tossing or the consulting of shoulder blades. They leave wide scope for interpretation, sometimes by the soothsayer, sometimes by the enquirer himself. Tarot is one example. Another is the currently popular *I Ching* or *Book of Changes,* an ancient Chinese classic. Both forms of divination call for the exercise of a faculty which we all know to exist but about which science has surprisingly little to tell us—intuition.

The tarot pack comprises 78 cards, of which 22 are Atouts (also called Trumps Major or Greater Arcana) and 56 ordinary cards (Lesser Arcana) divided into four suits—Rods (or Wands, Cups, Swords and Money (or Pentacles). Each suit consists of King, Queen, Knight, Page and ten numbered cards down to ace. The Atouts especially are steeped in symbolism, some of it deriving from as far back as ancient Egypt. Indeed, the tarot is sometimes referred to as the Book of Thoth, the Egyptian god of arts and sciences, who had the body of a man and the head of an ibis or baboon. The designs we know date back at least to the fourteenth century and though details have been changed in periodic revampings, the basic themes have persisted. The symbols used are among the most ancient known to man : the Sun, the Moon, the Lovers, the Magician, the Devil, the Tree of Life, intertwined serpents, which are a traditional badge of healing, and a serpent swallowing his own tail, which is an age-old symbol of unity. There are obvious links with astrology, numerology, Masonic symbolism and the ancient Jewish mystical symbolism of the Kabbala. There are also allusions to the vision of Ezekiel and in *The Waste Land,* T. S. Eliot associated the Hanged Man of the tarot with Frazer's Hanged God and tarot's Man with Three Staves with the Fisher King in the legend of the Holy Grail.

For purposes of divination, each suit has an underlying theme. The suit of Rods denotes enterprise, creation and work; Cups—love, happiness; Swords—hatred, war; Money—cash, business. The King represents a mature man, the Queen a mature woman, the knight a youth and the page a young boy or girl, but every card of every suit has a precise meaning, which does vary however from one interpreter to another. There are several systems of choosing and laying out the cards and the reading depends largely on their juxtaposition, each card being influenced by those around it.

As an example, we can take the system outlined by Mrs. John King van Rensselaer in her *Prophetical, Educational and Playing Cards,* (Hurst and Blackett, U.K., 1912). She says the King of Swords signifies a "dark bad man. A soldier, an enemy or one to be mistrusted." The Queen of Swords points to a "dark, wicked woman. A

57

gossip. A calumniator. Jealous" and the Cavalier to a "young dark man. An enemy. A spy." Ace of Swords refers to "commencement of enmity," four to "enemy defeated," seven to "enemy successful," ten to "uncertainty in the hatred" and so on. Mrs. Van Rensselaer goes on to show how even these brief stereotypes can be manipulated to produce a variety of interpretations. "The card is read in one way when it is required to reveal the character and in another when the social position or the thoughts of the enquirer are to be revealed. The same card signifies, under other circumstances, past or future events according to its position. A malignant card may be entirely changed if surrounded by benign cards. Thus, each condition must be given due weight when the cards are being consulted."

All this is still largely mechanical. It does not explain why some practitioners have a high reputation while others do not. If anyone could "read the cards" just by consulting a book, no one would repeatedly pay large sums to a favoured expert. Clearly an element of personal skill is indispensable. In what does this personal skill consist?

Nearly every expert agrees it is intuition. In his classic *Key to the Tarot* (Rider, U.K., 1920), Arthur Edward Waite puts it like this:

The value of intuitive and clairvoyant faculties is of course assumed in divination. Where these are naturally present or have been developed by the diviner, the fortuitous arrangement of cards forms a link between his mind and the atmosphere of the subject of divination, and then the rest is simple. Where intuition fails, or is absent, concentration, intellectual observation and deduction must be used to the fullest extent to obtain a satisfactory result. But intuition, even if apparently dormant, may be cultivated by practice. If in doubt as to the exact meaning of a card in a particular connexion, the diviner is recommended, by those who are versed in the matter, to place his hand on it, try to refrain from thinking of what it ought to be, and note the impressions that arise in his mind. At the beginning, this will probably resolve itself into mere guessing and may prove incorrect, but it becomes possible in practice to distinguish between a guess of the conscious mind and an impression arising from the mind which is subconscious.

In *Psychological Types* Routledge and Kegan Paul, U.K., 1923; McGrath, U.S.A. 1970), Carl Gustav Jung defines intuition as the psychological function which transmits perceptions *in an unconscious way.* Everything, whether outer or inner objects or their association, can be the object of this perception. Intuition has this peculiar quality: it is neither sensation, nor feeling, nor intellectual conclusion, although it may appear in any of these forms. Through intuition, any one content is presented as a complete whole, without our being able to explain or discover in what way this content has been arrived at. Intuition is a kind of instinctive apprehension, irrespective of the nature of its content. . . . Its contents . . . have the character of being given, in contrast to the "derived" or "deduced" character of feeling and thinking contents. Intuitive cognition, therefore, possesses an intrinsic character of certainty and conviction. . . .

It is also *irrational,* "not contrary to reason, but something outside the province of reason, whose essence, therefore, is not established by reason." That is why, in a scientific age, most laymen are suspicious, even derisive of intuition, though many scientists admit that "hunches" have put them on the track of some of their most important discoveries.

The successful card reader is, then, highly intuitive. From the moment a client enters his room, he is picking up clues from the client's dress, expression and manner of speaking, almost without being aware of it. Even the way the client sits down is relevant. Further clues follow from the answers to questions put by the reader and from the client's reactions to the first tentative readings. From his intuitive appreciation of the client's character, the diviner should be able to give a fairly accurate prediction as to whether a given course of action is likely to be favourable or unfavourable.

In *A Complete Guide to the Tarot* (Studio Vista, U.K., 1970; Crown, U.S.A., 1970), Eden Gray describes a sample reading given for Patricia, a married woman in her thirties whom he had previously met at a party. He sensed "a sadness or melancholy" about her. The first four cards indicated that she was intelligent and creative, with a tendency to dominate the lives of other people and had tried, unsuccessfully, to do this by spending too much money. The fifth card was "the Queen of Wands, reversed, a blonde blue-eyed woman who is in opposition to you. There is deceit here and jealousy." It struck an immediate response, "Yes, I know about her," said Patricia. "She works in my husband's office." The next two cards established that Patricia's way of life must change. "There is a chance that this blonde woman will cause your husband to leave you." To avoid trouble, Patricia must use her imagination and intuition. The

59

seventh card was the King of Cups, which had "fallen on the place of love, lust and the arts. Could this card be your husband?" Patricia said she thought it was. "He is an art director in an advertising agency in New York," she explained. Mr. Gray replied, "I feel that he is basically a very kind and generous man, as well as quite talented." The next card symbolized the master craftsman but as it was upside down, it meant her husband was failing in his job. "The pull on his affections is tearing him apart," said the reader. The next card indicated dissolution, perhaps of their marriage, perhaps of the husband's career, perhaps of both, but it was suggested that Patricia could help matters by changing her own materialistic attitude which had perhaps driven her husband to sacrifice his "artistic integrity." The final card indicated hope and courage. "Perhaps a little spiritual application would be good—prayer and meditation on the true meaning of life. I feel you will be helped—if you are sincere and see your husband as more than just a provider. . . . Love, tenderness and caring mean a great deal to him . . . there can definitely be a change for the better." A reading of the seven cards in the "qualifying pack" suggested that love and patience would pave the way for a reunion and possibly the birth of a child. Mr. Gray did not see Patricia again for a whole year. She then told him that she and her husband were happily together again and that she was pregnant.

Was his diagnosis and prediction just a coincidence? I don't think so. It seems clear that his intuition was working at full stretch throughout the reading. He had presumably summed her up as a materialistic type at the party and when a married woman in her thirties has a problem the odds are she is having trouble with her husband. As every marriage counsellor knows, there are usually faults on both sides, so it would not be difficult for someone with insight to realize that the woman's materialism was partly to blame. Earlier in his book, Mr. Gray advises readers to "try to make a running story about what you see in the cards in relation to the person for whom you are reading. . . . If after reading the cards, the Querent [enquirer] tells you that his question is not answered, ask him if the cards have perhaps dealt with a deeper question that he has been worrying about. I have found that people are sometimes a little timid about bringing out into the open what is really on their minds. . . . With a little digging and a sincere desire to help, you may uncover what is really bothering the Querent. . . ." With Patricia, he gets to the root of the problem much more quickly because she blurts out what is worrying her. He then explores the situation, using the cards as a starting point, and giving her eminently sensible advice. The inner need that had driven her to seek his help and the solemnity of the reading would tend to ensure that she heeded it. As for predicting the birth of her baby, Mr. Gray knew that she had an only child. It does not need psychic powers to divine the possibility of pregnacy when an attractive, fertile woman in her thirties is reconciled to her husband.

There are, of course, many other systems of cartomancy, or divination by cards. One using an ordinary pack is described by Mrs. van Rensselaer (*op. cit.*). After discarding the Two, Three and Five of each suit, the reader shuffles the remaining thirty-six cards, cuts them and hands them out to the enquirer, who cuts them three times. The reader then lays them out face upwards, consecutively, from left to right, in four rows of eight and one row of four, centred under the other rows. The enquirer is represented by the Ace of Spades, if male; by the Ace of Hearts, if female. Following the system devised by Mlle le Normand, the celebrated, nineteenth-century French card reader, Mrs. van Rensselaer lists four separate meanings for each of the other cards. These apply according to whether it lies above or below, to the right or the left of the enquirer's card. The closer it is, the stronger its influence. Once again, there is wide scope for interpretation. The King of Diamonds, for instance can stand for "Fortune from the sea. Enterprises successful. Misfortune. Loss." Meanings of the Ten of Clubs are "Happiness. Indifference. Trouble from outsiders. Slander."

Many other forms of divination relying heavily on the soothsayer's intuition and imagination have flourished over the years. Reading tea-leaves is a modern example. As with Rorschach ink-blot tests, different things can be read into the patterns by different people. Whatever the books may say, interpretation of a successful reader would largely depend on the impression he formed of the enquirer and his problem. So too would the advice offered. Ceroscopy was an ancient form of the same technique, with molten wax dripped into a vase of cold water so that the surface was covered with a pattern of tiny discs. In geomancy, the enquirer himself was asked to stab the earth at random with a pointed stick. The soothsayer then read the dots. Other ancient methods involved arranging the letters of the alphabet in a circle. They were then chosen by various methods. In gyromancy, the soothsayer danced round and round until he became so giddy that he fell on one. The process was then repeated. In dactylomancy, a ring was suspended by a thread, which was set on fire. When the ring fell, the soothsayers noted which letters it rolled over. In electromancy, a grain of wheat was placed by each letter and a cock set in the centre of the circle. A note was made of the letters from which the cock ate the grain. According to Waite (*The Occult Sciences,* Kegan Paul, London, 1891), a white, clawless bird which had been forced to swallow a piece of lambskin parchment inscribed with Hebrew characters was supposed to give the best chance of success, especially if the soothsayer opened the proceedings with a Latin prayer (*"O Deus Creator omnium, qui firmamentum pulchritudine stellarum formasti, constituens eas in signa et tempora, infunde virtutem tuam operibus nostris, ut per opus in eis consequamur affectum"*) and intoned two verses from the psalms (*"Domine, dilexi decorem domus tuae et locum habitationis tuae, Domine Deus virtutum, converte nos, ostende faciem suam, et salvi crimus"*) when he introduced the cock. Whether the letters were chosen by swooning, a rolling ring or a hungry cock, the soothsayer's job was to make up words from them and use these as the basis of divination.

All these methods used an extroverted intuition. The soothsayer was turning his powers on the apparatus, on the enquirer and on his problem in the hope of achieving a helpful synthesis. But there is another kind of intuition, by which we look inwards, not outwards. Many techniques of divination dispense with a soothsayer and call on the enquirer to use his own insight in drawing whatever conclusions are right *for him.* Books have often been used for this purpose (bibliomancy), especially Virgil and the Bible. The idea is to formulate a question and then open the book at random. The answer is supposed to lie in the first passage the enquirer reads. Occasionally, the prediction or advice is clear and accurate. Lord Falkland, Secretary of State, suggested that King Charles I try the *Sortes Virgilianae* (Virgilian oracle) while browsing in the Bodleian Library at Oxford. It was 1642, the year in which the Civil War started. The King's choice fell on Book IV of the *Aeneid* at line 615. Sadly, he read:

> at bello audacis populi vexatus et armis,
> finibus extorris, complexu avulsus Iuli
> auxilium imploret videatque indigna suorum
> funera; . . .

("But shaken by the armed uprising of a reckless people, driven from his territories and torn from the embrace of his [grandson] Julius, he begged for help and saw his friends undeservedly murdered.") This prediction was to prove only too true.

Moslems have similarly used the Koran and Christians the Bible. In his *Confessions,* St. Augustine tells how he was torn between the delights of the flesh and the claims of Christianity, when he heard a child singing a song with the chorus "Take it and read, take it and read." He hurried home and opened a book containing Paul's epistles. His eyes fell on Romans XIII; 13–14 : "Let us walk honestly, as in the day; not in rioting and drunkenness, not in chambering and wantonness, not in strife and envying. But put ye on the Lord Jesus Christ, and make not provision for the flesh, to fulfil the lusts thereof." The incident marked the turning point of Augustine's long drawn out conversion. Though he regarded bibliomancy as mere superstition when used to foretell the future, he held it in high esteem as a spiritual guide. So later did Bunyan, Wesley and other Christian leaders.

A form of divination which relies heavily on personal insight is that based on the *I Ching* or *Book of Changes,* which was compiled during the reign of the Chinese King Wen at the beginning of the second millennium B.C. from much earlier sources. Later additions suggest the material as a whole spans a thousand years. It was revered by Confucius (551–479 B.C.) and has recently come into vogue in the West. Paperback editions have appeared on both sides of the Atlantic and London shops sell bundles of yarrow stalks which were traditionally manipulated to consult the *I Ching* as an oracle. Alternatively, three coins can be tossed. Either way, a hexagram or symbol of six complete or broken lines is built up and explained by reference to interpretations in the book itself. These are complicated, metaphorical and allusive, mixing crisp practical advice with generalized observations about the sixty-four basic situations discussed.

P.K., if it exists, could influence the tossed coins or the manipulated yarrow stalks. More than any other method of divination we have so far discussed, however, the *I Ching* calls into play our insight into ourselves. It is not a rag-bag of fortune-teller's tags but an attempt to describe the eternal flux of nature which the ancient Greek philosopher Heraclitus of Ephesus (*c.* 540–*c.* 475 B.C.) summed up in the phrase "everything flows." At the same time, it seeks to illustrate the *un*changing laws that govern change and suggests a course of action It does not foretell our fate. It shows how we can master fate. Wherever we dip into the *I Ching* we are dipping into the stream of life and can find help by thinking over whatever passage we happen to light on. I had a personal example of this when I myself consulted it. After building up a hexagram by tossing coins, I turned to the interpretation and thought, "How appropriate." Only then did I notice that I had turned to the wrong interpretation. Leaving aside the possibility that my mistake was itself a product of P.K. or a meaningful psychological slip, I found the correct interpretation and after reflection, was surprised to find it was just as apt as the one I had mistakenly consulted.

A sceptic would probably regard this as clear proof that the *I Ching* is nonsense. I take the opposite view. *Wherever* we open it, the ancient oracle makes sense. Let us examine a passage which I am now choosing at random from the Richard Wilhelm translation, rendered into English by Cary F. Baynes (Routledge, U.K., 1951). The books falls open at situation 43, which is "Kuai—breakthrough (resoluteness)." The underying idea is "a breakthrough after a long accumulation of tension, as a swollen river bursts through its dikes, or in the manner of a cloudburst." Next comes a rhymed "Judgement", which reads in translation,

> Breakthrough. One must resolutely make the
> matter known at the courts of the king.
> It must be announced truthfully. Danger.
> It is necessary to notify one's own city.
> It does not further to resort to arms.
> It furthers one to undertake something.

The implications of the "Judgement" are then explained: the unavoidable need to fight for good against evil but only according to certain rules, rejecting compromise but combining strength with friendliness. We must not use direct force because we shall "ourselves get entangled in hatred and passion" and evil will have conquered. For this reason, it is important to look into ourselves to make sure that no passions remain to obscure reason. "In this way, finding no opponent, the sharp edges of the weapons of evil become dulled. For the same reason, we should not combat our own faults directly. As long as we wrestle with them, they continue victorious. Finally, the best way to fight evil is to make energetic progress in the good." Pithy verses with their accompanying commentaries fill another three pages, but it is clear from the sections quoted that the whole is a distillation of traditional wisdom that could give practical help on almost any problem posed, and the same is true of the interpretations of the other sixty-three hexagrams.

I say *could* give practical help because the nature of the enquirer and the spirit in which he turns to the *I Ching* are all important. In his introduction, Wilhelm says that "All individuals are not equally fitted to consult the oracle. It requires a clear and tranquil mind. . . ." The idea of manipulating yarrow stalks may seem strange to us but the yarrow was regarded as a sacred plant and presumably helped the enquirer approach the *I Ching* with the necessary seriousness. The procedure "works," according to Wilhelm, because it "makes it possible for the Unconscious in man to become active."

This is surely the essence. We shall get no straight answers from the *I Ching*. If we ask "Shall I win the football pools?" it will not answer "Yes" or "No," but however the yarrow stalks fall, it will plunge us into an all-embracing philosophy of life. If we reflect on this philosophy and use our subjective intuition to apply it to our own situation, we shall find guidance of a different sort. Depending on circumstances, we might be brought to ask ourselves, "Do I truly want to win the pools? Or am I happier as I am? Is the dream of wealth a fantasy which distracts me from the boredom and lack of satisfaction I feel in everyday life? Would it perhaps be better to devote the time, money and mental energy I now spend on the pools to tackling those problems directly?"

Wilhelm sums up, "In its judgements, and in the interpretations attached to it from the time of Confucius on, the Book of Changes opens to the reader the richest treasure of Chinese wisdom; at the same time, it affords him a comprehensive view of the varieties of human experience, enabling him thereby to shape his life of his own sovereign will into an organic whole and so direct it that it comes into accord with the ultimate tao [universal principle] lying at the root of all that exists." To put it another way, the *I Ching's* very comprehensiveness and, on occasion, vagueness enables the enquirer to find in it answers appropriate to the facts of a situation or to his own innermost needs. When he finally acts, he will do so with the full benefit of his reflection. Assuming he believes in the method, he can be *sure* that he is embarking on the right course. What more could one wish from any oracle?

5   Gazing into the Future

Crystal gazing, crystal vision, crystallomancy or scrying is now one of the less fashionable forms of divination, rarely to be found outside the fortune-teller's booth at the fairground, race-course or seaside promenade. Yet in an earlier generation, Waite (*op. cit.*) claimed it was "undoubtedly one of the most innocent, pleasing and successful methods of minor magical practice, and it is one which can be reproduced by an operator at the present day with considerable facility." All that was necessary was a sphere or ovoid of glass, crystal, water-green beryl or any other precious stone. Ancient books of magic insisted on an elaborate ritual requiring candles, compasses, a sword of pure steel, a hazel wand and a frame engraved with the words "Tetragrammaton" at the north, "Emanuel" at the east, "Agla" at the south and "Adonay" at the west, but Waite quoted approvingly the simplified rules advised by a "practised student of the subject."

These rules were, "Keep the crystal clean. Don't be too liberal in allowing strangers to handle it, except if you are going to look for them, when they ought to hold it in their hands for a few minutes. Hold the crystal between fingers and thumb, or on a table, if flat at the end. If the crystal appears hazy or dull, it is a true sign that you will see; the crystal will subsequently clear, and the forms manifest. If it be required to see events which are taking place at a distance, say, in Australia, look lengthwise through the crystal, when, if you can see at all, you are likely to accomplish your object." Visions rarely appeared immediately and various exponents have estimated that it took anything between five seconds and twenty minutes before the clouds dispersed and clear pictures formed. It was claimed by one adept that at least three people in ten had the gift of crystal vision.

Before we discuss its precise nature, we must be quite clear that the gift does in fact exist. There are innumerable well-attested cases. A crystal ball is not essential. Visions may be seen in small mirrors, cups or basins of water or wine, lakes or wells, polished stones, finger-nails, eyes, soap-bubbles or sword-blades. Jung describes the case of a jilted lover who stood on a bridge and gazed at the stars reflected in the river beneath. They seemed to him pairs of heavenly lovers forever linked together. He decided to join them and was found by police trying to break into a nearby observatory in the middle of the night.

In *Crystal-Gazing* (Rider, U.K., 1924), Theodore Besterman shows that the "speculatory art" has been practised in almost every age and culture from Egypt to the Congo, from Persia to Australia, from Malaya to Mexico, from Siberia to Samoa. He mentions springs at Patrae, Cyanae and Taenarum which were used for scrying by the ancient Greeks. Another method was to fill "certain round glasses with fair water about which they placed lighted torches : then invoked the question to be solved. A chaste and unpolluted boy, or a woman big with child, was appointed to observe with the greatest care and exactness all the alterations in the glasses : at the same time desiring, beseeching and also commanding an answer, which at length the demon (god) used to return by images in the glasses, which by reflections from the water represented that which should come to pass." The Romans, the British Druids, the Saxons and many of the peoples of mediaeval Europe are thought to have practised scrying and in 1467, William Byg of Wombwell, Yorkshire, confessed to using his crystal for the recovery of stolen property and was forced to recant, burn his books, and walk at the head of a procession through York Cathedral with a placard reading "Sortilegus" [Soothsayer] round his neck.

Giuseppe Balsamo (1743–95), better known as Count Alessandro di Cagliostro, was another adept. A Palermo, Sicily, grocer's son, he spent his early adult life wandering around Europe as a jobbing artist. He was a cheat and a charlatan and is best known for his part in the Diamond Necklace scandal, but he also had a genuine interest in alchemy, astrology and various forms of magic. In Courland, an independent principality south of the gulf of Riga, he used the young son of Chamberlain Count von der Howen as a scrying medium. At one public demonstration, the boy gazed into a globe-shaped carafe of pure water standing between two lighted candles and said he could see his sister clutching her breast and then embracing her soldier brother. The Count was puzzled because his daughter was in good health and his son on active service many miles away. When he returned home, he found that his son had been unexpectedly granted leave and that his daughter had severe heart pains at the time of the scrying. Cagliostro clinched his fame in Courland by predicting a man's death a month before he committed suicide and by having his boy medium call up the Archangel Michael.

The Englishman Dr. John Dee (1527–1608) had a more serious interest in scrying. Educated at Chelmsford Grammar School, St. John's College, Cambridge and the University of Louvain in Belgium, he won an international reputation as a mathematician, astronomer and geographer and kept up a lifelong correspondence with some of the leading scholars of Europe. He was also a cleric with extensive medical knowledge and made his name as an alchemist and astrologer while still a young man. He was asked by Robert Dudley to choose a propitious date for Queen Elizabeth's coronation. Tall, slim and bearded, he soon became a familiar figure at court and was on easy terms with Walsingham and Burleigh. More than once, the Queen visited his home at Mortlake. Unfortunately, his investigations aroused fear and suspicion among the ignorant and soon after his departure for the Continent, a mob broke into his home, smashed up much of his equipment and destroyed many of the 4,000 volumes in his library.

Dee probably became interested in crystal-gazing through his study of optics and on May 25th, 1581, wrote in his diary, "I had sight in Chrystallo offered me, and I saw." (Quoted by Charlotte Fell Smith in *John Dee,* Constable, U.K., 1909).

> However, he felt that he would make more progress by using a medium, and after contacting the angel Annael through a preacher called Barnabas Saul, he worked with a Mr. Edward Talbot who had been introduced by a friend.
> He (Talbot) settled himself to the Action, and on his knees at my desk, setting the stone before him, fell to prayer and entreaty, etc. In the mean space, I in my Oratory did pray and make motion to God and his good creatures for the furthering of this Action. And within one quarter of an hour (or less) he had sight of one in the stone. (Quoted by Smith, *op. cit.*)

The angel was Uriel, the Spirit of Light. In a series of sittings, it was ordered that Talbot and Dee work together, setting the crystal on a special table with a large seal in the centre and similar, smaller shields under each leg. The underside of each seal was to be inscribed with a mystical cross with the letters A G A L, initials of the Hebrew words meaning "Thou art great for ever, O Lord," set in the quarters. The upper sides must each carry a chequer-board of forty-nine squares inscribed with the seven names of God. In one of his appearances, the Archangel Michael presented Dee with a seal on a ring.

Towards the end of 1582, Dee discovered that "Edward Talbot" was really Edward Kelley, a former apothecary's apprentice of twenty-seven, who had been pilloried for forgery in Lancaster and charged with digging up a dead body at Walton-le-Dale, Lancashire, for the purpose of necromancy. After a row, the two were reconciled and any lingering doubts Dee may have had disappeared when a child angel appeared in the rays of the setting sun and presented him with a new crystal or "shewstone," which was "most bright, most clear and glorious, of the bigness of an egg." St. Michael also appeared and told him that he and Kelley must work together as master and man. They continued their work with the new stone, Dee a learned, other-worldly, almost saintly man of fifty-six, who was deeply respected at court and had secured the support of leading mathematicians for his scheme of calendar reform; Kelley disturbed, even violent, on the make, genuinely psychic but always ready to doctor his visions to his own advantage. They called up spirits both evil and good, and Kelley had premonitions of the execution of Mary Queen of Scots and the appearance of the Spanish Armada, four and five years ahead respectively.

Dee's fame was international. During a visit to England, Albert Laski, the dashing but impoverished Count Palatine of Siradia in Poland, called on him several times and finally invited him back to the Continent. Dee set off with his wife and three children, together with Kelley and *his* young wife. They travelled with Laski's party in a succession of small boats to Amsterdam, and thence to Emden, Bremen, Hamburg, Lübeck and Cracow, holding numerous sittings on the way. The Dees rented a house in Cracow and the Kelleys moved in with them but Kelley, never an easy partner, now threatened to give up scrying altogether.

More rows followed, which Dee patiently bore. Meanwhile, Laski had been travelling widely in an effort to raise money. Dee and Kelley were becoming desperate. Shuttling between Cracow and Prague, they tried to interest Rudolph II, Emperor of Austria, and then Stephen, King of Poland, in a project to discover the philosopher's stone, which would transmute base metals into gold. It was the age-old dream of the alchemists who were then highly influential in Prague, but Dee confidently believed that the secret would be given to him by the spirits seen in his shewstone. Both Rudolph and Stephen were sceptical. Kelley angrily threatened to return to England. Expelled from Prague by papal edict after popular disapproval of their dabbling in "magic," Dee and Kelley moved first to Erfurt and then to Cassel and Gotha. Finally, they all settled at Trebona Castle in Southern

Prediction and Prophecy

Bohemia under the protection of their new patron, Count Rosenberg.

Kelley was now convinced that he could gain more from his private alchemical experiments than from working as Dee's scryer but he seems to have been incapable of making a clean break. There were still more rows and threats. He even started to train Dee's seven-year-old son Arthur to scry in his place but the boy made little progress. Then came the most startling sitting of all.

A nine-years-old girl called Madimi had, said Kelley, appeared naked in the crystal. She had ordered them to share everything, including their wives. This was fine for Kelley, who hated his wife Joan. Dee, who loved his warm, capable wife Jane, was appalled. He rebuked Madimi but she insisted.

Dee debated with Kelley until two a.m. Finally, he gave in and broke the news to his wife, who was still awake. " 'Jane,' I said, 'I can see there is no other remedy, but as hath been said of our cross-matching, so it must needs be done.' " (Quoted by Smith, *op. cit.*). Mrs. Dee wept, implored, even raged. She had always disliked Kelley. Of all the discomforts and indignities brought on her by her over-trusting husband, this was the bitterest. Yet after a quarter of an hour, her loyalty overcame her repugnance. "I trust", she said, "that though I gave myself thus to be used, that God will turn me into a stone before he would suffer me in my obedience to receive any shame or inconvenience." (Quoted by Smith, *op. cit.*) Next morning, she and Mrs. Kelley insisted on a second scrying session for the arrangement to be confirmed. Madimi was adamant, and Dee composed a document promising obedience not in lust but in Christian charity. All four signed it. Dee thought of the agreement more as an expression of mutual love than a basis for action. He placed it on the altar of the castle chapel and prayed for God's help. Kelley's nerve broke at last. He ripped up the paper and blazed into a tantrum. The scrying was finally at an end. After further adventures, Dee returned safely home to England with his family and was later granted the wardenship of Christ's College, Manchester. He died at the age of eighty and was buried in the chancel of Mortlake church.

Meanwhile, Kelley continued his alchemical researches and used them as an entrée to the court of the Emperor Rudolph, who granted him a minor title. As Sir Edward, he found life as a courtier more exacting than his service with Dee. A jealous rival planted doubts in Rudolph's mind. Three times the Emperor called on Sir Edward to explain himself. Three times Sir Edward sent his excuses. He was arrested and imprisoned in the Castle of Pürglitz near Prague for two years. After a brief period of freedom, he was again arrested and shortly afterwards fell from a high turret. Did he jump or was he pushed? We shall never know. At forty, Sir Edward Kelley was dead.

Since Dee and Kelley, innumerable scryers have reported their experiences. They have seen visions on the surface of their crystal, as well as in it and behind it. They have watched figures move, heard them speak and in a few cases have marvelled at their brilliant colours. Most have appeared life-size. Many scryers prefer to shade their crystal with a black cloth to exclude reflections and refer to a milky cloud which clears away to reveal the image. A few, however, concentrate on reflections or highlights and allow their visions to grow out of these. Some seem to be fully conscious during scrying, others in a state of deep self-hypnosis. Many apparently drift into the no-man's-land between sleep and waking which everyone finds conducive to day-dreams. The evidence compels us to believe that they see *something* but what exactly is it? How does it get into the crystal? And where does it come from in the first place?

Besterman summed up his investigations into many kinds of scrying like this: "Scrying is a method of bringing into the consciousness of the scryer by means of a speculum [crystal] through one or more of his senses the content of his subconsciousness, or rendering him more susceptible to the reception of telepathically transmitted concepts, and of bringing into operation a latent and unknown faculty of perception." If we substitute the more generally accepted "unconscious" for "subconsciousness," this definition is hard to fault. Most of us have had the experience of seeing visions, if only fleetingly. I well remember travelling on a Manchester Corporation bus past a hoarding on which the name and trademark of a well-known petrol company were displayed. At that time, the company was running an advertising campaign which featured a nubile young woman in a cowboy hat flourishing a hose with a large nozzle. Although she did not appear on this particular hoarding, I distinctly "saw" her, complete with hat and hose. Within a fraction of a second, the picture faded and I found myself staring at the unadorned name and trademark of the petrol company. Clearly, my unconscious had carried the image of the young woman, which association had catapulted into consciousness and simultaneously projected on to the hoarding. It seems reasonable to assume that genuine scryers are able to bring unconscious material into consciousness and project it visually into their crystal. But of what does the unconscious material consist?

It could, of course, be literally anything. Some scryers have used their gift for the most trivial purposes, discovering in the crystal an unconscious memory of where they left a lost or mislaid object, such

71

as a doctor's prescription or bunch of keys. Others have told of night-marish visions in which they were chased by terrifying animals or murderous assailants. Clearly, they were projecting into the crystal unconscious anxieties of the kind usually revealed in dreams. The "spirits" of the Dee-Kelley experiments could be interpreted as personifications of mental elements, some good, some evil, which had previously failed to reach consciousness. These too may appear in dreams. There are many recorded cases of scryers seeing objects suggested by others, one of the most famous being that of Miss A. Goodrich-Freer, a well-known British scryer, who discovered her powers when as a child she was handed a crystal and told to look for soldiers. She saw soldiers. There have been clairvoyant scryers who were able to describe with uncanny accuracy events, of which they could not possibly have known, happening many miles away at the same moment as they saw them in the crystal. Typical of these was the Count von der Howen's young son who, as we noted earlier, worked with Cagliostro and saw in a carafe of water the return home of his soldier brother and his sister's heart attack. Telepathic scryers are different again : they have seen events about which other people have been thinking and as with the clairvoyants, we must assume that knowledge of these events came into their unconscious by means which we do not yet understand and were then projected into the crystal.

In his book, *The Making of Religion* (Longman, U.K., 1898; AMS Press, U.S.A., 1971), Andrew Lang, a former president of the Society for Psychical Research, who made a special study of scrying, described a case which seemed to combine both telepathy and clair-voyance. The scryer was "Miss Angus." She lived with her family in Scotland and one evening, they invited to dinner an Englishman who was visiting the town. "He dined with her family," writes Lang,

> and about 10.15 to 10.30 p.m. she proposed to look into the glass for a scene or person of whom he was to think. He called up a mental picture of a ball at which he had recently been, and of a young lady to whom he had there been introduced. The lady's face, however, he could not clearly visualise, and Miss Angus reported nothing but a view of an empty ballroom, with a polished floor and waxed lights. The gentleman made another effort and remembered his partner with some distinctness. Miss Angus then described another room, not a ballroom, comfortably furnished, in which a girl with brown hair drawn back from her forehead, and attired in a high-necked white blouse, was reading, or writing

letters, under a bright light in an unshaded glass globe. The description of the features, figure and height tallied with Mr. —'s recollection; but he had never seen this Geraldine of an hour except in ball dress. He and Miss Angus noted the time by their watches (it was 10.30), and Mr. — said that on the first opportunity, he would ask the young lady how she had been dressed and how employed at that hour in December 21st (1897).

On December 22nd, he met her at another dance, and her reply corroborated the crystal picture. She had been writing letters, in a high-necked white blouse, under an incandescent gas-lamp with an unshaded glass globe. She was entirely unknown to Miss Angus, and had only been seen once by Mr —. Mr. — and the lady of the crystal picture corroborated all this in writing. We clearly have a case in which some of the information for the crystal vision could have been telepathically "transmitted" to the scryer while the rest could only have been perceived directly by the unconscious mind.

Perhaps the most interesting cases of all are those where scryers have apparently been able to see visions of events that were still in the future. These cases cannot be explained by telepathy, by intuition or even by psychokinesis. The best of them predict events so unlikely that we can rule out the possibility of the scryer's making hopeful guesses. They are not vague generalizations but precise and detailed accounts.

One such case was reported to the Society for Psychical Research by Sir William Barrett, F.R.S., a former president of the society, in 1923 (*Journal of the Society for Psychical Research,* 1923–24.) The scryer was Miss Nell St. John Montague who explained that she had called on a friend identified as Mrs. R. on April 14th, 1920. Mrs. R. had a guest, whom she called Mrs. Holt, and this Mrs. Holt was eager to have a crystal reading. Fortunately, Miss Montague lived close by, so a servant was sent round to collect her crystal ball and when it arrived, Mrs. Holt was asked to hold it. "When I took it from her hands and looked into it," said Miss Montague, "I experienced a terrible shock." Seeing her consternation, Mrs. Holt insisted on an explanation. "I warned her as delicately as I could that a gruesome tragedy was before her, an awful deed which would make her a widow almost immediately. To her relief, Mrs. Holt laughed it off but Miss Montague jotted down a note of her vision.

I can see a tall fair man, rather bald, pacing up and down a small room, evidently a smoking room, close beside the desk is a telephone, he is excitedly taking up the receiver and speaking into it, he opens a drawer in the desk and holds an object taken from it in his right hand—it is a revolver—again he speaks into the receiver excitedly and watches the closed door on the left eagerly. Once more he speaks into the receiver, and for a moment points the revolver in the direction of the door—apparently listening for someone to come—he makes a gesture of angry despair, and for the third time takes the receiver in his left hand, whilst his face, working with frenzied emotion, seems to shout into the telephone—he waits once more, pointing the revolver at the door—he turns his face and seems to stare out of the crystal, there is a tragedy of despair in his eyes. With a sudden gesture he looks once more at the door and shakes his head as though giving up hope of it opening to admit someone for whom he seems to be waiting. He raises his right hand and staggers back, the revolver is now pointing at his own head—then I see blood everywhere gushing. A woman comes into the room, the same woman who is in the room with me now [*i.e.* Mrs. Holt], only in the picture she wears a loose wrapper, she lifts his head—blood is everywhere.

Three days later, Mr. R. called on Miss Montague with a message from Mrs. R. He was in a hurry. Mr. Holt, he explained, had rung him three times within minutes and wished to see him immediately, as "he wanted to take him with him." Miss Montague remembered the crystal vision. She urged Mr. R. not to go. He did not understand her alarm and was anxious to be on his way, but she kept him arguing for some fifteen minutes, after which he rang Mr. Holt on Mrs. Montague's telephone. There was no reply. He left immediately, and Miss Montague went to see her doctor, Dr. Sloan Chesser, with whom she had an appointment, telling her maid she could be reached there in case she was wanted. No sooner had she arrived than she was called to the telephone. It was Mr. R., phoning from the private hotel where Mr. Holt lived. On ringing the doorbell, he said, he had heard a shot and shortly afterwards was told that Mr. Holt had shot himself. When found he was lying with a revolver in his hand.

The circumstances of Mr. Holt's death corresponded with the account given by Miss Montague of her crystal vision. The three telephone calls, the expectation of a visitor, the suicide by revolver were all clearly predicted. They are not the sort of details that a charlatan would be likely to hit on by chance and even if we supposed that Miss Montague's intuition was so highly developed that she could sense in Mrs. Holt an unspoken, perhaps not fully conscious, fear that her husband was in imminent danger of killing himself, the three telephone calls and the expectation of a visitor who failed to arrive could not possibly have been in Mrs. Holt's mind for Miss Montague to intuit.

Can we really be sure that Miss Montague did see the vision prior to Mr. Holt's suicide and did not fabricate, or imagine, it later? Sir William investigated the case fully. He found that Mr. Holt, who was thirty-eight, had served in the Army in France and had also been in Dublin during the Irish rebellion. He had suffered from shell-shock and was clearly disturbed at the time of his suicide. For some reason, he felt the need of a friend to join him in death and had chosen Mr. R. for the role. These facts are confirmed in a news report published in the *Daily Mail* for Monday, April 19th, 1920. As for Miss Montague's vision, no witness was produced to show that she had revealed the details in advance but Mrs. Holt told Sir William in an interview witnessed by the Society's research officer that Miss Montague had predicted "that she would be a widow within two days," and when Sir William asked to see the notes which Miss Montague said she had made immediately after the sitting, she was able to produce them. They were, said Sir William, "hastily written in pencil, but are word for word exactly as she has transcribed them in her narrative."

Could the notes themselves have been written after the event? This is obviously *possible* but there was ample evidence that Miss Montague had been seriously worried on the morning of April 17th. Dr. Chesser recalled that there had been a telephone call for her during the consultation and Mr. R. confirmed in writing her account of what happened. "An April 17th, 1920," he wrote, "when I called on Miss Montague, I told her I was going to see Mr. Holt; she implored me not to go and kept me talking for nearly a quarter of an hour. Then I left and drove to Mr. Holt's house. After ringing his front door bell, I heard the report of a pistol. . . . I owe my life to Miss Montague's warning." Finally, both Miss Montague and Mr. R. attended a meeting of the Society and, says Sir William, answered very fully and satisfactorily the numerous questions asked by the members. Thus there is no conclusive evidence that Miss Montague saw in the crystal all the details which she later said she had seen (as there would have been, for instance, if she had deposited her notes with an independent witness *before* the suicide), but nevertheless, there is strong circumstantial evidence in her favour. At the very least, she prophesied to Mrs. Holt that her husband would shortly die.

Prediction and Prophecy

The Holt case is far from isolated. Almost all of us have first-hand, or good second-hand knowledge of predictions that came true. As a student, my own wife consulted a fortune-teller "as a joke" and was told she was in love with another student, myself, who would shortly ask her to marry him. Three months later, I did so. A friend of mine described a visit to a West London clairvoyant, now dead, who was long famous for the accuracy of her predictions.

She had a tiny flat and her "waiting-room" was the kitchen. It was filthy. There was a pile of unwashed pots in the sink and grease-stains all over the floor. It was quite a sight to see all these well-dressed women sitting around. Several wore mink coats. When your turn came, you had to go along to her bedroom at the end of the passage. It was as dirty and untidy as the kitchen with piles of books, tatting, household linen covering most of the floor. She herself was sitting up in bed, a frowzy old woman who kept taking swigs of gin from a bottle on her bedside table.

Despite the squalor of the "consulting room," clients returned again and again, some of them over a period of twenty years or more. Many introduced their friends:

I took in an Italian girl who was living in North London with her widowed mother. As soon as she saw her, the old woman said, "Your father died recently" and when my friend nodded, she added, "He was drowned." This was true and though you might think it pretty far-fetched for her to have hit on both death and drowning, which is a pretty unusual way to die these days, she could have made an intelligent guess. My friend was still pretty distraught and she looked Italian and had a fairly strong Italian accent. Her father had, in fact, been a passenger on an Italian cruise liner which had recently sunk and there had been a good deal of publicity about it. So the old lady could have put two and two together.

But then she went on to tell my friend about the future and this time, there could be no possible explanation. "I don't want to distress you, dearie," she said, "but your mother's going to have an accident pretty soon and she won't live very long afterwards. I see you've also got a brother?" My friend said she had, and the old woman went on, "He won't live much longer than your mother. But I *can* say that nothing unpleasant is going to happen to you personally and that you'll make a new home for

yourself across the water." My friend came out of the consultation absolutely shaken but she couldn't really believe it was all
going to happen. Her mother was elderly but reasonably fit and
there seemed no reason why she should die. Her brother was
hundreds of miles away in Italy and in the best of health. Yet
everything the old woman said came true. First her mother fell
down the stairs of their London flat, broke a thigh and died soon
afterwards in hospital. Six months later, her brother was killed
in a car crash in Italy. My friend could see no future for herself
in Britain and she went to join some relatives in America. When
last I heard from her, she was successfully building a new life
for herself "over the water."

Some present-day crystal-gazers have gone on to predict public
events as well as private. One of the best known is the American
Mrs. Jeane Dixon of Washington, D.C., who has scored a remarkable number of hits since a gypsy sensed her prophetic powers and
presented her with a crystal ball when she was only eight years
old. A year later, she was advising Marie Dressler against opening
an hotel and insisted she persevered with her career. Miss Dressler
did so and became one of America's best-known actresses. Later,
she advised film actress Carole Lombard against travelling by plane.
Miss Lombard ignored her and shortly afterwards died in a plane
crash. She went on to foretell President Roosevelt's election victories
and his death; Sir Winston Churchill's election defeat after the war;
the murder of Gandhi; the communist revolution in China; the
election victories of Presidents Truman and Eisenhower; the succession of Bulganin and Khrushchev in the U.S.S.R.; Dag Hammer-
skjold's plane crash; Marilyn Monroe's suicide; and the assassina-
tions of U.S. Senator Robert F. Kennedy and of the black moderate
leader, Martin Luther King. In recent years, Mrs. Dixon's most
famous prediction was that of President Kennedy's assassination.
Justine Glass tells the story (*op. cit.*). As long ago as 1952, Mrs.
Dixon had a vision while sitting in St. Matthew's Cathedral,
Washington, in which she "saw" a blue-eyed Democrat win the
Presidential election of 1960, only to be assassinated during his
term of office. No one can claim that Mrs. Dixon conveniently "remembered" her prediction after the event. On May 13th, 1956,
writer Jack Anderson published an interview in *Parade* magazine,
in which he reported, "As for the 1960 election, Mrs. Dixon thinks
it will be won by a Democrat. But he will be assassinated in office."
For the next seven years, Mrs. Dixon had further premonitions of

the President's death, some of which she mentioned to friends of his family. They became more and more precise, referring first to a shooting and then to a bullet in the head. On November 22nd, 1963, the day on which he made his fatal ride through Houston, Texas, she had a breakfast-time vision of a White House covered with black drapes. She even foresaw that the assassin would be a man with a six-lettered name of two syllables. The first letters would be "Os" and the last letter "went straight up." It was a fair stab at "Oswald."

No power that we have yet discussed could possibly explain a prediction so precise in its details. We can reasonably assume that the visions came from Mrs. Dixon's unconscious. But how did they get there? Unless we assume she was a female Mephistopheles controlling Lee Harvey Oswald, by some mechanism that transcended time and space, psychokinesis does not come into it. Nor could it be claimed that her prediction acted by suggestion. After all, President Kennedy did not will his own death actively or passively and there is no evidence that he even knew of Mrs. Dixon's prediction. Intuition is ruled out because the first vision in 1953 came far too early for there to be the remotest evidence for even the unconscious mind to work on. Telepathy takes place only in the present and clairvoyance is the apprehension of remote objects or happenings, again in the present.

Does this mean that man possesses some faculty whereby he can see into the future? If so, can we prove it exists, other than by anecdotal evidence? Can we produce its effects under laboratory conditions?

Once again, it must be emphasized that we are investigating phenomena that lie on the boundaries of human experience. While many scientists would agree that their existence has been proved beyond reasonable doubt and that they cannot yet be explained by the known laws of science, some insist that it is only a matter of time before new discoveries will place them within accepted chains of cause and effect. Others, equally reputable, believe we are dealing with a human faculty which orthodox Western science has tended to ignore or discredit, the power of precognition—the ability to know about things *before* they happen. But what is the evidence for precognition, other than striking but admittedly unscientific examples of the kind we have already discussed?

As with P.K., the story starts at Duke University, North Carolina, U.S.A., where Dr. Joseph Banks Rhine and his wife Dr. Louise E. Rhine studied psychic, E.S.P. or "psi" phenomena throughout the 1930s. Besides P.K., they were interested in clairvoyance, the ability to see mentally things and happening that are out of sight, and also in telepathy, the direct transference of thoughts from one person to another without any help from the known senses. In passing, it is worth noticing that it is sometimes very difficult to distinguish between the two. If I mentally see a bus in the next town, how can I tell whether I am "seeing" it direct or reading the mind of someone in the next town who is seeing the bus physically with his eyes?

Rhine evolved techniques for distinguishing between the two and carried out tests with ordinary playing cards. These proved unsatisfactory. Most people have preconceived ideas about certain cards. The ace of clubs is considered unlucky, and so too is the four of clubs ("the devil's bedstead"). The nine of diamonds is widely known as "the Curse of Scotland," perhaps because the Earl of Stair, who was partly responsible for the massacre of Glencoe, had nine lozenges on his arms. It was found that these preconceptions interfered with clairvoyant or telepathic messages (if there were any) and Rhine looked for an alternative. He devised a pack of twenty-five cards, five of which were marked with a cross, five with a star, five with a circle, five with a square and five with wavy lines. They became known as Zener cards and worked well. Rhine and his colleagues conducted many carefully controlled experiments which seemed to show that at least some people had the power of clairvoyance and/or telepathy.

One of the many British scientists following Rhine's work with interest was Dr. S. G. Soal, senior lecturer in pure mathematics at Queen Mary College, University of London and a former president of the Society for Psychical Research. At first Soal was sceptical. He himself had been carrying out a series of experiments with Frederick Marion who was then well known as a music-hall telepathist. In one of them, Marion was given the Queen of Diamonds from a newly-opened pack of cards and after handling it for a few moments, left the room. Soal picked out five more cards at random, laid them face down on a table and called Marion in again. Marion lightly touched the back of each card and turned one up. It was the Queen of Diamonds. Any music-hall audience would have been convinced. But not Soal. In *Modern Experiments in Telepathy* (Faber, U.K., 1954; Yale U.P., U.S.A., 1954), he and his co-author F. Bateman state, "We soon discovered by means of certain tests that what Marion recognized was the actual piece of pasteboard which he had previously touched, and not the value on the face of the card. . . . His constant tapping on the backs of the cards as they lay on the table suggested that he was examining the contact which the different parts of the card made with the wooden surface." Soal tried further experiments in which Marion was not allowed to touch the cards on the table. He was consistently successful but this time it was suspected that he had flexed the chosen card slightly when first handling it. This enabled him to distinguish it from the others on the table. With cards of four-millimetre millboard, which he was allowed to touch on the table, he succeeded nine times out of seventeen, far more often than could be expected by chance, but when the millboard cards were placed in individual envelopes, he failed completely. "Recognition must have been by touch," concluded Soal.

Undeterred by his failure to prove that Marion had clairvoyant or telepathic powers, Soal now tried to reproduce Rhine's American experiments. He tested many different kinds of volunteer including self-styled clairvoyants, trance mediums, an automatic writer, a professional hypnotic subject, Frederick Marion, four members of a Welsh family and London University students from America, China, Egypt, India and most of Western Europe. Basil Shackleton, a well-known photographer, volunteered his services. Then thirty-six, he said he had not come "to be tested but to demonstrate telepathy." He was always astonishing his friends, he claimed, with his gift for guessing cards. Mrs. D. A. Stewart, wife of a consulting engineer, also took part. Her husband claimed she had psychic powers. Soal even invited Mrs. Eileen Garrett, a New Zealand medium, who had been one of Rhine's star performers. In clairvoyance tests at Duke University, she had scored 888 hits out of 3,525, the odds against this happening by chance being 100,000,000,000 to 1. Her results in telepathy tests were even better—336 correct out of 625. In London, Soal used the same strict conditions insisted on by Rhine. He ran both clairvoyance tests and tests in which either clairvoyance *or* telepathy could have been used. He did not test for telepathy alone. Over five years, 16 people made 128,350 guesses, all to no avail. The experiments were a total failure. Mrs. Garret's results were totally insignificant and though Mrs. Stewart's were a little above average, they did not mean very much when lumped in with the others.

"Until the autumn of 1939," wrote Soal of himself (*op. cit.*), "he still believed that it was practically impossible, at any rate in England, to find persons who could demonstrate E.S.P. by guessing at the figures on the Zener cards. He drew attention to this record of persistent failure by articles in the Press, and by lectures given to the British Psychological Society in London and in Glasgow, and to the Society of Psychical Research. In November, 1939, this growing scepticism received a shock. . . ."

Unknown to Soal, a time-bomb was ticking away in the archives of his score-sheets. It was to be revealed by Whateley Carington, a scientist with a highly original mind who was himself passionately interested in psychical research. He is best known as the author of a famous experiment in clairvoyance simultaneously involving 741 people in Holland, America and Great Britain. Every night, for ten nights, Carington selected at random a page of Webster's International Dictionary and noted the first object mentioned. His wife made a drawing of it and placed it in his locked study overnight. The 741 subjects then tried to "see" the drawing mentally and reproduced it on a sketch block. The whole process was repeated ten times, and the blocks returned to Carington who tore off the drawings, coded them, shuffled them and passed them to a colleague for comparison with the originals. He had no dates to guide him and gave them a score of 1, ½ or 0 according to their likeness. The number of hits was not significant. But Carington made a surprising discovery. An object chosen for a particular day tended to appear on the days immediately before and after. Some of the distant "artists" were apparently able to "see" both forward into the future and back into the past. It was just as though a pianist had a built-in bias which gave him a tendency to strike not the right note but one immediately above or below it.

Carington discussed these findings with Soal who found them "striking," although he had reservations about Carington's statistical methods. Carington then suggested that Soal reviewed the results of his previous five years' work with Zener cards, looking not for direct hits but for near-misses. In other words, could at least some of Soal's subjects have failed because they had been seeing not the target card but the one that came immediately before or immediately after it? Soal was overwhelmed by Carington's persistence. "It was in no very hopeful spirit," he wrote (*op. cit.*) "that Soal began the task of searching his records for this 'displacement' effect."

Soal turned first to the records of Mrs. Stewart, one of the very few subjects who had achieved better-than-chance results. As he checked through her scores for precognitive hits, *i.e.* those corresponding to the *next* card coming up, and postcognitive hits, *i.e.* those corresponding to the previous card, his excitement mounted. On chance alone, he could have expected 192 of each in the first thousand. In fact, she had 221 postcognitive hits and 225 precognitive hits. "To the amazement of the experimenter," her results on the second thousand were even better—221 postcognitive and 232 precognitive. Soal claimed that the odds against this happening by chance were more than a million to one.

With renewed enthusiasm, he went on to review the records of his other subjects. For almost a month he found nothing of interest. Then in late December, 1939, he came to the score-sheets for Basil Shackleton, the photographer who had been tested in February and March, 1936. In 800 guesses, Shackleton had scored 195 postcognitive hits and 194 precognitive hits, when only 153·6 of each could have been expected by chance.

For the purposes of our own investigation, we are interested in precognition rather than postcognition. In other words, the guessers' ability to predict the next card coming up, not divine the one that has just passed. The question Soal now had to face was whether the so-called precognitive scores really showed precognition, or could the guessers have mentally seen, in the present, the next card which was already waiting to be turned up? To prove precognition, he would have to show that his subjects were not doing this but foretelling the future contents of the card-turner's mind.

Five years of experiments with Mrs. Stewart were highly successful in showing the workings of straightforward telepathy and also of postcognitive telepathy. But they gave little or no evidence of precognitive powers. The breakthrough came with Shackleton. After a year's Army service, he had been discharged on health grounds and by the end of 1940 was once again working as a photographer, this time from a studio in the basement of 51, Shaftesbury Avenue. Soal secured as his assistant Mrs. K. M. Goldney, M.B.E., Assistant Regional Administrator at W.V.S. headquarters in London, who was an experienced psychical investigator. They arranged a long series of experiments with the cards and other apparatus on a table in the studio while Shackleton wrote down his guesses at a desk in an ante-room. There was no possibility of Shackleton or an accomplice seeing the cards. Nor was it possible for any of the experimenters to give him clues consciously or unconsciously. Both Shackleton and the person manipulating the cards were closely watched throughout the experiments and none of those involved had any idea which card would turn up next.

Soal himself, or a colleague, prepared random lists of the numbers one to five and these were handed at the very last moment to an "experimenter" sitting at one side of the table in the studio.

At the other side, behind a three-foot screen pierced only by a small opening, sat the "agent" who shuffled the five target cards and placed them face downwards in a row inside a cardboard box. The experimenter took the first of the random numbers and held up to the opening a board marked with the same number. The agent then glanced briefly at the corresponding card in the box, letting it fall back into place almost immediately.

If the first random number was two, for example, the experimenter held up a board marked "2" to the opening and the agent glanced at the second card from the left. The experimenter then called out the number of this particular try (there were twenty-five in each run) and in the next room, Shackleton wrote his guess on a tabulated score-card. The experimenter then held to the opening a board corresponding with the next random number, and so on.

Later the form of the experiment was varied slightly. Instead of using random numbers, the experimenter drew a counter from a bag or bowl, dropping it back after each call. At times too, the rate of call was doubled. It is worth noting that the experimenter, not the agent, shouted each call to Shackleton. He did not know the card to which the random number or counter referred, so he could not have given hints by his tone of voice. The agent did not speak.

The results of the experiments were exciting. In the tests with random numbers Shackleton guessed the card immediately following the one being called 1,101 times out of a possible 3,789, rather more than 325 times than could be expected by chance. With counters, he made 439 correct precognitive guesses out of 1,578. This was 118 better than chance. In both series, his guesses for the cards which had been or were being called were of no significance. Still more interesting was the effect of doubling the rate of call. Instead of predicting the card immediately following, he tended to guess the one after that, putting him two ahead of the game. This happened 84 times out of 265, more than 30 above chance, in one series of tests; and 236 out of 794, nearly 77 above chance, in another. Again, there was nothing significant about his scores on other cards.

The Soal-Goldney experiments, as they have come to be called, covered many more aspects of E.S.P. Trials were made with non-random numbers and with two agents at once, sometimes acting together, at other times "sending" different cards. Checks were made as to whether the subject's health affected his results and whether he himself could tell in advance whether or not he was likely to be successful. Mrs. Stewart was tested in an X-ray chamber, behind a lead screen and 200 miles away in Antwerp. At one stage, Shackleton suddenly developed postcognitive powers and in one remarkable series at double the usual speed, he tended to be two cards ahead of the game for part of the time and two cards behind for the rest. Only two questions need concern us, however. Were the experiments sound? If so, did Shackleton's precognitive scores mean that he was able to foresee events that were still in the future?

Numerous attempts have been made to discredit Soal and Goldney, some of them highly technical criticisms of his statistical methods. It must suffice here to say that these criticisms have never been generally accepted. The other main line of attack has been to suggest that the experiments were unscientific because of the possibility of fraud. It does not help to point out that Soal and Goldney had no motive for fraud. Neither had the perpetrator of Piltdown Man nor the discoverer of the "Hastings Rarities" in ornithology. It seems incredible, however, that Soal could have gone on faking his procedures or doctoring the results, with or without an accomplice or accomplices, for a whole ten years without being detected.

Still harder to explain on the cheating principle is the origin of the experiments. Until the end of 1939, Soal was highly sceptical of ever achieving successful E.S.P. results in Britain. It was only after Carington persuaded him to review his previous records back to 1936 that he came upon the evidence of precognition that led him to embark on the subsequent experiments. Can we really believe that he would lock up carefully faked results for three years before allowing himself to be persuaded that they should be brought to public notice? Alternatively, can we believe that he doctored the records only when he came to review them in 1939? Why should he? If he wanted to run a series of experiments on telepathy or precognition, he hardly needed the justification of earlier work.

For all practical purposes, we can take it that the Soal-Goldney experiments were soundly conceived, honestly conducted and reliable in their results. But do those results necessarily imply precognition? Soal himself has pointed out (*op. cit.*) that if Shackleton had the gift of clairvoyance, with or without telepathy, he could have "seen" the list of random numbers as well as the cards. By relating them, he could have known exactly which card was going to be "transmitted" next. Alternatively, he could have seen into the minds of both experimenter and agent by telepathy. Admittedly, these would be remarkable feats but no more remarkable than seeing into the future. Even when counters were used, the experimenter could have picked out the next counter with his right hand before replacing the current one with his left. Clairvoyance could again have given Shackleton his clue.

There are two objections to this theory. A series of carefully designed experiments showed that Shackleton was not clairvoyant. Also, he had a remarkable capacity for keeping two jumps ahead of the game when the rate of call was doubled. Even if the experimenter momentarily had one counter in his left hand and another in his right, Shackleton could not deduce which he would pick out next by either clairvoyance (which he did not have anyway) nor by telepathy. But could it be that he himself *influenced* the experimenter to pick a particular counter out of the bag? Again, careful experiments were devised to test whether this was possible. The results were inconclusive.

Soal himself states (*op. cit.*) that the possibility of Shackleton's "being influenced by a future event, *i.e.* the image which was to enter the agent's mind in about three seconds' time, has much to support it." This would explain why he was two jumps ahead of —or sometimes behind—the game, not just one, when the rate of call was doubled. It would also explain why he was equally successful with his precognitive guesses on the first three or four tries in each run using random numbers. Ruling out clairvoyance, he could know about the upcoming numbers by telepathy with the experimenter but he could not know to which cards they referred because the agent herself did not know until she had turned them up during the course of the experiment. Soal concluded (*op. cit.*) "Carington's experiments and those of Soal and Goldney strongly suggested, even if they did not prove, that a person might be aware of the future content of another person's mind without the use of rational inference based on present knowledge."

How is it possible for someone to see into the future in this way? Is our usual conception of time too limited? What other theories have been suggested to explain such anomalies? We shall examine some of these theories in Chapter 7. First, we shall consider a form of precognition that many of us have experienced at some time or another—that found in dreams.

6   Perchance to Dream

The methods of prediction we have discussed so far are non-rational. They are not against reason. They are outside it. They depend on chance and intuition, on strange forces buried in the unconscious and on some little-understood faculty that seems to transcend our usual ideas about time. What of the men and women who pride themselves on their rationality and dismiss oracles and crystal-gazing, tarot and the *I Ching,* as superstitious nonsense? Can they really exclude these unknown quantities from their lives?

Try as they will, they cannot make their lives entirely reasonable. In dreams at least they plunge uncontrollably into a world where the familiar mingles with the fabulous, where the living speak with the dead, where the accepted laws of cause and effect no longer apply, where space contracts and time expands, giving us an insight not only into the past and present but seemingly into the future.

In early times, men had no difficulty in accepting the prophetic quality of dreams. We read in the Old Testament how Gideon's victory over the Midianites was forecast by one of his men who dreamed that a cake of barley bread had fallen on to the Midianite army and had knocked down one of its tents (Judges vii). When Joseph was a captive in Egypt, Pharaoh consulted him about his dream of seven fat kine being eaten by seven lean kine. Joseph correctly predicted that seven years of plenty would be followed by seven years of famine (Genesis xl, xli).

The Greeks and Romans also believed that dreams could be used for divination. According to the Greek historian Herodotus (*c.* 484–424 B.C.), King Croesus of Lydia dreamed that his son Atya would be killed by a sharp-pointed weapon. He forbade Atya to fight or even to take part in military training but Atya resented this molly-coddling and he begged for permission to join a boar hunt. Croesus gave in but insisted on placing him under the personal supervision of Adrastus, the leading huntsman. Ironically, this very precaution was the cause of his death. At the climax of the hunt, Adrastus flung his spear at the boar, missed and killed Atya.

Several Roman emperors, including Julius Caesar, Tiberius, Domitian and Caligula died after warning dreams, and Julian described in a letter to his physician a dream symbolically foretelling his succession as emperor two years in advance. Origen, Tertullian and other Christian Fathers were equally certain that the future might sometimes be revealed in dreams and in his *Confessions,* St. Augustine describes a dream of his mother, Monica, predicting his conversion nine years before it took place. "It seems that divination by dreams is not unlawful," wrote St. Thomas Aquinas in his *Summa Theologica.* "It is the experience of all men that a dream contains some indication of the future. Therefore, it is vain to deny that dreams have efficacy in divination." (Quoted by Norman Mackenzie in *Dreams and Dreaming,* Aldus Books, U.K., 1965; Vanguard, U.S.A., 1965.)

If chance dreams can be used for prediction, why not deliberately plan them? The modern psychotherapist says to his patient, "Perhaps you will have a dream that will throw light on your problem," and the ancients too were well aware of the powers of suggestion. Caves, temples and gloomy vales were thought to be especially conducive to prophetic dreams. In Egypt, the temples of Isis at Philaw, Thoth at Khimunu and I-m-hotep at Memphis were highly favoured. In one famous dream I-m-hotep appeared to Mahituaskit, a suppliant seeking a cure for her sterility, and directed her to give her husband a potion brewed from a plant she would find growing by a certain fountain. If she slept with him the same night, she would be sure to conceive. The Greeks had similar dream oracles. That of Trophonius at Lebadea required the suppliant to bath and anoint himself before descending into a cave with a honeyed cake in his hand. Next morning, he described his dream to priests who interpreted it to him. There were other dream oracles at Oropus and Epidaurus.

Folk wisdom has always taught that dreams of the future can be self-induced. "Place a piece of wedding-cake under your pillow and you will dream of your future husband," was the age-old advice to village girls. Keats described an equally simple ritual in his poem *The Eve of St. Agnes:*

> They told her how, upon St. Agnes' Eve,
> Young virgins might have visions of delight,
> And soft adorings from their loves receive

Prediction and Prophecy

> Upon the honeyed middle of the night,
> If ceremonies due they did aright:
> As, supperless to bed they must retire,
> And couch supine their beauties, lily white;
> Nor look behind, nor sideways, but require
> Of Heaven with upward eyes for all that they desire.

Whether or not these methods worked, we simply do not know. Clearly, there is no evidence that would satisfy a modern investigator and many of the stories we have recounted were probably myths or anecdotes with little if any basis of truth. With the exception of the Emperor Julian's prophetic dream, all are written down *after* the events they were supposed to have predicted. They could have been shaped with the wisdom of hindsight. Nevertheless, they do show that a belief in the prophetic power of dreams has existed among intelligent people from the beginnings of history.

What of more recent times? Here, the evidence, though far from watertight, is more reliable. There are many well-authenticated accounts of dreams bearing an uncanny resemblance to future events, and *they were reported before those events took place*. One of the most striking concerns the assassination of Abraham Lincoln (1809–65).

Shortly before his assassination, he was discussing dream prophecies with his wife and two or three friends. He recalled those mentioned in the Bible but said that he himself was sceptical. He confessed, however, that a recent dream had been troubling him and Ward Hill Lamon, who was among those present, thought it so striking that he made notes on it immediately afterwards. Lamon reported the dream in Lincoln's own words in his *Recollections of Abraham Lincoln, 1847–1865* (edited by Dorothy Lamon Teillard, Cambridge U.P., U.S.A., 1911).

About ten days ago, I retired very late. I had been up waiting for important dispatches from the front. I could not have been long in bed when I fell into a slumber, for I was weary. I soon began to dream. There seemed to be death-like stillness about me. Then I heard subdued sobs, as if a number of people were weeping. I thought I left my bed and wandered downstairs. There the silence was broken by the same pitiful sobbing, but the mourners were invisible. I went from room to room; no living person was in sight, but the same mournful sounds of distress met me as I passed along. It was light in all the rooms; every object was familiar to me; but where were all the people who were grieving as if their hearts would break? I was puzzled and alarmed. What could be the meaning of all this? Determined to find the cause of a state of things so mysterious and shocking, I kept on until I arrived at the East Room, which I entered. There I met with a sickening surprise. Before me was a catafalque, on which rested a corpse wrapped in funeral vestments. Around it were stationed soldiers who were acting as guards; and there was a throng of people, some gazing mournfully upon the corpse, whose face was covered, others weeping pitifully. "Who is dead in the White House?" I demanded of one of the soldiers. "The President," was his answer; "he was killed by an assassin." Then came a loud burst of grief from the crowd which awoke me from my dream.

A few days later, Lincoln's body was indeed lying on the catafalque. He had been shot through the head by John Wilkes Booth, a crazed actor, while watching a play at Ford's theatre in Washington, D.C.

It could be argued that Lamon may have added details to his account of the dream after the lying-in-state had taken place and that its self-dramatizing tone doesn't match Lincoln's character or other examples of his speeches or writing. Yet even if it has been "worked up" by Lamon, it had an underlying ring of truth and one feels that Lincoln did indeed have a dream about his own death. It could be said, of course, that it was an expression of his anxiety that such a thing *might* happen. He lived in a time of violence and was hated as well as loved. On the other hand, he is reported to have had several other dreams which enabled him to predict Union victories at Antietam, Gettysburg and elsewhere.

Even more striking was the experience of John Williams, a Cornish mining engineer, who woke three times on the night of May 2nd or 3rd, 1812, and each time told his wife of a remarkable vision. Next day, he discussed it repeatedly with his friends in Falmouth. In one account, quoted from manuscript by R. L. Megroz (*The Dream World*, John Lane, U.K., 1939; Dutton, U.S.A., 1939), he wrote:

I dreamed I was in the lobby of the House of Commons (a place well-known to me). A small man, dressed in a blue coat and a white waistcoat, entered, and immediately, I saw a person whom I had observed on my first entrance, dressed in a snuff-coloured coat with metal buttons, take a pistol from under his coat and present it at the little man above-mentioned. The pistol was discharged, and the ball entered under the left breast of the person at whom it was directed. I saw the blood issue from the place where the ball had struck him, his countenance instantly altered, and he fell to the ground. Upon enquiry whom the sufferer might be, I was informed he was the Chancellor.

It seems that this reference to the Chancellor puzzled some of Williams's friends. They pointed out that the Lord Chancellor would not be in the House of Commons. His son-in-law then suggested that Chancellor could mean Chancellor of the Exchequer, a post then held by Spencer Perceval (1762–1812) who was also Prime Minister.

So much alarmed and impressed was I that I felt much doubt whether it was not my duty to take a journey to London and communicate upon the subject with the party principally concerned. Upon this point, I consulted with some friends of mine on the following day. After having stated to them the particulars of the dream itself and what were my own feelings in relation to it, they dissuaded me from my purpose, saying I might expose myself to contempt and vexation, or be taken up as a fanatic. Upon this, I said no more, but anxiously watched the newspapers every morning as the post arrived.

On the evening of May 13th, no account of Mr. Perceval's death was in the newspapers, but my second son, returning from Truro, came in a hurried manner into the room where I was sitting and exclaimed, "O father, your dream has come true! Mr. Perceval has been shot in the lobby of the House of Commons; there is an account come from London to Truro written after the newspapers were printed." The fact was Mr. Perceval was assassinated on the evening of the 11th.

At this distance in time, it is not possible to check Williams's story at first hand but it was then taken seriously enough for him to be interviewed by some of the commissioners of the navy. All the details were accurate, even to the colours of the coats and waistcoats. We know that he saw an artist's impression of the murder, so it is possible that the finer points crept in during subsequent retellings of his story, but even allowing for this, it is still remarkable that he dreamed of the incident more than a week before it happened. Falmouth is more than 250 miles from London and in those days, there was no radio, television, telephone or even electric telegraph. Nor was he even interested in politics. "I had no leisure to pay any attention to political matters," he wrote, "and hardly

knew at that time who formed the administration of the country."
In any case, the assassination of a British prime minister is so rare
an event that not even Perceval's bitterest enemy would be likely
even to dream of it happening. Assuming that Williams actually
had the dream he claimed, and there is every reason to believe he
did, there is no easy way of accounting for it.

As a final example, let us take a dream described by the late
Dr. J. C. Barker, consultant psychiatrist at the Shelton Hospital,
Shrewsbury. In his book *Scared to Death* (Muller, U.K., 1968; Dell,
U.S.A., 1971), he tells of an American woman who had a dream
while recovering from an anaesthetic in 1941. "I could see events
to come in the Second World War," she wrote. "I foresaw the
invasion of Africa by allied troops. I saw the great Armada at
sea. I saw the penetration of Italy from the south-west. Then I
arrived in Germany in my dream! I saw a field marshal, one of
the German General Staff. I had no reason to identify him, but I
did see and speak to him and appeared to know him. This dream
was so vivid that I told it to my husband at once and also to two
friends who called at the hospital."

The dream came true in a remarkable way. As an employee of
the American War Department, the writer was appointed secretary to General George Patton, commander of a Task Force for
the invasion of Africa. "I was the only woman permitted in the
map room and knew the whole scheme of the war," she said. "I
was last to bid good-bye to General Patton before he took off to
rendezvous with his staff on the U.S.S. *Augusta* in mid-Atlantic."

Later, as Head Secretary of the War Crimes Commission, she
was present at the pre-trial interrogations of German war criminals
in Nuremberg, Germany. Field Marshal Keitel was the first to be
interviewed and as he entered the room, he turned to the remote
corner of the hall where she was sitting and bowed. She recognized
him immediately as the field marshal she had dreamed about four
years before. Though he sat with his back to her, he turned round
soon afterwards. "He stared at me, not in wonder but somehow
in recognition. When he left the room he made another bow, and
afterwards in the courtroom at Nuremberg, Keitel always looked
for me and nodded."

The dream interested Barker because so little of it could be
explained away. Presumably, Keitel might first have bowed to the
woman out of politeness or "perhaps she reminded him of someone he knew." Possibly, she could have unconsciously willed him
to look at her. But these are mere details. The fact is that in 1941,

Prediction and Prophecy

even before America had entered the war, she was able to foretell
not only the invasion of Africa, an unlikely enough happening from
the American point of view, but a meeting four years ahead with
a German field marshal in Germany. The odds against this happening by chance seem remote.

I say "seem" deliberately. Clearly, chance does have a part to
play. But how great? Recent research suggests that it is far more
extensive than we have realized.

The breakthrough came with the development of the electroencephalograph machine by Hans Berger of Jena University, Germany in the early 1930s. He discovered that electroencephalograph
recordings (E.E.G.s) showed changes in the minute electric currents
given off by the brain (brain waves) during sleep. Dr. Nathaniel
Kleitman, who was studying sleep at the University of Chicago,
recorded the brain waves of volunteers who spent the night in his
laboratory. They were wired with devices to measure heart rate,
breathing, blood pressure and temperature during sleep, and had
electrodes plastered to their temples, to their foreheads and around
their eyes.

It is unnecessary to describe in detail all the discoveries made
by Kleitman and his colleagues but for our purpose, the most important was that changes in the brain waves, as shown in E.E.G.s,
indicated differing "depths" of sleep during the night. These came
in cycles of some ninety minutes, starting with deep sleep that
became progressively lighter until the sleeper plunged back into
the initial deep sleep of the next cycle, and so on. During the light
sleep, which could last anything from a few minutes to half an hour
or even longer, E.E.G.s showed that there were periods when the
sleeper's eyes darted from side to side or flicked up and down
(Rapid Eye Movements or R.E.M.s). At the same time, pulse and
respiration rates speeded up. Could this increased bodily activity
be associated with dreaming?

There was only one way to find out. Volunteers were woken during both R.E.M. and non-R.E.M. periods and asked. Only a tiny
proportion of those woken in non-R.E.M. periods reported dreams
(and it has been suggested that even these were memories of earlier
dreams), but those woken during R.E.M. periods nearly always did
so. This was a revolutionary discovery. It meant that we could say
with a fair degree of certainty whether or not a man was dreaming
just by looking at his E.E.G.

Further research suggested that most of us dream for about
ninety minutes each night, a fifth of our total sleeping time. The

92

dreams come in three to five R.E.M. periods scattered evenly through the night. The first may be short, perhaps as little as five minutes, but later ones get gradually longer and the final one may extend to three-quarters of an hour. The amount of time spent dreaming does not vary with sex or intelligence and we all seem to *need* dreams. If we are deprived of dreaming time by being repeatedly woken during R.E.M. periods, we have extra R.E.M. periods next time we sleep. This does not happen if we are woken during non-R.E.M. periods.

What of the people who say they "never have dreams"? Two Brooklyn doctors, Arthur Shapiro and Donald Goodenough, took eight men and women students who claimed they never dreamed and eight who said they did. For three nights, all sixteen were kept under observation. Both groups had similar cycles and when roused during R.E.M. periods, *all* reported dreams. It seems likely then that there is no such person as a non-dreamer, though clearly there are some who forget their dreams so efficiently as to believe they never had them.

The implications are staggering. Every night, in Britain alone, some fifty million people each dream through three to five R.E.M. periods totalling approximately ninety minutes. We know from experience how one dream merges into another, so it would not be unreasonable to estimate that each person has at least ten separate dreams a night. This gives us collectively something like 172,500,000,000 dreams a year. (A comparative figure for America would be 730,000,000,000.) Each of these contains an indefinite number of people, places, objects and events, some of them purely imaginary, some taken from memory and some recalled from a past we thought we had forgotten. Many combine all three. So the sum total of dream objects and happenings is almost infinite in both number and variety.

The implications for any theory of dream prediction are obvious. Take any event, however remote and unexpected, and it is almost certain that someone, somewhere, has had a dream sufficiently like it, in some details, at least, as to convince him that he has the gift of prophecy. If he has spoken, or better still, written about it in advance, other people also believe he has the gift of prophecy. Everyone forgets the hundreds of thousands of millions of dreams that do not "come true."

Dr. Barker recognized this difficulty when he appealed through Peter Fairley, Science Correspondent of the London *Evening Standard,* for premonitions of the disaster that shook the South Wales coal-mining village of Aberfan in 1966. On October 21st, a slag heap cascaded down a mountain and killed 166 villagers, 128 of them children buried alive in Pantglas Junior School. After the appeal had been nationally syndicated, sixty correspondents claimed foreknowledge of the tragedy, thirty-six of them in dreams. Yet Barker's report in the *Journal of the Society for Psychical Research* (vol. 44, no. 734), is unimpressive. Among the dreams confirmed by witnesses as having been told to them *before* the events, the most convincing was of children trying to get out of a room, then "hundreds of people all running to the same place. The looks on people's faces were terrible. Some were crying and others holding handkerchiefs to their faces." Other correspondents described "screaming children buried by avalanche of coal in mining village" and "school, screaming children and 'creeping black slimy substance'." There were two references to the name Aberfan and one to Aberredven but none of these was confirmed. One dream specifically referred to Bognor, Sussex and another was originally associated by the dreamer with Australia. The most moving was recorded in a statement made to a local minister by the parents of a ten-years-old victim who had already had a premonition of death: "The day before the disaster, she said to her mother, 'Mummy, let me tell you about my dream last night.' Her mother answered gently, 'Darling, I've no time now. Tell me again later.' The child replied, 'No, Mummy, you *must* listen. I dreamt I went to school and there was no school there. Something black had come down all over it."

In his somewhat inconclusive discussion, Barker commented: "The principal difficulty is that few of the premonitions are in any way specific. Most of them might be regarded as rather vague prognostications of doom, and with 50 million or so people in the country dreaming several dreams a night, it would indeed be surprising if they did not produce a few dozen premonitions of doom amongst them. Nevertheless, the Aberfan disaster was an extremely unusual one so that dreams resembling it are likely to be fairly improbable."

I wonder. All the elements mentioned are fairly common in dreams. A school may be associated with anxiety and especially with those beastly examinations which we are so often required to undergo in dreams. Alternatively, it may be a place where we learn how to make progress in our psychic life. Children may represent aspects of ourselves that need to grow up. They scream because they dislike the idea. Similarly, a death may symbolize an aspect of ourselves that is dying or, according to Freud, it could be a wish fulfilment of a death unconsciously desired, either of ourself or of someone else. As for the blackness that blots out the scene, this could be a screen thrown up by the unconscious to prevent us from remembering things too painful to face, even in a dream. The fact that a school, with its overtones of anxiety, is blotted out, often among scenes of terror, fits in well with this interpretation. On the whole, then, it is not so improbable that among the hundreds of millions of dreams experienced in the weeks and months before the Aberfan disaster, a few should have included scenes combining such common dream ingredients as school, children, terror and blackness.

Can we say then that *any* dreams are prophetic? I believe that they are, and in several different ways. Jung, for instance, pointed out that some dreams seem to be "an anticipatory combination of probabilities which may coincide with the actual behaviour of things but need not necessarily agree in every detail" (quoted by E. A. Bennet in *What Jung Really Said,* Macdonald, U.K., 1966; Schocken, U.S.A., 1969). By revealing tendencies in the mind, they may foreshadow future events, ideas, discoveries. One of the most significant dreams in Jung's own life was of being in his study on the first-floor of a beautiful old house. The style was eighteenth-century but when he went down to the ground floor, it seemed to be two centuries older and the cellar was clearly Roman. He was wondering what all this meant when he noticed a square stone with a ring in the corner. Raising it, he found a ladder leading down to a still lower level, rather like a cave or tomb, packed with skulls and ancient pottery. He woke up with the feeling that he had made a great discovery.

Freud, whom Jung consulted, concentrated on the skulls and suggested that the dream revealed an unconscious wish that someone should die. Jung was not satisfied. The house, he felt, represented his own personality and the various floors previous levels of human culture. After years of reflection, he came to believe that the cave represented the deepest and most ancient part of the unconscious mind. Until then, Jung had broadly agreed with Freud that the unconscious was a part of the mind containing ideas, feelings and memories which we had banished from consciousness because we could not bear to face them. We normally became aware of them only through dreams, by means of therapeutic techniques such as psychoanalysis and by noting inexplicable errors, lapses of memory and other quirks of behaviour. Jung developed the idea that the unconscious contained not just this personal material, which was unique to the individual, but also collective material common to the whole of humanity. It consisted of archetypes, inherited patterns rather like instincts, forming images and symbols which we can trace in the art, religion and mythology of all peoples, at all periods of history. The idea of the collective unconscious is not universally accepted but Jung believed it was his greatest single contribution to psychology. And it was anticipated by his dream of the house with the skulls in the cellar.

Jung himself pointed out that many other important scientific discoveries have been similarly anticipated. One of the most famous is that of the molecular structure of trimethyl benzene by the German chemist August von Stradonitz Kekulé (1829–96). After months of fruitless thought, he was dozing in a chair when he dreamed that the atoms were dancing in front of him, some of them forming long, snake-like chains. Suddenly, one of the "snakes" swallowed its own tail. In a flash of inspiration, Kekulé realized that he had found the solution to his problem. Benzene's molecular structure was basically a ring. "Let us learn to dream, gentlemen," he advised colleagues at an 1890 convention of scientists.

Others who learned to dream were Jerome Cardan (1501–76), an Italian physician and mathematician who foresaw the detailed scheme of his best-known book, *De Subtilitate Rerum*; William Blake (1757–1827) who was shown a new method of engraving by his dead brother; and the American Assyriologist, Dr. H. V. Hilprecht, who was given the clue that led to the decipherment of fragmentary cuneiform inscriptions of a Babylonian priest.

Dreams have proved even more fruitful in the arts. Perhaps the best-known case is that of the poet Samuel Taylor Coleridge (1772–1834), who in 1787 was convalescing in a remote Somerset farmhouse. After taking opium for a "slight indisposition," he fell asleep in his chair while reading in *Purchas's Pilgrimage* of the Khan Kubla who "commanded a palace to be built, and a stately garden thereunto. And thus ten miles of fertile ground were enclosed with a wall." In the next three hours, he dreamed he had composed between two and three hundred lines of poetry which he hurried to write down when he woke up. A "person on business from Porlock" disturbed him and when he later tried to finish them, he was unable to do so. "With the exception of some eight or ten scattered lines and images," he wrote, "all the rest had passed away like the images on the surface of a stream into which a stone had been cast." A dream, then, gave us the exquisitely haunting *Kubla Khan,* even if "a person from Porlock" deprived us of a further two hundred lines.

1. The Sanctuary of Apollo at Delphi. Here the oracle gave judgement on a wide variety of queries and problems

2. Roman augurs

3. Astrolabe (above) and astrological forecasts (below) derived from observation of the moon, both Assyrian

Dieu se sert icy de ma bouche
Pour t'anoncer la verité,
Si ma prediction te touche
Rends grace à sa Divinite

4. Nostradamus

5. Mother Shipton

7. Dr John Dee

6. Joanna Southcott

8. In Britain, with its variable climate, it is impossible to forecast the weather with 100 per cent accuracy. Yet we spend millions of pounds every year working out forecasts, and use the most elaborate equipment

9. Tarot cards

10. In this experiment to test telepathy the experimenter holds up a random number to the aperture, indicating to the agent on the other side which card she should select. The percipient, who is in another room, then tries to record the symbol displayed on the card selected. The agent is used as a precaution against leakage of information to the percipient

11. Would you accept an analysis of your personality or a prediction of your future from a computer? This "Astroscope" in a London store provides such information from personal details fed to it on a punch card

12. Palmist

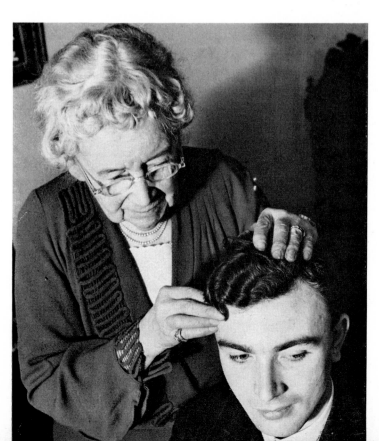

13. A phrenologist tries to predict a young man's future by feeling the bumps on his head

14. In the USA one Hallowe'en custom is for young girls to retire to a little used room with a candle, apple and clock. At 11.45 p.m. they start eating the apple by candlelight and finish at exactly midnight. If they then look in the mirror, they are supposed to see the face of their future husband

15. Water diviner

Giuseppe Tartini (1692–1770) was a brilliant violinist, theorist and teacher but he was also the composer of a famous sonata called *The Devil's Trill.* This too was the result of a dream in which the devil played on his violin. Tartini told Joseph Lalande (1732–1807), the French astronomer, "I heard him play with consummate skill a sonata of such exquisite beauty that it surpassed the most audacious dreams of my imagination. I was delighted, transported, enchanted." When Tartini woke, he tried to reproduce the sonata on his own violin. It was impossible. "The piece I composed, *The Devil's Trill,* was the best I had written, but how remote it was from the one in my dream."

Nearer our own time, the novelist Robert Louis Stevenson (1850–94) described how he systematically cultivated his dreams to give him the raw material for his stories. Each night's instalment followed on directly from the previous night. He was probably helped in this by his tuberculosis. He was often too feverish to enjoy any but the lightest sleep which would be rich in dream-producing R.E.M. periods. The lack of deep sleep probably made it easier for him to remember his dreams on waking, but he paid a heavy price for their vividness and continuity. He felt he was leading a double life. His night fantasies became so compelling that they almost overshadowed his normal, day-time self. Yet this internal struggle itself produced a dream which foreshadowed one of his most successful books. Desperate for money, he had been wondering how he could work up the theme of split personality into a saleable novel. "For two nights, I went about racking my brain for a plot of any sort," he wrote in *Across the Plains,* "and on the second night I dreamed the scene at the window, and a scene afterwards split in two, in which Hyde, pursued for some crime, took the powder and underwent the change in the presence of his pursuers. All the rest was made awake, and consciously." He was, of course, referring to *Dr. Jekyll and Mr. Hyde.*

These anticipatory dreams relate to the future in the sense that they produce concrete results when the dreamer wakes up. In the relaxed state of sleep, our minds are apparently able to select and arrange in meaningful patterns material not only from the part of our mind that is conscious when we are awake but also from the unconscious. Our intuition also seems to work better. It creates, or at least points the way to, a future springing directly from the existing contents of our minds.

This happens too in diagnostic dreams. It sometimes happens that a man dreams he has cancer of, say, the jaw, only to be reassured by his doctor that he has no such thing. Yet some months later, he does indeed develop cancer of the jaw, proving that the dream was right and the doctor wrong. The reason seems to be that the mind can sometimes detect early indications of bodily disease and reveal them in dreams long before they can be diagnosed by the most sensitive methods yet known to medical science.

(We must be careful here. As we have seen before, dreams cannot be interpreted rigidly as many naïve "dream books" suggest. A single symbol can have many different meanings according to the circumstances of the dreamer and often the right one can be determined only by painstaking analysis, if at all. A dream of cancer could simply mean that the dreamer has been worrying about cancer, perhaps because someone he knew died of it at the same age. A Freudian might interpret the dream as a death-wish, while a Jungian might regard the cancer as the symbol of a complex, an emotionally charged repression of which the dreamer is not directly aware.)

In *Dreams and Nightmares* (Penguin, U.K., 1954; Penguin, U.S.A., 1971), the distinguished psychologist Dr. J. A. Hadfield mentions another type of dream which is essentially diagnostic. He quotes an example from the *Proceedings of the Society for Psychical Research* (VIII, 400):

> Mr. Brighten, sleeping on board a yacht at anchor, dreamed of a voice warning him of being in danger of being run down by another vessel. He woke and went on deck, but finding everything quiet and in order, although fog had come on, turned in again and went to sleep. The dream was repeated and he again awoke and went up on deck. He was rendered so anxious by the dream—and by the fog—that this time he went aloft, just in time to see above the fog another vessel bearing down on him. He shouted to the captain of this other vessel, who put his helm over and thus avoided a collision.

As Dr. Hadfield points out, there is probably a straightforward explanation for this type of "prophecy." When we sleep, our sense organs do not switch off. We know this because we often find on waking that we have incorporated a real noise, such as the ringing of an alarm-clock, into the structure of a dream. We have clearly "heard" it at some level of consciousness. This type of hearing is highly selective. It ignores irrelevant noises like the patter of rain on the window or clanks from the central heating system, so that our sleep is not broken unnecessarily. Yet it is extremely sensitive to noises that *are* important to us. A mother will wake at the slightest whimper from her child. A doctor is unlikely to sleep through the ringing of his telephone.

It is known that the throbbing of a ship's engine can sometimes be heard many miles away at sea. It is also known that fog plays strange tricks, and a sound that is audible one moment can disappear the next and then come back louder than ever. Dr. Hadfield suggests that the Brighten case can be explained in this way. "In other words," he says, "Mr. Brighten's premonition was probably the natural inference from a sensation subconsciously perceived."

Even when we are awake, the unconscious part of our mind takes in a mass of information of which we are not consciously aware. Dreams may give us access to this too. One man was puzzled by a dream in which a trusted friend handed him a counterfeit coin. Shortly afterwards, this same friend cheated him in a business transaction. His unconscious mind had stored up nagging doubts about his friend's honesty but he was unwilling to acknowledge this consciously. Once his conscious mind was asleep, his unconscious was free to give its message in a dream.

Similarly, a couple had made up their minds to pay a large sum for a house when the husband dreamed that the seller had dropped his price by £500. They held off and a few days later, the dream came true. Again, the husband's unconscious mind had picked up in the seller's attitude signals too slight for the conscious mind to register. His unconscious thought them important enough to bring them to notice in a dream.

A friend of mine spent days searching for a lost bunch of keys and then dreamed they were behind books in a rarely used cupboard. Next morning, he looked in the cupboard and there they were. Probably he will never know why his conscious mind should have erected a barrier against remembering this while waking. The reason could well be some painful association with cupboards, or keys, dating back to his early childhood. In sleep, the barriers tumbled down and the unconscious was free to help him.

Can we cultivate this faculty? "Sleep on it" has always been good advice for those faced with a difficult choice. The answer may come in a dream or in a quiet conviction on waking. If we try to bully our unconscious—"I *must* have a dream, I *must* have a dream" —we are more likely to paralyse it. If we tell ourselves casually, "Perhaps a dream will give me the answer," we may well find that we too have the gift of "prophecy."

Prediction and Prophecy

What of dreams that predict a future that could not possibly be deduced from facts that were already known or subconsciously perceived? Here again, several explanations are possible, each of them valid in particular cases. Superficially, it may seem almost miraculous that as early as 1863, the Prussian President, Otto von Bismarck (1815–98), had a dream which clearly prophesied the success of a policy which at that time was hazardous in the extreme, the unification of Germany under Prussia. His support of Russia in suppressing the Polish uprising had alienated his own Parliament. The invasion of Denmark set him at odds with almost every other nation in Europe. Austria, Prussia's rival for the German leadership, was thought to be the stronger. "In the worst days of the struggle," wrote Bismarck, "from which no human eye could see any possible escape, I dreamt that I was riding on a narrow Alpine path, a precipice on the right, rocks on the left. The path grew narrower, so that the horse refused to proceed, and it was impossible to turn round or dismount, owing to lack of space. Then, with my whip in my left hand, I struck the smooth rock and called on God. The whip grew to an endless length, the rocky wall dropped like a piece of stage machinery and opened out in a broad path, with a view over hills and forests, like a landscape in Bohemia; there were Prussian troops with banners. . . . I woke up rejoiced and strengthened."

Both then and later, Bismarck chose to regard the dream as prophetic. It did in fact come about that, against all the odds, he succeeded in uniting Germany under Prussian leadership. Yet it seems easier to interpret the dream as a simple case of wish fulfilment. Freud believed that virtually all dreams were wish fulfilments and though few psychologists would now take so exclusive a view, even fewer would deny that such dreams are common. A starving man has visions of a banquet. A man with money troubles dreams of winning the football pools. Someone with career difficulties dreams he has been granted the longed-for promotion that will solve all his problems. Bismarck too faced difficulties. On one side, the precipice indicated that he was in imminent danger of falling from power; on the other were the rocks of world opinion. The road ahead was blocked, until it was miraculously opened for him in the dream. The fact that he succeeded in real life was coincidental. He might just as easily have failed, just as other dreamers have found on waking that there is no real-life banquet, pools win or promotion.

Not everyone believes in telepathy, the power of one mind to perceive what is happening in another mind without the help of the bodily senses. If it does exist, it might explain some of the most puzzling dreams of all.

In his *Occult Phenomena* (Burns and Oates, U.K., 1957; Newman Press, U.S.A., 1959), Alois Wiesinger, O.C.S.O., quotes from Moser's *Okultismus* Bishop Dr. Joseph Lanyi's own account of a dream apparently predicting the murder of Archduke Franz Ferdinand, which set in motion the events leading to the First World War. Lanyi, his former tutor, was at Grosswardein in Hungary; Ferdinand, three hundred miles away in Ilidze. The Bishop wrote:

At a quarter past three on the morning of June 28th, 1914, I awoke from a terrible dream. I dreamed that I had gone to my desk early in the morning to look through the post that had come in. On top of all the other letters there lay one with a black border, a black seal and the arms of the Archduke. I immediately recognized the latter's writing, and saw at the head of the notepaper in blue colouring a picture like those on picture postcards which showed me a street and a narrow side-street. Their Highnesses sat in a car, opposite them sat a general, and an officer next to the chauffeur. On both sides of the street, there was a large crowd. Two young lads sprang forward and shot at their Highnesses. The text of the letter was as follows: "Dear Dr. Lanyi, Your Excellency, I wish to inform you that my wife and I were the victims of a political assassination. We recommend ourselves to your prayers. Cordial greetings from your Archduke Franz, Sarajevo, June 28th, 3.15 a.m." Trembling and in tears, I sprang out of bed and I looked at the clock which showed 3.15. I immediately hurried to my desk and wrote down what I had read and seen in my dream. In doing so, I even retained the form of certain letters just as the Archduke had written them. My servant entered my study at a quarter to six that morning and saw me sitting there pale and saying my rosary. He asked whether I was ill. I said: "Call my mother and the guest at once. I will say Mass immediately for their Highnesses, for I have had a terrible dream." My mother and the guest came at a quarter to seven. I told my mother the dream in the presence of the guest and of my servant. Then I went into the house chapel. The day passed in fear and apprehension. At half-past three, a telegram brought us news of the murder.

Lanyi's dream impresses by its detail. Even if he had a generalized fear for the Archduke's safety, he could not have imagined so accurately the circumstances of the assassination. Nor, in the ordinary way, could he have had foreknowledge. Yet Wiesinger suggests he *did* have foreknowledge, not of the execution itself but of the plans for it. He bases his argument on seemingly unimportant discrepancies between Lanyi's account and the assassination itself. The dream was accurate in pinpointing the spot where the shots were fired and also in showing a general sitting facing the Archduke. But it was inaccurate in showing two assassins (there was only one) and also in placing an officer next to the chauffeur ("he was standing on the left-hand running-board").

Wiesinger finds both the similarities and the errors significant. The junction of Appel Quai and the narrow street into which the procession turned was an automatic choice for the murder because the Archduke's car would have to slow down there. As for the position of the general, this would have been included in the official plans of which the conspirators might well have known. Wiesinger suggests that they may have originally intended to use two gunmen not one. Before the attempt, they had every reason to think that the officer would be sitting next to the chauffeur, because that was the position allotted to him in the plans. He stood on the running board only because of an earlier, unsuccessful bomb attempt on the Archduke that same morning.

According to Wiesinger, then, Lanyi's dream did not give a preview of the assassination itself. It showed only what the conspirators expected to happen *at the time of the dream*. From this, he concludes that the dream was not predictive but telepathic. In other words, Lanyi was not foreseeing a future event. He was seeing into the minds of conspirators *before* the event.

Assuming we believe in telepathy, such a theory is possible but hardly convincing. Wiesinger's account bristles with phrases like "it may well be that . . ." "it is quite likely that . . ." and "it was no doubt . . . ," then culminates in the stark assertion "it was *in fact* a very remarkable case of telepathy" (my italics). He offers no evidence at all to show that the conspirators had previous knowledge of the arrangements for the procession, though admittedly they may well have done so. Nor is there anything to indicate that the conspirators originally planned to post two gunmen, not one, at the murder junction. Yet if we reject his theory of telepathy, what are we left with?

After examining some hundreds of dreams, I find that the great majority have no conceivable reference to the future. Most of those that do can be explained as wish fulfilments or, more commonly, as the recovery and re-arrangement of existing facts, feelings and intuitions, so that the dream points the way to the solution of a problem or to the outcome of trends whose elements are already present. In a few cases, too, telepathy is certainly a possibility. There remains, however, a tiny minority of dreams that do not fit into any of these categories. They include the dreams concerning President Lincoln, Spencer Perceval and Field Marshal Keitel mentioned earlier in this chapter. I, personally, would add Bishop Lanyi's dream of the Sarajevo murder. None of these dreams can be dismissed as coincidence, and the wealth of accurate detail precludes mere wish fulfilment, however disguised. As the details were most unlikely to be in anyone's mind at the time of the dream, telepathy can also be ruled out. Once again we are forced to ask ourselves what we mean by "present," future" and "past." Could it be that our everyday idea of time is incomplete? Could time have more aspects than we dream of when we measure out our days in hours, minutes and seconds and make sure we are punctual for appointments by checking our watches? In the next chapter, we shall go more deeply into this question of time, to see whether we can find some explanation not only for dreams that foretell the future but also for precognition and other techniques of prophecy and prediction.

7 Tomorrow and Tomorrow and Tomorrow

We now come hard up against the question of time. What exactly is it? In everyday life, we regard it as a single, one-way path along which we move like sandwich-men between two slitless shutters. One of them hides the view ahead; the other blocks off the view behind. We can neither see into the future nor take a backward glance at the past. We are aware only of an ever-changing, infinitely narrow slice of life which we call "the present." Everyone, and everything, in the whole universe is walking exactly in line with us and, allowing for difference in position, experiences exactly the same "present."

To suggest that anyone in the here and now can have knowledge of an event that has not yet taken place offends this commonsense view. It also blows sky-high the old-fashioned insistence on cause and effect. How can we even be aware of the existence of something of which our senses give us no evidence? Apparently, too, prediction destroys the possibility of free will, for if the future can be foreseen, it must be predetermined. And if it is predetermined, there is nothing we can do to change it.

We need not be surprised then at the uneasiness and scorn with which many people, both laymen and scientists, treat the whole subject. Yet a moment's thought will show that time is much more complicated than it sometimes seems. We shall see that there are a number of theories which could allow for glimpses into both future and past. Before we look at them, it is worth noting that everyday time too has puzzling features.

It seems to slow down and speed up. When we are making love, talking with friends or working on some absorbing project, it "stands still." An hour slips by without our being aware of it. But five minutes can seem an eternity when we are having a tooth filled or waiting for an interview with the bank manager. It could rightly be said that these impressions are subjective. But more difficulties arise when we try to measure time objectively. We might relate it to the motion of some natural feature, defining a day as the period of time that elapses between sunrise and sunset. Yet such a measurement is useless because it changes from season to season. On a highly sophisticated level, archaeologists have sought to date the remains of ancient objects made of organic materials by the use of radiocarbon techniques. It is known that living matter takes up a radioactive isotope of carbon known as Carbon 14 which is produced by the action of cosmic rays. It also takes up non-radioactive Carbon 12 in a constant proportion to the Carbon 14. This process stops when the plant or animal dies and though the Carbon 12 remains, the Carbon 14 decays at a known rate. By finding the ratio of Carbon 14 to Carbon 12 in the remains of a dinosaur or a piece of ancient timber, we can pinpoint the moment of death. Or so it was thought. Now, however, it is known that there are variations in the cosmic rays producing the Carbon 14 in the first place, so that the original ratio was *not* constant. So some Carbon 14 dates are too late and others too early.

Could it be that animals have the secret of measuring time? Cats become uneasy when feeding time approaches and we know that this is not simply a result of domestication because wild creatures show similar tendencies. They seem to have a biological clock that, depending on the species, tells them when it is time to eat, drink, sleep and mate. Yet there is nothing objective about it. The mechanism can be slowed down or speeded up by various means, as was shown by Karl von Frisch, the bee expert. When he gave his bees a chemical, they set off for their feeding grounds too early; when he kept them in a refrigerator, too late. So "nature" is no more reliable than man as a time-keeper. She too can be upset by outside influences.

In practice, we use the movements of the earth, moon and sun. It takes a *day* for the earth to make one complete revolution on its own axis; a *month* for the moon to make one complete revolution round the earth; a *year* for the earth to make one complete revolution round the sun. Even then, there are anomalies. None of these movements is regular. Measured in this way, the year does not consist of an exact numbers of days, so we are forced to have Leap Years with extra days to maintain the score. Again, the moon revolves round the earth approximately every $29\frac{1}{2}$ days so the lunar months do not correspond with the calendar months. As 365 is not divisible by 12, even the calendar months have to be of differing lengths.

Dividing the day into twenty-four hours is comparatively simple.

Prediction and Prophecy

We do it artificially by means of the clock, a device which works reasonably well for everyday purposes and if we take enough trouble, we can build one that is accurate to very fine tolerances indeed for scientific work. Yet the clock itself creates problems. It seems convenient, though it is not strictly necessary, for clocks all over the world to register the same time for corresponding points in the day. When the sun is directly overhead, for instance, we like to see the hands of the clock pointing to twelve noon. Since the earth revolves, we can achieve this only by putting our clocks forward or back according to our longitude. Strictly speaking, we should adjust them a few seconds for every mile we travel east or west but this is clearly impractical and we compromise by dividing the world into time zones, each of which covers approximately fifteen degrees of longitude. As we pass from one to the other, we put our clocks backwards or forwards by a whole hour. Base time is that of longitude zero degrees which runs through Greenwich, England (Greenwich Mean Time). Norway is one hour fast on Greenwich, Turkey two hours, Aden three and so on. In the same way, Iceland is one hour slow on Greenwich, the Azores two and Greenland three.

Apart from local variations adopted by some countries to give them more daylight during working hours, the system of time zones brings another complication. If we fly right round the earth, we gain or lose a whole day depending on whether we have been travelling eastwards or westwards. So the International Date Line is drawn through the Pacific Ocean. If we cross it from east to west, we gain a day on the calendar. If we cross it from west to east, we lose a day, or, in practice, have a day of the same date twice. This arrangement keeps us in line with the calendar but once more shows that time and dates are relative, not absolute.

Science itself leads us into even stranger channels. The American physicists Albert Michelson and Edward Morley discovered as early as 1887 that the speed of light was constant. In 1905, Albert Einstein went on in his Special Theory of Relativity to refute Sir Isaac Newton's classic statement that "Absolute, true and mathematical time, of itself, and by its own nature, flows constantly without relation to anything outside itself." Einstein showed that there was no such things as absolute time. It was meaningless to say that events at a distance from each other happened simultaneously unless you also said who was observing them.

This becomes clear when we consider the stars. The nearest is four light years away, which means that it takes four years for its light to reach earth. So we are not seeing that star as it is now. We are seeing it as it was four years ago. Other stars are hundreds, thousands, millions and even hundreds of millions of light years away. If their planets supported living beings that could see Earth in detail, they might now be watching the American War of Independence, the Black Death or the Crucifixion of Christ. *For us,* our present is simultaneous with their past. *For them,* our present is still in the future.

The implications are startling. If we could travel from the earth on a spaceship at the speed of light, time would stand still for us. Leaving on January 1st, we should continue in January 1st indefinitely. If we exceeded the speed of light, we should overtake light signals sent out before we left. Looking back at the earth, we should see history turning backwards. If we could build spaceships fast enough and cameras powerful enough, we could make a film of the Crucifixion, return with it to earth and show Jesus' agony on television.

Einstein's Special Theory and his later General Theory of Relativity (1911) are still debated by scientists. They are far too abstruse for discussion here but two points are worth noting. Einstein further eroded our "commonsense" ideas by arguing that time is affected by mass. In other words, if we could place a clock on a body whose mass was greater than earth's, it would run more slowly than an identical clock on our own planet. He also argued that time is affected by relative speed. A man leaving earth for a lengthy space trip at or around the speed of light would find that time virtually stood still for him. He would return to earth only a little older, yet find that hundreds of years had gone by. It is no longer possible to dismiss such a theory on "commonsense" grounds and in its favour we now know that biological mechanisms can be slowed down or speeded up by chemicals or by changes in temperature. It is not inconceivable that travel at the speed of light would also have a slowing down effect. Theoretical arguments have been advanced on both sides and as yet there is no sign of agreement. Einstein could be wrong. But he could just as easily be right.

We have sketched out these aspects of time because they are taken seriously, if not always agreed, by orthodox scientists of the highest qualifications and integrity. Yet are they any more extraordinary than the notion that we here on earth may sometimes catch glimpses of our own future? One of the men who thought not was John William Dunne, a former Army officer and aeronautical engineer whose interest was sparked off by a series of extraordinary dreams.

In his book *An Experiment with Time* (Faber, U.K., 1934; Macmillan, U.S.A., 1938), he describes how he first became aware of some faculty he was then unable to explain. While staying in a Sussex hotel, he dreamed that his watch had stopped at 4.30, roused himself to check and found that his watch was not in its usual place by his bed but on a chest of drawers across the room. It had indeed stopped at 4.30. He assumed that this had happened the previous afternoon, that he had placed it on the chest of drawers and that he had then forgotten about it. The dream was simply an unconscious memory. He rewound the watch and went back to bed. Next morning, he checked the watch against the hotel clock and was astonished to find it was only a couple of minutes slow, the time it took for him to get out of bed, find it and rewind it during the night. This put the incident in a totally different light. Alone in his room, he had no possible means of knowing the time. So apart from its being highly unlikely that he had forgotten that his watch had stopped the previous afternoon, it was improbable in the extreme that he should have woken exactly twelve hours later. The obvious explanation was that he woke when he did because he unconsciously noticed in his sleep the sudden absence of ticking. How then could he have dreamed it was 4.30? Looking back on the incident, he concluded it was because he had foreseen the act of looking at his watch on the chest of drawers.

Among many other examples of his predictive dreams, two more are worth mentioning. While in camp with the 6th Mounted Infantry during the Boer War, he dreamed that he was standing on a mountain.

The ground was of a curious white formation. Here and there were little fissures, and from these, jets of vapour were spouting upward. In my dream, I recognized the place as an island of which I had dreamed before—an island which was in imminent peril of a volcano. And, when I saw the vapour spouting from the ground, I gasped, "It's the island! Good Lord, the whole thing is going to *blow up*!" For I had memories of reading about Krakatoa, where the sea, making its way into the heart of a volcano through a submarine crevice, flushed into steam, and blew the whole mountain to pieces. Forthwith, I was seized with a frantic desire to save the four thousand (I knew the number) unsuspecting inhabitants. Obviously, there was only one way of doing this, and that was to take them off in ships. There followed a most distressing nightmare, in which I was at a neighbouring island, trying to get the incredulous *French* authorities to despatch vessels of every and any description to remove the inhabitants of the threatened island.

The camp, near Lindley in the Orange Free State, was completely cut off from the outside world and it was some time before the next batch of newspapers arrived from England. The main headline in the *Daily Telegraph* read: "Volcano disaster in Martinique. Town swept away. An avalanche of flame. Probable loss of over 40,000 lives." A smaller headline followed: "A mountain explodes." The story confirmed most of the details in the dream. Martinique is French and an eye-witness described how the volcano Mont Pelée seemed to "split open." Many of the survivors were taken by boat to nearby islands. The only major inaccuracy in Dunne's dream was the figure of 4,000 dead, as against the *Telegraph's* 40,000. Dunne has an interesting explanation for this. He says he misread the newspaper account and believing it too mentioned the figure 4,000, repeatedly quoted it to his friends as an added point of similarity. It was only when he checked the reference fifteen years later that he noticed the discrepancy. Moreover, the true death roll was quite different.

The fact that Dunne admits the error makes his account all the more credible, but suggests that he had foreknowledge of the newspaper story rather than of the event itself. This opened up a disturbing possibility, which he himself points out. He could have read the newspaper story first and then *imagined* that he had dreamed about it. In other words, he could have been a victim of "identifying paramnesia," a well-known mental phenomenon which must always be considered as a possible explanation for any precognitive dream or vision.

From then on, he took care to eliminate identifying paramnesia by carefully noting his dreams on waking. He could then be sure they came *before* subsequent events and not after them. Several of his dreams were apparently prophetic and in the autumn of 1913, he saw a high railway embankment which he knew from personal experience was just north of the Firth of Forth Bridge in Scotland. A northbound train plunged down the embankment and when he tried to "get" the time, he had an impression that it would be in the spring. Next morning, he described the dream to his sister who said later that she had the impression that he had settled on March. He himself thought he had mentioned the middle of April. Whichever it was, the dream came true reasonably on time. On April 4th, 1914, the northbound *Flying Scotsman* was derailed near Burntisland shortly after crossing the Forth Bridge. It plunged twenty feet down an embankment and came to rest on the golf links below. This was a clear case of the event following the dream. "Identifying paramnesia" is excluded by his sister's confirmation.

Prediction and Prophecy

Altogether, Dunne had about twenty dreams that were apparently precognitive. They were spread over some fifteen years. He realized that, like everyone else, he remembered only a tiny proportion of his dreams and if some of these had hinted at future events, it seemed reasonable to suppose that some of those he had forgotten had done so too. He reasoned that if he had precognitive dreams, other people might also have them, indeed that it was normal to do so. Why then were they so rarely reported? He concluded that most of us simply do not notice them. We accept that dreams incorporate material from the past but the idea of their drawing also on the future is so alien to our whole way of thinking about time that we do not even consider the possibility.

The only way to test this theory was to record dreams regularly and compare them with future events. Dunne devised a technique which has become standard for most later dream-researchers. You keep a pencil and note-pad by your bed and *immediately on waking* jot down brief, perhaps single-word, notes of the main incidents. You then go back over the notes, filling out each incident with as much detail as you remember. It sounds easy but the amount of will-power needed is considerable. Half awake, you tell yourself that the dream is obviously unimportant and not worth recording, or you persuade yourself, in the face of all past experience, that you will remember the dream later in the day and that it is safe to go back to sleep. All such temptations must be resisted. The mind automatically deletes almost all of our dreams within minutes. The only way to retain them is to jot them down *immediately on waking*.

When he started experimenting systematically, Dunne had no clear success until the eleventh day. He was out shooting (in real life) and realized he might have strayed from the area for which he had a permit. At that moment, he heard two men approaching from different directions, apparently urging on a dog. Naturally, he was frightened and beat a swift retreat. He was able to slip through a gate in the boundary wall before the men saw him. Though unpleasant, the episode seemed of little significance but that evening, he glanced through his dream book and noticed at the end of the previous night's record, a pencilled note "Hunted by two men and a dog." He had forgotten that he had ever had such a dream.

As a result of this experience, he laid down the most important rule of all for dream-watchers. Mentally, we must turn time upside down. We must think of the events of the day and compare them with our dreams of the previous few nights, pretending that the dreams came after the events. Our minds are so much more ready to accept that dreams embody material from the past that they will be much more alert to similarities if we carry out this simple deception.

Dunne persuaded half a dozen friends and relatives to make a record of their dreams. He suggested to one woman, who claimed she never had any, that she wrote down her thoughts on waking and then worked out why she was thinking them. She too was then able to recall dreams and like all the others, quickly found that they contained references to the future. There was no obvious reason why precognition should be restricted to dreams. Dunne chose at random from his club library books he had never read, concentrated on their titles and *avoiding conscious associations,* allowed words and images to form spontaneously in his mind. These were written down. In most cases, they corresponded too closely with passages in the books to be explained away by coincidence. One day, he had a vision of an umbrella standing upside down on its handle with its point in the air. He could find no connection with the book he was working on but a few days later saw an old lady using an umbrella as a walking stick. It too was upside down. She held the point in her hand and tapped the handle along the pavement.

These experiments were by no means scientific. Some of them could be explained by clairvoyance or psychokinesis or even unconscious memory. Presumably it was possible that the old lady had previously made the mistake of walking with her umbrella upside down and that Dunne had unconsciously noticed her. Yet after allowing for all possible objections, there seemed at least a *prima facie* case for precognition. Moreover, all the people asked to experiment apparently had the faculty. It seemed normal not *abnormal* as so many psychical researchers had implied. Nor is it impracticable to trace all examples of precognition in dreams because of the time factor. We often notice past references as far back as childhood. Yet to trace future references over a similar span, we should have to keep detailed records and check them against the happenings of each day for the rest of our lives. By restricting his view to a few days ahead and comparing the number of clearly identifiable future references with the number of clearly identifiable past references during a similar number of previous days Dunne tentatively concluded that our dreams contained as many future references as past references.

He went on to devise a theory of time to account for his experiences. It was based partly on the ideas of C. H. Hinton who had written a highly original monograph entitled *What is the Fourth Dimension?* as long ago as 1887. Hinton pointed out that all objects have the three dimensions of length, breadth and thickness. They must also have a fourth dimension, time. We cannot conceive of a cat, dog, table or mountain which exists for no time. It would not exist at all. But what is this time?

The other three dimensions extend to infinity—length above and below the observer, breadth to his left and right, thickness in front and behind. These extensions are always present, even beyond the range of our senses. A traveller on a ship in the middle of the Pacific Ocean sees the sea stretching to the horizons all round him, where it seems to disappear. We have all followed, at least on television, the launching of a space rocket which soon passes from sight in the vertical dimension. Hinton believed that time extended in a similar sort of way. Unless we take a fundamentalist view, we must conclude that it stretches backwards through the epochs measured by historians, archaeologists, geologists and astronomers into an infinite past. Similarly, it must stretch forwards into an infinite future.

Dunne, following Hinton, believed that what we call the present is simply a cross-section of all the objects and events existing at a particular point in time. Later, we shall see another cross-section, then another and another. . . . We see them only one by one. Those we have already seen become memories. Those ahead are hidden. Together, they form into a continuously moving picture, just as though we were projectionists flashing in rapid succession the pictures of one present after another on to our own consciousness. We cannot wind back the film. We can only remember what we happened to notice. We do not know what is to come in later frames.

Can we say then that the future exists before we become conscious of it? If it doesn't, asks Dunne, where does it come from? The only answer is that it is being continuously created, as we move along the time dimension. And this, he thinks, is "a very strange proposition, and one for which we have no evidence whatsoever." He prefers to think it exists all along.

Dunne also points out that our consciousness is continuously moving along the dimension of time so that successive presents move into the past, which is always growing. We call this movement the passage of time, which, he says, "must be timeable." This Time 1, as he calls it, can, however, only be timed from a fifth dimension at right angles to the fourth. The fifth dimension is Time 2. A second consciousness or Observer 2 travels along Time 2. Observer 2 can see not just the present of Time 1 but also its past and a part of its future. But this is not the end of the matter. We need yet another dimension to time Observer 2 travelling along Time 2, so we have Time 3 and

Observer 3, which require a Time 4 and Observer 4, and so on to infinity. All these different observers are contained in the same self. At infinity, an "Absolute Time" will comprehend all the pasts, presents and futures of the other Times.

He worked out this theory of Serialism in complicated mathematical formulae and intended it to be a "theory of the universe." He applied it to dreams by asking us to imagine an Observer 2 who sometimes took over when the attention of Observer 1 wandered during sleep. Observer 2 could see into Observer 1's future. Hence the mixture of past and future experiences that mingle in our dreams. They are, of course, both distorted for psychological reasons but Dunne believed that the time shifts were an integral part of them.

I have oversimplified Dunne's ideas but not, I hope, twisted them. They are notoriously difficult to explain and in his *Man and Time* (Aldus, U.K., 1964; Doubleday, U.S.A., 1964), J. B. Priestley tells how Dunne himself, an old friend of Priestley's, expounded them to the cast of Priestley's own play on the theme of time, *Time and the Conways*. They were, says Priestley, "a cast that always played well but never better than when they were pretending to understand what he was telling them."

Priestley admired Dunne for his freshness of approach, his boldness of attack, his total lack of crankiness. Most of us have had experiences which do not conform to the "commonsense" view of time and Dunne made it possible for us to discuss these without recourse to mysticism or abstruse philosophy. "Nobody now can seriously examine the Time problem without taking Dunne's work into account," says Priestley. "He has still to be praised as one of our great originals and liberators."

Yet he disagreed almost totally with Dunne's theory, pointing out that it was built on a basic confusion between time as an abstract dimension in the same category as length, breadth or thickness and time as a movement of successive presents along this dimension. Dunne's notion of "taking time" to move along this dimension is what we normally mean by "time." In rejecting this, he was drawn into Serialism with its onion-skin layers of new times and observers to travel along them, so that Absolute Time was reached only at Infinity. Like most of us, Priestley finds this hard to believe.

Nor was Dunne able to solve the problem of free-will and determinism. Priestley quotes a dream mentioned by Dr. Louise E. Rhine in the American *Journal of Parapsychology*. The dreamer saw herself on a camping holiday with her year-old baby. She was about to wash some clothes in a stream when she found she had left the soap behind and leaving her baby on the shingle, went off to get it. When she returned, she found her baby lying face downwards in the water, dead. She woke up sobbing. Shortly afterwards, she was in fact on a camping holiday with her baby and went to wash some clothes in a stream. She realized she had no soap. She was about to get some, leaving her baby behind, when she remembered her dream. The scene was identical. She snatched up her baby and carried him to safety.

The account suggests that the dreamer had a true vision of the future and as a result was able to save her baby's life. But how could she have seen a true picture if the baby did not in fact die? How is it possible for us to intervene in a future that is predetermined?

In Dunne's terms, the Observer 2 part of the woman's mind was able to look ahead and see what was in store for her in Time 1. When she awoke, Observer 1 was back in control but was able to remember Observer 2's glimpse into the future. When she went camping in real life, the memory of the dream reactivated Observer 2 who was able to intervene and change what happened in Time 1. It seems a neat way of resolving the difficulty but does it make sense? Priestley thinks not. As Dunne himself admitted, if Observer 2 sees something lying ahead in Time 1, it must exist. If it fails to materialize, what exactly is it? Dunne gives no satisfactory answer.

Priestley himself had been interested in the time problem long before he read *An Experiment with Time*. In his own life, he occasionally experienced, as most of us have, those moments of entrancement which seem to take us outside the relentless advance of everyday time. They may come when we are listening to music, reading a poem, exploring an ancient cathedral. While looking at the dead fish on a fishmonger's slab, he once had a cosmic vision of the sea and everything contained in it. He had another experience of the odd way in which time works when writing his most difficult plays: *Dangerous Corner, Time and the Conways, An Inspector Calls, The Linden Tree*. They were packed with technical problems but carried along on a wave of creativity, he was able to write them in a week or, at most, ten days. These were among his best plays—*Dangerous Corner* was also his first. Yet they took far less *time* than "very faulty or even abortive plays."

Priestley does not offer a tightly buttoned mathematical theory to account for his experiences. He admits that he does not know the answer to some of the questions raised but he is convinced that time is much more complicated, even here on earth, than our "common-sense" suggests. In an attempt to distinguish between the various aspects, he follows Dunne in giving the name Time 1 to everyday, passing time, a concept adequate and even necessary for practical life, but from then on his ideas are looser and rather different. Priestley's Time 2 takes over in visions, premonitions and most commonly of all in dreams. It offers glimpses of the future. And here we come up once again against the conflict between determinism and free will. If we can foresee the future, it must be predetermined. If it *is* predetermined, how can we change it, as, for instance, the American woman who saved her baby from drowning in the stream succeeded in doing?

Priestley shows that there is a way out of the dilemma. In effect, he asks: "Just because some of the future is predetermined, why should it all be?" We accept this view without question in everyday matters. I know that a year from now the sun will rise every morning, that it will shine down on the part of Earth in which I happen to live and that my home town will look much the same as it does now. But then uncertainty creeps in. I *expect* that I shall still be living in the same house but I might win the football pools and so have the choice of moving to a better house. I *expect* to be alive and well but I could have a fatal accident or illness and whether I do so will be decided at least partly by my own carefulness and whether I consult a doctor in time. Priestley points out that Time 2 predictions in dreams may in fact be predetermined but that parts of what we think are predictions are not predictions at all, just elaborations of the imagination. Returning once more to the American woman who saved her baby from drowning, we could say that the scene by the stream was predetermined but the rest of her dream was "a dramatization of not unusual maternal anxiety." It was a warning of *possible* danger. On this theory, it would seem that Time 2 gives us the "set and characters" but "the action comes out of imagination." These actions cannot come out of Time 1 nor yet out of Time 2, which only foresees the future of Time 1. They can come only from a Time 3, the part of the mind "where the creative imagination has its home and does its work." It was in Time 3 that he was able to write *Dangerous Corner* and the other plays so quickly.

Yet Priestley is dissatisfied with this theory, mainly because there seems to be no difference in texture between the parts of a dream that are predetermined and those that are imaginary. There is no logical reason why there should be but he feels it odd. The alternative, which he prefers, is to assume a future "already shaped but still pliable, yielding—in these instances, though obviously not in many others—to will and action. It is as if ahead of us in Time 1 were shapes, moulds, patterns, possibilities, seen as definite events in certain of our dreams; and into some of these shapes, moulds, patterns, there arrives the material substance that actualizes them, hardening them into world history." He suggests that this may be the reason why pre-cognitive dreams rarely seem to deal with events of average impor-tance, but nearly always of "the terrible and the trivial." It is pre-cisely the terrible and the trivial which "are nearly always outside our control. So that it is they in nine cases out of 10, at least, that will be revealed in precognitive dreams because they are there to be revealed."

Priestley's views on time are highly personal, owing more to intuition than to physics and mathematics, and in the present state of our knowledge, this is no bad thing. He gives us a theory that cannot be proved but goes nearer than most to explaining what many of us *feel* about this complex subject. Before leaving it, let us take a look at the light in which some other thinkers of various kinds accounted for this phenomenon of the future, as well as the past, somehow existing in the present.

From Langland to Tennyson, poets have "dip't into the future" with their visions and in "Burnt Norton", T. S. Eliot suggests that all time is co-existent :

> Time present and time past
> Are both perhaps present in time future,
> And time future contained in time past.

Some mystics have felt the same. Meister Eckhart was a Dominican monk who came of an aristocratic German family and graduated as a doctor of theology in Paris in 1302. Among the few other things we know about him are that he held at various times the offices of Prior of Erfurt, Vicar of Thuringia and Prior of Strasbourg and died shortly before being condemned as a heretic by a papal Bull of 1329. His sermons and other works give him a foremost place among the great German mystics. Yet, allowing for the difference of terminology, his view of eternity is similar in many respects to Priestley's Time 3. In his *Sermon on the Just Man and Justice* (trans-lated by James M. Clark and John V. Skinner in *Meister Eckhart*, Faber, U.K., 1958; Philosophical Library, U.S.A., 1959), he says,

> When man is raised up above time into eternity, he works there one work with God. Some people ask how man can do the works that God did a thousand years ago and will do a thousand years hence, and they do not understand it. In eternity, there is neither "before" nor "after." For this reason, what occurred a thousand years ago and what will happen a thousand years hence and what

happens now are all one in eternity. Therefore, what God wrought a thousand years ago, what He will do in a thousand years and what He is doing now is nothing but one work. Therefore the man who is raised up above time in eternity works with God what God worked a thousand years ago and what He will work a thousand years hence. And this is for wise people a matter of knowledge and for the ignorant a matter of belief.

In a completely different way, the German philosopher Immanuel Kant (1724–1804) undermined conventional ideas of time. Briefly, he believed that we could *know* nothing about "things in themselves" and all we had to go on were sense impressions of them—the sight of a table, the sound of an explosion, the smell of turpentine, the feel of silk and so on. We cannot experience time in this way, says Kant. It is a form of "intuition." Unless we presuppose there is such a thing as time, we cannot say whether things exist at the same time or at different times. So past, present and future are all in the mind. It would seem, therefore, that these might happen in a different order if the mind somehow changed gear.

More recent theorists have suggested much the same idea. P. D. Ouspensky, the Russian writer, believed that time itself had three dimensions, the third of them containing "unactualized possibilities," —the might-have-beens of life. This, at least, is a neat way of disposing of events dreamed of but avoided because the dreamer was given prior warning. Usually, says Ouspensky, we do not see the future at all. He explains why in *Tertium Organum* (Routledge, U.K., 1957; Roydon House, U.S.A., 1971).

Our psychic life proceeds upon some definite plans (of conscious-ness or matter) and never rises above it. If our receptivity could rise above this plane it would undoubtedly perceive *simultaneously,* below itself, a far greater number of events than it usually sees while on a plane. Just as a man, ascending a mountain, or going up in a balloon, begins to see *simultaneously* and *at once* many things which it is impossible to see simultaneously and at once from below—the movement of two trains toward one another between which a collision will occur; the approach of an enemy detachment to a sleeping camp; two cities divided by a ridge, etc. —so consciousness rising above the plane in which it usually functions, must see simultaneously the events divided for ordinary consciousness by *periods of time.* These will be the events which ordinary consciousness *never* sees together, as *cause and effect;* the work and the payment: the crime and the punishment: the movement of trains toward one another and their collision: the approach of the enemy and the battle: the sunrise and the sunset: the morning and the evening: the day and the night: spring, autumn, summer and winter: the birth and the death of a man.

The angel of vision will enlarge during such an ascent, the *moment* will expand.

Mr. H. F. Saltmarsh, a distinguished and highly sceptical psychical researcher said much the same thing in rather different words. He pointed out that what we call the present is not, except for scientists, a point without length or breadth. It occupies a space of time, however minute. It must extend slightly into the past, slightly into the future. Now most apparent glimpses into the future seem to occur when we are not in a normal state of consciousness. They come in dreams when we are asleep, and in visions or flashes of intuition when ordinary waking consciousness seems to be transcended. Saltmarsh suggested that the present occupies a wider space of time in the sub-conscious, giving us access to both future and past, just as a man peeping through a hole at a moving picture of a fox running across a screen would know before a man looking at the same picture through a smaller hole, that the fox was being chased by hounds. For this man, he could predict what was coming on the screen next. The necessities of everyday life require us to give our full attention to what is immediately under our noses and it would make for total confusion if we tried to cope with the events of too wide a time span. On the conscious level, therefore, our knowledge is restricted, but when we are relaxed, tired or asleep, the sub-conscious may take over and allow us to see a much wider range of time, both past and future.

Professor C. D. Broad of Cambridge University suggested a rather similar theory. Normally, we think of time as a one-dimensional line leading from the past through the present to the future. But suppose time had a second dimension so that it was not a line but a plane. We could then explain apparent predictions as glimpses of the future seen "across country" to our right and left. It would be as though ordinary passing time was a car driven along a straight road with high hedges. At right angles to this road are numerous cross roads representing future events. In normal states of consciousness, we cannot see what is happening on them until we reach a junction where they cross our road. But suppose there were occasions, perhaps in sleep or states of trance, when the hedges were down. We could then look diagonally ahead and see what was happening on the crossing roads before we reached the point where they intersected our normal time track. We could see into the future.

Such theories are only theories. They explain only *how* we might be able to see into the future, assuming it somehow co-existed with the present. But even if we accept that the future can be foreseen, we need not believe that it exists already. Attempts have been made to explain prediction by comparing the human mind with a highly complicated computer. If we assume that the universe works only by the known rules of cause and effect, it follows that the causes of every future event exist here and now in the present. Given a mind sensitive enough to pick up all these causative influences through the senses of sight, sound, taste, smell, touch and others which we do not yet know about, it would be able to sort and interpret them, so as to predict their future effects. It would presumably be doing this all the time but for practical reasons would not normally give us such a torrent of information for fear of confusing us. To some extent, we accept this view. If we hear the doorbell ring we know from previous experience stored in our personal computer that some-one will be there when we open it. However, when we apply the theory to remoter predictions, it is hard to credit. Dunne, for instance, claimed that he foresaw a newspaper account of an earthquake that happened at the other side of the world. Clearly the causes existed long in advance : the state of the earth's crust in Martinique, the character of the victims and rescuers that caused them to act as they did (though this dodges the question of free will), the elaborate machinery for reporting the news, printing it and shipping the papers to South Africa. Knowing the fallibility of the human mind, one simply cannot believe that it could pick up such a mass of informa-tion with the necessary degree of accuracy (after all, Dunne *mis*read the report when it actually appeared, taking 40,000 for 4,000) and then interpret it all so precisely as to foresee the actual phrases the *Daily Telegraph* headline writers would use in presenting it.

In their book *Modern Experiments in Telepathy* (Faber, U.K., 1954; Yale U.P., U.S.A., 1957), S. G. Soal and F. Bateman put forward yet another theory. It was devised by Dr. G. D. Wassermann, a mathematical physicist of Durham University, who helped them in some of their precognition experiments. Dr. Wassermann suggested "that world events have pre-existing mental patterns, and that it is these patterns, and not the events themselves, which we contact. . . . Themselves timeless, these patterns are in the process of realizing themselves in time. Perhaps . . . the latent patterns of all possible events pre-exist—both those that will be realized and those that will never become actual." He thinks that an infinity of mental patterns is associated not only with the particles of living matter but with every fundamental particle in the universe. The evolutionary process suggests the pre-existence of well-defined patterns which realize themselves bit by bit at the moments when appropriate molecular assemblies become available. It is difficult to suppose for instance that the neurons of the speech centres in man were the result of chance mutations alone. Wassermann thinks that natural selection and chance mutations are insufficient to explain evolution; there is in addition a tremendous drive inherent in the patterns themselves, which are pushing towards physical embodiment against all obstacles. ". . . There is no creation but only a development of patterns which are eternal and indestructible. According to this view, the behaviour of the molecules in a human body is only partly determined by the laws of quantum theory; there are superimposed on these quantum effects psycho-kinetic influences produced by the urge of striving patterns. The only meaning that could be given to human freedom is that we are free when our desires are in harmony with the unconscious urge of the developing patterns. It may be that we are unconsciously in touch with the mental patterns of all possible events in the universe, but an avoidance drive prevents the vast majority of such patterns from becoming conscious. Those patterns which have achieved realization in time appear to us as memory but only rarely do the unfulfilled patterns of future events escape the vigilance of the avoidance drive and reach the level of consciousness."

Again, this can be criticized as "just a theory" and so it is. But at the moment, we know almost nothing of the true nature of time.

Eventual agreement, if it is ever reached, will result from the successful testing of an hypothesis at least as revolutionary as any we have yet examined. Meanwhile, it is important to keep a completely open mind. The fact that we regard prior knowledge of the future as inconceivable does not mean it is impossible. As Dr. Hadfield points out (*op. cit.*), discoveries and inventions we now take for granted were once greeted with derision by leading scientists. When Professor Tait, the physicist, was told of the invention of the telephone, he snorted, "It is all humbug, for such a discovery is physically impossible." In 1878, a learned member of the French Academy of Science was so affronted by a demonstration of Edison's phonograph that he accused the demonstrator of tricking them with ventriloquism. Even when, six months later, he was allowed to inspect the machine, he refused to believe that a thing of metal could reproduce the human voice. Ten, a hundred or perhaps a thousand years from now, historians of science will perhaps be writing of the time when distinguished scientists and philosophers were silly enough to believe that foreknowledge of the future was equally absurd.

8 Our Prophetic Stars

Today, astrology is easily the most popular method of foretelling the future. Millions who never have prophetic dreams, never visit palmists and have never even heard of scientific experiments in precognition turn automatically to their favourite newspaper astrologer every morning of their lives. In 1968 the *Sunday Times* published an Opinion Research Centre poll which showed that three-quarters of the women and half the men in Britain regularly read their horoscopes. Interest was higher among the "unskilled working class" (70 per cent) than among the "professional and managerial class" (58 per cent). Perhaps the most surprising finding was that horoscopes were especially popular with the 21-24 group. More than three-quarters regularly consulted them. As we have seen, newspaper astrology has probably become more, not less popular, since the Opinion Research Centre poll was taken.

Nor does interest end with newspapers. Sales of paperbacks with an astrological slant run into eight figures a year. They cover everything from straight instruction to astrological cooking and sex. Numerous magazines ranging from the trivial to the learned are published in Britain, America, France, Germany, India and many other countries. At least one, sold in both Britain and America, has a circulation of some quarter of a million. *Old Moore's Almanack*, published continuously since 1697 when it was launched by Dr. Francis Moore to promote sales of his medicines, has a British circulation of 1,300,000 and a readership almost four times as great. Overseas editions are published in America, Australia and Canada.

Computerized horoscopes can also be bought. So too, can long-playing records giving a whole year's predictions. In Britain, the Post Office telephone service offers a two-and-a-half minute recording consisting of a general forecast and a special birthday forecast, both of which are changed daily. The only charge is the price of a phone call to Birmingham. When the scheme started in May, 1972, astrologer Maurice Woodruff admitted, "It is impossible to give detailed horoscopes for all twelve signs of the Zodiac in such a short time. But I am sure the service will be a great help, particularly to people who rush impulsively into things."

According to Derek Parker, whose wife Julia is herself a well-known astrologer and secretary of the Faculty of Astrological Studies, more and more businessmen are consulting astrologers before taking important decisions. In his *Astrology in the Modern World* (Taplinger, U.S.A., 1970), he says that one well-known woman practitioner "works in an advisory capacity for over fifty companies, some of them bearing internationally known names. There is an initial basic fee of 100 guineas for a consultation at which she collects the information she requires about the company and its officers; she then works on various charts and eventually gets a good general picture of the company's astrological personality. She is then in a position to give advice on particular contingencies for which her fee may be from 25 guineas upwards."

Collectively we must be spending millions of pounds a year to learn about our future from the stars. But how far do we really believe in astrology?

Again, there is little hard information. One of the few thorough surveys was undertaken by Geoffrey Gore and reported in his *Exploring English Character* (Cresset, U.K., 1955). Of 4,983 readers who filled in a questionnaire in *The People* newspaper, a half said that they regularly read its astrologer, "Lyndoe," and another 39 per cent that they read him "occasionally." Four out of five also regularly or occasionally read other newspaper horoscopes. Yet only 20 per cent of those who read horoscopes thought there was "something in" them and a third were "uncertain." The rest, 44 per cent, were total sceptics. Only 3 per cent regularly acted on the advice given and a further 22 occasionally did so. Nearly three-quarters totally ignored it.

It seems, then, that millions regularly consult the stars by one means or another just in case there may be "something in it." Few people are willing to confess themselves believers, though the evidence suggests that collectively, we have enough faith to spend large sums of money on it. The same is apparently true of business astrology. Derek Parker (*op. cit.*) confesses that it is difficult to produce concrete evidence because the astrologers concerned rightly refuse to reveal the names of their clients and the businessmen themselves are unwilling to come out into the open, presumably because it would be bad for their reputations. "In fact, an astrologer is often retained semi-privately by a member of the board of a company, and the account will show his fees as paid to a 'business consultant'. He will sometimes be brought the astrological data of two or three companies and will have to inspect the charts of the members of rival boards, and of the companies themselves, before advising on a take-over. He will have to advise, also, a propitious time to make contact, and for the signing of papers."

Of the numerous celebrities and businessmen who consult astrologers, I have been able to find only two who were brave enough to confess it. In a *Daily Mail* article by Anthea Disney (August 17th, 1971), Mr. Harry Rosenthal, owner of the Foremost Travel Agency in London, was quoted as saying, "For six years, I have been going to Maurice Woodruff. He is reliable. I recently sold a hotel on his advice, and later was able to buy a far better one offered to me out of the blue, just as he'd predicted." Roger Moore, the actor, was said to have been warned off buying a house by his astrologer, Ivor Dean. "I liked the place so much," Mr. Moore was quoted as saying. "But I found out afterwards how horribly swindled I would have been if I'd gone ahead. If I hit a problem tomorrow, I would phone three people straight away—my agent, my bank manager and Ivor Dean."

Even though so few of us admit that we believe in astrology, many of us do so at least partly and from the numbers who read newspaper horoscopes, it seems obvious that we should *like* to believe in it. There is a good reaon for this. Only a minority now have an active religious faith or even a well thought out alternative, such as humanism. The majority feel themselves adrift in a world ruled by chance alone. Even in a welfare state, death and disaster are forever hovering in the wings, ready to pounce at the most unexpected moments. We feel desperately insecure. Millions turn to astrology because it offers a total system of which our earth is an integral part. Nothing happens by chance. It happens because it is "in our stars." Moreover, astrology uses some of the most powerful symbols known to man—the sun, the moon, the planets, virile animals such as the goat, the lion and the bull; the fish and the virgin which had deep religious significance long before the advent of Christianity. These appeal to the irrational, instinctive side of our nature which technology denies but cannot destroy. The fascination of astrology for so many young people should not surprise us. It is one way of filling a need which, they feel, they can no longer satisfy by orthodox religion.

These trends are reflected in the paradoxical history of astrology. Broadly speaking, it prospered as a science when so much of nature was inexplicable. It almost died when the Age of Enlightenment briefly promised that everything could be explained by Reason. It took on a new life when this promise was found to be false. Now, with both reason and organized religion on the retreat, it flourishes as never before.

Almost all ancient civilizations, including those of India, China, Egypt and even the Americas tried to find a meaning in the stars. Our own system of astrology is descended directly from that of Babylon, which also influenced Indian ideas and dominated those of Egyptian astrologers. Living in a land of immense plains and brilliantly clear skies, the Babylonian priests were ideally placed to study the movements of the heavenly bodies. They did so from high towers, specially erected for the purpose, and kept detailed records which they compared with events on earth. They quickly discovered that the position of the sun corresponded closely with the growing cycle and the state of the rivers and when they found that there were approximaely twelve full moons during a complete cycle of the sun, they had the basis of a calendar. They could predict accurately in which moon, or month, it was propitious to sow and reap. They knew exactly when they could expect flood or drought, hot days or comparatively cool days. Apart from the sun and moon, they distinguished two kinds of heavenly bodies. The stars, which seemed to revolve round the earth but did not change their position relative to each other, formed a sort of back-cloth for five others, which wandered in more complex fashion—the planets Mercury, Venus, Mars, Jupiter and Saturn.

If the sun and moon could together influence the earth, it seemed logical to suppose that the planets could do so too. At first, they thought that planets themselves had this godlike power. Later, they came to believe that various gods worked through the planets. They had different names from those used by us but their attributes were similar. Mars, which has a ruddy tinge, was ruled by an angry, war-like god. Venus, which rose early in the morning, heralding the birth of a new day, was the domain of a goddess representing all that was feminine in life. The system was next extended by the marking out of the Zodiac, an imaginary band whose centre line was the ecliptic or apparent orbit of the sun. The Zodiac extended some eight degrees on each side of this to take in also the apparent movements of the planets and was divided into twelve equal parts or signs. These too corresponded with our own. Each took its name from the constellation in the ascendant, that is, rising over the eastern horizon at dawn during the period in question.

It is interesting to note that the constellations themselves were named not because of their shapes. The names symbolized events which happened when they were in the ascendant. In *The Astrologers and their Creed* (Hutchinson, U.K., 1969) Christopher McIntosh explains that the signs were thought of as aspects of the sun and moon. The stars were likened to a flock of sheep and as the first sign opened the year as the sun opens the day, its brightest star was thought of as the Ram (Aries) which leads the flock.

> Aquarius, the Water Pourer, is the Sun in his capacity as a rain-giver. This is because of the heavy rainfall that occurred in Babylonia in January—the time when the Sun was in Aquarius. The alternation of night and day is reflected in the way in which the constellation figures are associated alternately with the Sun and Moon, or night and day. Thus, whilst the first sign, Aries, is a day sign, the second, Taurus, is a night sign. The horns of the Moon lead to an obvious association with those of a bull. And so the alternation continues round the zodiac. Today the divisions between day and night signs has been transformed into a division between positive and negative signs.

The Babylonians also allotted to each sign an element—earth, air, fire or water—which we still recognize. By the fourth century B.C., the Babylonians were casting personal horoscopes.

After the conquest of Babylon by Alexander the Great, astrology was widely practised in Greece and the system elaborated still further. Birth charts were divided into twelve segments or "houses," each representing some part of life such as personality or career. Also, each sign was placed under the "rule" of a planet or of the sun and moon combined and due regard paid to the "aspects," the relative positions of the planets on the birth chart. Again, these refinements are still in use. In the second century A.D., Claudius Ptolemy, a mathematician of Alexandria, wrote his *Syntaxis,* a highly learned work of astronomy that set out an ingenious theory whereby the entire universe was said to revolve around the earth.

The early Roman emperors sharply stimulated belief in astrology. Until then, it had been largely regarded as the province of orientalized Greeks, though it was by no means unknown under the Republic. When the future Emperor Augustus was born, a scholar called Publius Tigidius Figulus announced that the baby would one day rule Rome and eighteen years later, the astrologer Theogenes confirmed the prediction. Not surprisingly, Augustus became a lifelong believer and even had his birth sign, Capricorn, inscribed on a coin. Rome swarmed with astrologers. Some were obviously charlatans and he had them expelled.

He was also aware of another danger that was to haunt his successors too. If an astrologer predicted an emperor's death, those who hoped to take his place would be tempted to hasten the process. In A.D. 11, Augustus made it an offence publicly to predict death. Later emperors were more devious, using astrologers when it was convenient but keeping them in constant fear for their own safety. In his *Annals* (translated by Michael Grant, Penguin, London, 1956), Tacitus gives a graphic description of Tiberius's dealing with Thrasyllus, the learned Greek who had taught him about astrology in Rhodes.

> He tested Thrasyllus' knowledge in this way. When seeking occult guidance, Tiberius would retire to the top of his house, with a single, tough, illiterate ex-slave as confidant. Those astrologers whose skill Tiberius had decided to test were escorted to him by this man over pathless precipitous ground; for the house overhung a cliff. Then, on their way down, if they were suspected of unreliability or fraudulence, the ex-slave hurled them into the sea below, so that no betrayer of the secret proceedings should survive. Thrasyllus, after reaching Tiberius by this steep route, had impressed him, when interrogated, by his intelligent forecasts of future events—including Tiberius's accession. Tiberius then inquired if Thrasyllus had cast his own horoscope. How did it appear for the current year and day? Thrasyllus, after measuring the positions and distance of the stars, hesitated, then showed alarm. The more he looked, the greater became his astonishment and fright. Then he cried that a critical and perhaps fatal emergency was upon him. Tiberius clasped him, commending his divination of peril and promising he would escape it. Thrasyllus was admitted among his closest friends; his pronouncements were regarded as oracular.

Astrology was not just a superstition of the unthinking. It was embraced by many of the most intelligent and learned. There was a widespread belief that the entire universe was joined together in over-riding harmony: men and gods, earth and the heavenly bodies. The Stoics especially elevated astrology almost into a religion. It powerfully influenced both Gnosticism, a collection of beliefs based on the assumption that salvation comes only from knowledge revealed to the initiated, and to a lesser extent, the neo-Platonism of Plotinus.

Yet there had always been an undertow of doubt. The idea that man's destiny was controlled by outside influences affronted the early Republican ideal of self-reliance. The poet Lucretius, the soldier-dictator Julius Caesar and the lawyer-politician Cicero all remained sceptical. So later did the writers Pliny and Juvenal.

Prediction and Prophecy

Astrology also failed to satisfy the emotional needs of the people. As a belief by which they could live, it was too rigorous, too rational. It made men pawns in the cosmic game, condemning them to oblivion after their brief and meaningless spell on earth. Many turned to mystery religions such as Mithraism and the worship of Bacchus, Aesculapius, Cybele or Isis. These provided an outlet for the instincts and feelings which astrology tended to deny.

At first, Christianity tolerated astrology but in the long run, it was hard to reconcile Christian doctrine with the view that human destiny was controlled by the heavenly bodies. In his *Confessions,* St. Augustine called astrologers "impostors." He quoted Jesus' words to the cripple he had cured, "Sin no more, lest a worse thing come unto thee." He went on, "This truth is our whole salvation, but the astrologers try to do away with it. They tell us that the cause of sin is determined in the heavens and we cannot escape it, and that this or that is the work of Venus or Saturn or Mars. They want us to believe that man is guiltless, flesh and blood though he is and doomed to die despite his pride. Instead, they have it that the blame is to be laid on the Creator and Ruler of the Heavens, and the stars, none other than our God, himself the very source of justice." (From *Confessions,* translated by R. S. Pine-Coffin, Penguin, U.K., 1961; U.S.A., 1961.)

During the Dark Ages, the flame of learning was kept alight in Christian Europe almost exclusively by the church. As astrology was now officially out of favour, it was almost forgotten. However, Arab scholars kept the subject alive and it was from their manuscripts that interest revived, especially in the school of Chartres. The renaissance of classical learning added to this interest and after a long period of doubt, during which an astrologer called Cecco d'Ascoli was burnt at the stake, the church finally came to terms with astrology. After all, a star had heralded the birth of Jesus and later, he himself had prophesied, "And there shall be signs in the sun, and in the moon, and in the stars; and upon the earth, distress of nations . . ." (Luke xxi:25). Most churchmen followed St. Thomas Aquinas in concluding that heavenly bodies did in truth exert an influence over men's characters and deeds. However, this influence could be counteracted by the human will and predictions could therefore come true only in general terms.

Astrology boomed as never before. Kings, princes, merchants, even popes consulted astrologers. The leading scholars of the day studied the stars. As we have seen, the Englishman Dr. John Dee was asked to choose by astrology a propitious day for Queen Elizabeth i's coronation. Doctors used astrology for predicting the course of an illness and for deciding the moment at which a leech was to be applied. They blamed the stars for diseases ranging from syphilis to the plague and even today we speak of "influenza," because it was then thought to be caused by an astral influence.

The death knell of astrology as an accepted science sounded in 1543. In that year, a Polish scholar called Nicolas Copernicus published his *De Revolutionibus Orbium,* which sought to show that the earth was not the centre of the universe but simply one of the planets revolving round the sun. Later astronomers, including Galileo, agreed with Copernicus and though it took some two hundred years for the implications to be understood and accepted, it was clear that no serious thinker could continue to believe that the earth was the centre of the universe. Many of the assumptions on which astrology was based were seen to be untenable. After violent controversies, it was written off as a mere superstition by the philosophers and scientists of the eighteenth-century "Enlightenment."

Unlike alchemy, astrology did not die. It was kept alive by scholars with a taste for the occult. It was practised among the ordinary people who were always ready to pay a few pence for a horoscope, even though astrologers were frowned on by authority. In England, they were liable to be prosecuted under the Vagrancy Act of 1824 which, even now, states that "every Person pretending or professing to tell Fortunes . . . to deceive and impose on any of His Majesty's Subjects . . . shall be deemed a Rogue and vagabond . . ."

As successive Education Acts brought mass literacy, astrology flourished alongside the popular press and widely advertised patent medicines. Robert Cross Smith was the first to appeal to this growing public with his *Prophetic Messenger,* first published in 1827. He wrote under the name of Raphael. Lieutenant Richard James Morrison, a retired naval officer, wrote several books on astrology, including an annual *Herald of Astrology* under his pen name Zadkiel.

Raphael and Zadkiel were the best-known of several astrologers writing for this popular market. Though sometimes sensational in their approach, they were basically serious. Alfred John Pearce, who died in 1923 at the age of eighty-three, was the author of a standard text-book containing nearly 500 closely printed pages of instructions, examples, statistics and anecdotes of successful predictions. "Tycho Brahe not only carefully studied the comet of 1577 as an astronomer," he wrote, "but as an astrologer predicted, from its appearance, that: 'In the North, in Finland, there should be born a Prince who should lay waste Germany and vanish in 1632.'

Prediction and Prophecy

Gustavus Adolphus, it is well known, was born in Finland, overran Germany, and died in 1632." Pearce, who was the third editor of *Zadkiel's Almanac,* claims that he himself "clearly foretold the following great earthquakes:—Kuchan, 1893; San Francisco, 1906; India, 1905; Valparaiso, 1906; Italy and Messina, 1908–1909. Moreover, these forecasts saved many readers of *Zadkiel's Almanac* for 1905, 1906, 1908 and 1909 from being involved in the horrors of these awful catastrophes." He quotes a "fan" letter from a Captain A. T. Banon who wrote to him from the Punjab after the Indian earthquake of 1905 : "I have come to the conclusion that your theory, electric telluric currents, as to the cause of earthquakes is correct; and that the scientific orthodox theory is incorrect."

In the Edwardian era, an astrologer known as Alan Leo was much better known than Pearce. His real name was William Frederick Allen and he used the techniques of salesmanship picked up during his early life as a commercial traveller to sell both the *Astrologer's Magazine,* which he launched in 1890, and more especially the personal horoscopes he advertised in it. In the first three years, he sold 20,000 at a shilling a time. These were individually prepared by his staff of nine in the same way that motoring organizations prepare road routes for their members. He broke down all the analyses he had ever written into separate paragraphs, which were duplicated and filed. His assistants worked out which were appropriate for each enquirer, clipped them together and sent them off.

Leo's books and those of his contemporary Sepharial sold in large numbers. Even so, astrology remained a minority interest until well after the First World War. Some devotees tried to keep it scientific but many preferred it with an occult flavour, especially those who came to it through the Theosophical Society of Madame Blavatsky and Annie Besant, or through the breakaway Anthroposophical Society of Rudolf Steiner. In Britain, Germany and America, the Theosophical Society, whose doctrines are tinged with Eastern mysticism, was a major influence in spreading interest.

Astrology broke into the mass media in 1930. With a characteristic flair for scenting what the public was ready for, the editor of the *Daily Express* asked R. H. Naylor to cast a horoscope for Princess Margaret who had been born on August 21st. Naylor scored some remarkable hits. The Princess would have "extreme originality of mind, an unconventional vein . . . a vivid emotional nature." He predicted that "events of tremendous importance to the Royal Family and to the nation will come about near her seventh year and these events will indirectly affect her own fortunes." He forecast a sudden marriage "about the 24th or 26th year." As we now know, King Edward VIII abdicated just before she was seven and her father, the then Duke of York, became King George VI. These events had such an effect on her own fortunes that despite her undoubted "originality of mind, unconventional vein and vivid emotional nature" she was virtually forced by her position to break with Group Captain Peter Townsend, whom most people had expected her to marry, when she was twenty-six.

At the time, Naylor's article was simply entertaining journalism but it helped win him a regular place in the *Sunday Express*. In his very first column, he scored a sensational success. British aircraft, he said, were in great danger. On that very day, October 5th, 1930, the R101 airship crashed at Beauvais, France. This coup virtually forced other newspapers to run horoscope columns and they have done so ever since. In 1941, a Mass-Observation survey explained the appeal of astrology in the uncertain conditions of the time as a reassurance to the majority who lacked "deep ideological or theological belief" that there was "some sort of pattern for events to follow." Mass-Observation thought it filled a passing need and would decline after the war. It has not declined, presumably because he majority still lack "deep ideological or theological belief" to sustain them in the uncertainties of peace.

But is this belief justified? Can the relative positions of the heavenly bodies really give us an insight into either the present or the future? If so, how?

Few serious astrologers would defend newspaper horoscopes, except as harmless entertainment (and as a way of making money for themselves). By their own rules, predictions for all readers born under a particular sign can have very little in common. They are forced to generalize in a way which may, with luck, intuition and intelligent guesswork based on current events and the time of the year, mean something to a fair proportion of the readers under each sign. Anyone can make a quick test of their objective truth by comparing the prediction of the various newspapers on a particular day.

Here are those given for my own sign, *Virgo* (August 22nd-September 22nd) for Sunday, April 9th, 1972, complete and unedited:

Sunday Express (David Saxby): "Friends and neighbours take a prominent part in family issues. A major upward trend occurs in your work."

Prediction and Prophecy

Sunday Mirror (Constance Sharp): "Career prospects a bit dodgy. Sit tight until they improve. If you must make a move, Tuesday is the best day."
News of the World ("Stargazer"—Dorothy Adams): "Big developments in working life with unexpected gains. Your prestige rises to dizzy heights. Love life is exciting. LUCKY NUMBER 11."
Sunday People (Lyndoe): "A tendency to rush decisions should be avoided. One would expect some temperamental reactions from a friend. People connected with your work provide help."

Do these make sense? It is hard to reconcile "a major upward trend" in my work with "career prospects a bit dodgy." If I can hope for "unexpected gains" and prestige rising "to dizzy heights," I am unlikely to avoid my alleged "tendency to rush decisions."

Lyndoe does score one hit. On this particular Sunday, he advised his readers how they should "get away from it all." Virgoans were lumped with Taureans and Capricornians. Those of us born under these signs, he said, "frequently make a big show of being hard-headed and practical. Deep down, however, there is a liking for the gentler, more beautiful things in life. So they should relax by studying nature, visiting art galleries." Was it only a coincidence that I had just taken up bird-watching and had always found enjoyment in visiting art galleries? I am beginning to understand why so many people read their horoscope regularly!

An individually prepared horoscope is quite different. The astrologer needs to know not just the place and date of birth but the time as well. This is usually taken to be the moment when the baby first cried. If the baby was born unconscious, it is the time when the cord was cut. The astrologer then draws a plan of the sky showing the positions of the sun, moon, stars and planets as they were then. In the "equal house" method, which is commonly favoured in Britain, he starts with a blank chart, consisting of two concentric outer circles and a smaller inner circle representing the earth. The space between the inner and the first outer circle is then divided into twelve segments of thirty degrees. These represent the "houses," which are numbered anti-clockwise from one to twelve, starting with the segment between eight and nine o'clock. The astrologer now consults an "ephemeris" or astrological almanac, which details the positions of the heavenly bodies as seen from various places on every day of the year. He finds out which sign of the Zodiac lay over the eastern horizon at the time of birth and at what angle. He marks this angle by a line drawn between the two outer circles of his chart and then marks off the other signs in order. The positions of the sun, moon and planets are then plotted. All this involves laborious calculation.

The birth chart or horoscope is then interpreted to give the client's general disposition and life tendencies. Basically, these are determined by the relative positions of the sun, moon and planets. Their influence may be weak or strong, depending on where they lie and how they are affected by each other. Systems of interpretation differ and astrologers themselves make further modifications in the light of experience. Generally speaking they agree that the houses relate to separate aspects of life:

> First – character.
> Second – money.
> Third – communication, immediate family.
> Fourth – home, parents.
> Fifth – children, sex, the instincts.
> Sixth – health.
> Seventh – marriage, relationships outside the family.
> Eighth – death.
> Ninth – travel, the inner life.
> Tenth – career, position in the world.
> Eleventh – friends.
> Twelfth – illness, afflictions.

The twelve personality types corresponding to the zodiacal signs are also generally agreed. They are:

Aries – irritable, aggressive, perhaps with strong powers of leadership, *e.g.* Bismarck, Van Gogh.

Taurus – practical, equable but furious when provoked, *e.g.* George Washington, Sigmund Freud.

Gemini – of lively intellect, creative, but can be fickle, *e.g.* George Bernard Shaw, John F. Kennedy.

Cancer – undemonstrative, tenacious, sensitive but can be devious, effeminate, *e.g.* Lord Byron, Frederick Wolfe (alias Baron Corvo).

Leo – resolute, outgoing, uncomplicated but can be haughty and over-ambitious, *e.g.* Dumas père (author of *The Three Musketeers*), Mussolini.

Virgo – studious, aloof, industrious, perhaps country-loving, *e.g.* Lyndon B. Johnson, Tolstoy.

Libra – good-tempered, amiable, high principled, balanced but can be vacillating, *e.g.* Erasmus, Gandhi.

Prediction and Prophecy

Scorpio – vigorous, sexy, ambitious, can be reserved and thoughtful but also rancorous, *e.g.* Napoleon Bonaparte, Mata Hari, Edith Piaf.

Sagittarius – jovial, active, intellectual but also physical, traditionally the hunting type, *e.g.* Theodore Roosevelt, Sir Winston Churchill.

Capricorn – phlegmatic, stubborn, subtle, can be somewhat humourless, *e.g.* Emperor Augustus, Woodrow Wilson.

Aquarius – amiable, peaceful, idealistic, given to "doing his own thing," *e.g.* Charles Dickens, Abraham Lincoln.

Pisces – dreamy, artistic, usually lively but can be moody, *e.g.* Chopin, Nijinsky.

These basic character types can be affected, emphasized or even negated by the ways in which they are influenced by the sun, moon and planets. Here, interpretation becomes highly complex, calling for both knowledge and experience. It is not surprising that astrologers with a reputation for hitting on the truth are in great demand.

Apart from innumerable charlatans and semi-amateurs, there are possibly several hundred full-time professional astrologers in Britain. They are extremely serious about their work and may even have completed the exacting two-year examination course of the Faculty of Astrological Studies. A single analysis may take many hours, even days, depending on the information requested by the client. Fees are necessarily high with leading practitioners charging up to twenty-five guineas for a full forecast. In America it could easily be one hundred dollars. (The type of forecast offered for £1 or less is unlikely to consist of anything more than duplicated generalizations.)

Considering the work involved, these fees are not excessive but they suggest that the people paying them have a genuine problem for which they have been unable to find help elsewhere. Work and marital difficulties are commonly brought to the astrologer. Some people want to know about their health or the possible outcome of some project. Mundane astrology is the branch that studies the fortunes of corporate bodies such as business firms or whole nations. Electional astrology concentrates on identifying the best time for starting a new undertaking.

No serious astrologer claims that he can make a detailed prediction of a future event. He cannot say whether we shall win the football pools next month or drown when a sudden gust of wind capsizes our sailing dinghy. He does claim that he can identify *tendencies* in our lives, periods when luck is running with us and our schemes have a good chance of success; periods that could prove disastrous, if we took unecessary risks. He deals in rhythms rather than notes, themes rather than plots.

But does it work? There are innumerable anecdotes. In recent years, astrologers have correctly forecast, or so they claim, the first moon landing and the death of President Kennedy. On the Sunday before Hitler's deputy, Rudolf Hess, flew to Britain on May 10th, 1941, Gypsy Petulengro forecast in the *Sunday Chronicle,* "Hitler's right hand man will die this week." Editor Jimmy Drawbell explained later that Petulengro would have been exactly right if a sub-editor had not changed his copy. The original copy read, "Hitler's right hand man will be *lost* this week," but the word "lost" was altered because it was thought unclear.

Such anecdotes prove little. Assuming the facts are correct, and there is no reason to doubt them, they could be variously explained by suggestion, intuition, clairvoyance, telepathy, precognition or just pure chance. Dealing in tendencies rather than in detailed forecasts, the astrologer is in an impregnable position. If he predicts a period of disaster, and no disaster happens, he can say to his client, "That was because you were forewarned. You took the necessary precautions and averted the danger." If the client breaks his leg, goes bankrupt or loses his entire family in a road accident, the astrologer can say, "But of course, it was in your stars."

Is astrology then anything more than what the psychologists call "a delusional system," an elaborate scheme of false beliefs such as we see, in an extreme form, in schizophrenics? Is it any more sane than believing that you are Napoleon, that the hospital is your palace and that the doctors and patients are your loyal subjects.

No one could possibly deny that some at least of the heavenly bodies profoundly affect us both collectively and individually. The sun is the most important single influence on our climate. It sets the pattern of our agriculture. It affects our food, clothes, building styles, working hours, the time and manner of our holidays, and even our mental states at different times of the year. Millions of us feel vaguely depressed in the depth of winter. In spring, our fancy turns to love or pilgrimage. We are equally familiar with the moon's influence on tides.

We are now finding that the sun, moon and even some of the other planets have effects that were inconceivable a hundred, or even fifty years ago. Sun spots come in cycles of roughly eleven years. At their peak, they may cause severe electrical storms, blot out short-wave radio transmissions, increase the likelihood of aurorae and interfere with magnetic compasses. We know too that these peaks tend to occur when the planet Mercury is on the opposite side of the sun from the earth. By working out the future position of Mercury, then, we can predict the likelihood of bad weather, displays of the Northern Lights and interference on our short-wave radio.

We also know that mean earth temperatures fall when Mercury or Venus is on the far side of the sun and rise again as these planets come back on to the near side. Temperatures also have a tendency to fall sharply at the time of the full moon. Research in Spain, America and Australia has shown that rainfall is also affected by the phases of the moon.

Now all these discoveries have been made by reputable scientists. They were based on observation and though they show tendencies only, they can be verified statistically. Some, but not all of them, can now be explained in terms of radiation, discharges of electrically charged particles and effects on the ionization of atmospheric layers. Yet would they have been any less true if they had been noted by Babylonian astrologers working with limited data, little statistical expertise and no knowledge of radiation, but blessed with a large share of that intuition which the best modern scientists admit is indispensable in making discoveries? Can it be that astrology is built on intelligent hunches which science willl ultimately prove to be true?

This may be so in some cases, but on the whole, it seems unlikely. Astrology is not consistent in itself. Leaving aside differences of interpretation and even of basic practice, it goes by assumptions that do not make sense *on its own terms*. It is not inconceivable that the sun, moon and planets could influence a baby's development through radiation, streams of electrically charged particles or agencies of whose existence we are as yet unaware. But why should the moment of the first cry be chosen as the one and only point at which they operate? If they do have an effect, it must operate continuously, first on the ovum and spermatozoon before they unite, then on the foetus during pregnancy and finally during the process of birth, which may last many hours. What is so important about the first cry?

It could, perhaps, be argued that a horoscope drawn up at this time is interpreted according to a tradition that in practice takes account of these other influences. Here, another difficulty arises. Modern astrologers still draw up horoscopes on the principle of the ancient Zodiac, which linked signs to fixed stars. A person born at the spring equinox, which is about March 23rd, was an Aries because at that time, the constellation containing the star Aries was in the ascendant. For at least two thousand years, it has been known that the fixed stars do not keep an unchanging position relative to the apparent path of the sun. They slip back at the rate of some thirty degrees every two thousand years. Around the time that Jesus was born, the spring equinox entered Pisces, a coincidence much commented on. Now it is moving into Aquarius. Hence, the "Age of Aquarius," another happy coincidence because the free, individualistic, revolution-qualities associated with the sign appeals strongly to the so-called "hippie" generation. Most astrologers have ignored this movement, allowing their horoscopes to be "out" by two whole signs. They admit this but say it does not matter. The signs themselves, not the position of the fixed stars, they claim, are the important factor. "The inference from this is clear," says Christopher McIntosh (*op. cit.*): "either the astrological tradition became obsolete as soon as the precession began to affect the alignment of signs and constellations, or else the qualities attributed to the signs are not connected with the stars at all."

Even more puzzling is the practice of "progression." A birth chart points only to inborn character and tendencies, and clients often ask astrologers for more precise indications. Logically, the only way of doing this would be to add to the horoscope all the influences affecting it minute by minute, hour by hour, day by day, year by year right up to the time for which the prediction is required. This is clearly impossible. Instead, many astrologers "progress" the birth chart by one day for every year of life. If a client asks for information about his forty-fifth year, the astrologer casts a horoscope for a date forty-five days ahead of the day of birth and bases his predictions on this. He cannot say why he should do so. He just says that it works in practice.

How can we test this claim? If it proves valid, how can we explain it?

Proof is not easy. It means different things to different people. The cold statistics required by scientists would have little interest for most of the people who consult astrologers. Even if the statistics proved unfavourable, devotees would still go on believing. Conversely, the fact that thousands of clients have complete faith in their astrologers and are willing to back that faith with large sums of money, means nothing to scientists. It could, they say, be wishful thinking. Or the astrologer might only be giving good advice arrived at by either common sense or intuition. Astrologers themselves admit they are often called on to give psychological support to people in distress.

There can be no figures then, or even agreed criteria, to show how valid the claims of astrology are from the client's point of view. Numerous attempts have been made, however, to correlate earthly phenomena with the positions of the heavenly bodies. Rupert Gleadow quotes one of these in his *The Origin of the Zodiac* (Cape, U.K., 1968). "Up to the present," he writes, "the best figures produced have been those of Donald A. Bradley in a very thorough publication called *Profession and Birthdate* (Llewellyn Publications, U.S.A.). Working on the published birth dates of 2,492 American clergymen, Mr. Bradley found for the sun's position between 79 degrees and 109 degrees of tropical longitude, a probability ratio of — 4.54, which is rated at odds of well over 100,000 to 1 against the result being merely accidental. This was supported by odds of nearly 1,000 to 1 for the frequency of Mercury in Aries, and about 30 to 1 for Mars or Venus in Aries and Leo respectively."

In France, Michel Gauquelin made a somewhat similar discovery. A graduate in psychology and statistics, he has worked at both the French *Centre National de Recherche Scientifique* and in the Psychophysiological Laboratory of Strasburg University. Though not an astrologer, he had been interested in the subject all his life and like other scientists, was only too well aware of the failure of astrologers to provide statistically convincing proof of their system. He decided to run his own tests and examine the birth charts of tens of thousands of successful men in several European countries. Two main points emerged. First, the moon and the planets Mars, Jupiter and Saturn appeared in them far more frequently than could be accounted for by chance. Secondly, there was a correlation between the planets on the birth charts and the subjects' professions. Soldiers tended to have Mars in a strong position, as did doctors and sportsmen, whereas Jupiter was prominent in the charts of actors and politicians. These correlations cut across national boundaries. Gauquelin explained them not in terms of traditional astrology but by the effect of planetary influences on pre-natal labour. After examining the birth charts of fifteen children and their parents, he found striking resemblances, especially when those of the parents also had features in common.

Once more, we are left with an inconclusive result. Gauquelin had apparently discovered regular correspondences between his subjects' birth charts and subsequent professions. He could not prove a causal connection. It was simply that the two patterns corresponded.

We often notice inexplicable patterns in everyday life. We call them coincidences. We rightly blame most of them on chance. Sometimes, too, we find that apparently unconnected events have a common cause which we had overlooked. But some coincidences seem impossible to explain by chance and try as we might, we cannot find any causal connection. Why is it, for instance, that *every* President of the United States elected at intervals of twenty years since 1840, has died in office? They are:

1840. William Henry Harrison. Died 1841.
1860. Abraham Lincoln. Assassinated 1865.
1880. James A. Garfield. Assassinated 1881.
1900. William McKinley. Assassinated 1901.
1920. Warren G. Harding. Died 1923.
1940. Franklin D. Roosevelt. Died 1945.
1960. John F. Kennedy. Assassinated 1963.

No other American president has been assassinated and only one other has died in office, Zachary Taylor, who was elected in 1848 and died two years later.

Another unexplained coincidence concerns "odd" and "even" years in British weather. In August 1968, Mr. N. E. Davis of the Meteorological Office, Strike Command, High Wycombe, Buckinghamshire, reported on a review he had made of weather records from 1880 to 1967 at twenty-two weather stations from Stornoway to Scilly. Taking into account mean temperature, total rainfall and total sunshine, he found that the best summers occurred in two separate cycles. In "odd" years, the cycle peaked every ten to twelve years, with "highs" in 1945, 1947 and 1959, and "lows" in 1941, 1953 and 1965. "Even" years peaked only every thirty-four years, with "highs" in the periods 1898-1906 and 1932-40 and "lows" in 1888, 1922 and 1956. With even years running at their maximum in the period 1966-74 and odd years due to peak in 1971, he predicted the odds of at least one very good summer at 98 per cent during the years 1968, 1970, 1972, and 1974. There was a 78 per cent possibility of two very good summers. It was also extremely likely that one of the years 1969, 1971 and 1973 would have a very good summer. At this writing (December 1971), Mr. Davis still stands by his prediction.

Now there is no reason why good and bad summers should occur in these mysterious cycles that themselves differ according to whether the year is odd or even. Nor is there any reason why American presidents elected at intervals of twenty years should regularly die in office. All we know is that they have done so without exception since 1840. Can it be that there is a similar, inexplicable correspondence between the position of the heavenly bodies and events on earth?

One man who thought there might be was Dr. Carl Jung. He used the word synchronicity to describe "the simultaneous occurrence of two meaningfully but not causally connected events." In his paper on "Synchronicity: An Acausal Connecting Principle" (*Collected Works,* vol. 8, Routledge, U.K., 1960), he gives as examples J. W. Dunne's prophetic dreams (See Chapter 7) and Professor J. B. Rhine's work on telepathy at Duke University, North Carolina, U.S.A. In card-guessing experiments, Rhine showed that some people consistently scored above chance expectation when asked to guess which card had been turned up by an experimenter hidden by a screen and sometimes sitting in another room. As an everyday example, Jung quotes a case cited by the celebrated French astronomer, Camille Flammarion.

> A certain Mr. Deschamps, when a boy in Orleans, was once given a piece of plum-pudding by a M. de Fortgibu. Ten years later, he discovered another plum-pudding in a Paris restaurant, and asked if he could have a piece. It turned out, however, that the plum-pudding was already ordered—by M. de Fortgibu. Many years afterwards, M. Deschamps was invited to partake of a plum-pudding as a special rarity. While he was eating it, he remarked that the only thing lacking was M. de Fortgibu. At that moment, the door opened and an old, old man in the last stages of disorientation walked in: M. de Fortgibu, who had got hold of the wrong address and burst in on the party by mistake.

Jung chose astrology as a field in which it might be possible to verify the principle of synchronicity statistically. He believed that recent scientific discoveries had given "some prospect" that astrology might eventually be explained on orthodox scientific lines but "there are still large areas of uncertainty." ("On synchronicity," *op. cit.*) It was impossible to test the claims of astrology in predicting character because there was no way of measuring it objectively. Instead he chose the *fact* of marriage as a touchstone. He collected at random the horoscopes of 483 married couples in batches of 180, 220 and 83, examining them for 50 different correspondences which should, by tradition indicate marriage. In astrological jargon, they included all the conjunctions or oppositions of the sun, moon, Venus, Mars, the Ascendant and the Descendant. He then took the 966 individual horoscopes and paired them with all the partners to whom they were *not* married. This gave him 32,220 unmarried couples. He examined the paired horoscopes of these unmarried couples for similar correspondences and compared the frequency with which they occurred with his previous findings. Both were expressed in terms of percentages.

Not all the traditional correspondences worked out. The best results came when the moon on the horoscope of one married partner was in conjunction with the sun on that of the other, when the moon was in conjunction with the moon and when the moon was in opposition to the sun. The average incidence of all three aspects spread over the 483 married pairs was 7·4 per cent, which compared with 5·3 per cent for the 32,220 unmarried pairs. Taking the best results in each group of married pairs separately, the results showed odds over chance of 1,000 to 1 (180 couples), 10,000 to 1 (220 couples) and 50 to 1 (83 couples).

Jung admits that scientifically the results can be explained as "mere chance." But "that anything so improbable . . . should occur at all, however, can only be explained either as a result of an intentional or unintentional fraud, or else as precisely such a meaningful coincidence, that is, as synchronicity." The attitude of the researcher, which was hopeful and expectant had, he thinks, a profound influence. He goes on to suggest that the mind cannot be bound by time and space and that both are relative to the mind.

He concludes, "Causality is the way we explain the link between successive events. Synchronicity designated the parallelism of time and meaning between psychic and psycho-physical events, which scientific knowledge so far has been unable to reduce to a common principle. . . . [It] is a modern differentiation of the obsolete concept of correspondence, sympathy and harmony. It is based not on philosophical assumptions but on empirical experience and experimentation."

How then can we sum up the present state of astrology?

Whether or not they believe in all its claims, more people read their horoscopes or consult astrologers than at any time in history. They pay good money to do so. This may be little more than an instinctive reaction against materialism, technology and our twentieth-century tendency to neglect the feeling and intuitive sides of our nature. Possibly, too, devotees are comforted at least temporarily by the suggestion that they are not alone in life but are guided by a Higher Power, albeit an impersonal one, operating through the influence of the stars. Also, those who consult astrologers personally may benefit profoundly from psychological support and intuitive understanding that may have little to do with astrology as a method of predicting the future.

But *can* astrology predict the future?

Reason clearly shouts, "No;" another part of our nature whispers "No, but . . ." When we consider it impartially, there are so many imponderables that it is impossible to make a once-for-all judgement on the present evidence.

The literal-minded scientist (and that does *not* include all, or even a majority of scientists) is in a highly vulnerable position. The history of science shows over and over again that yesterday's superstitions are today's truths, and vice-versa. Over the centuries, a number of astrological theories, particularly to do with weather, have been proved true and henceforth became not astrology but "science." Moreover, science itself no longer insists that everything can and must be explained on a "cause-and-effect" basis. Jung (*op. cit.*) quotes Sir James Jeans as saying, "Radioactive breakup appeared to be an effect without a cause, and suggested that the ultimate laws of nature were not even causal." In modern microphysics, light may appear as *either* a wave *or* composed of particles, depending on the experimental set-up. We cannot objectively measure the behaviour of sub-atomic particles because the measuring apparatus affects the result. In other words, we cannot completely separate what is observed from the mind of the observer. Objectively is a meaningless concept.

Moreover, we now have evidence, though some scientists dispute it, that phenomena such as telepathy, psychokinesis and precognition can be reproduced under laboratory conditions. It is, of course, admitted that they cannot be reproduced at will. But unless we presuppose a world-wide conspiracy of experimenters, which is far harder to accept than the published results, we are left with a residue of happenings that simply cannot be explained by any known scientific principle.

And that seems to be the current position of astrology. Objectors could rightly argue first that it cannot be shown to work by any principles known to science and secondly that the experimental evidence is far from sufficient to accept it on its own terms. The first objection is true but irrelevant. The second is also true but does not explain those insights into the future that so many clients are sure they receive when consulting a skilled (or should we say wise) astrologer. The case is not proven, either way. What we need is not closed minds but further enquiry.

9   Water, Oil and Precious Metals

While most of us glance at our horoscopes at least occasionally, only a minority admit that they take astrology seriously. It is exactly the opposite with dowsing, rhabdomancy, water divining or water witching, as it is called in America. Few of us ever need to employ a water diviner. Yet almost all of us, except dedicated scientists, have a sneaking feeling that some people have a gift which enables them to predict where water can be found. Dowsers still practise their craft in areas where lack of water is a problem.

Some years ago, a friend of mine called Richard Serjeant moved his mink farm to the Isle of Purbeck in Dorset. His new property had no mains water supply and though the fire brigade made regular deliveries, his animals' lives depended on water. What would happen if his farm was cut off by bad weather? An official of the local Agricultural Executive Committee suggested he have a well dug and introduced him to a water diviner.

In his book *Mink on my Shoulder* (Hale, U.K., 1966; T. Allen, U.S.A., 1966), Serjeant tells how the official made it sound "a simple routine job," but he himself had no previous experience of dowsers. "The thought of a water diviner coming on to my land and actually discovering water many feet below the surface smacked almost of magic," he wrote. However, he suppressed his doubts and the diviner turned out to be "an ordinary sort of man who might have been a salesman or an insurance agent."

The diviner worked with the traditional hazel twig, which was shaped like a "Y" with a short stem. Grasping the branches firmly in his hands, he walked up and down the field, holding it out before him. Suddenly, it twitched violently downwards. He made a mark and continued. Altogether, the hazel twitched eight times.

The diviner claimed that there was water under each of these spots but he was unable to say whether the underlying strata were soft enough to dig through. He could, however, give an estimate of the depth at which the water lay. He walked slowly towards the stake marking his first find and scraped his heel in the grass as soon as he began to feel pressure on his hazel stick. He then measured the distance to the stake, some forty feet, which was equivalent to the depth at which water could be found. Checks on the other water sources showed that one, which was also nearest the house, lay at only twenty feet. This was where Serjeant decided to try.

Keeping his fingers crossed, he called in the well-diggers. They spent three days digging through nineteen feet of clay. Then they hit sandstone. There was no sign of water and Serjeant began to have doubts, but he told them to keep on. For three more days, they inched their way through the solid rock. Still, the well was dry. Next morning, Serjeant got up early to think things over. Unless the diggers struck water soon, he would have to call a halt. He decided to give them one more day. He walked over to the well and looked down into it. "A glassy surface reflected back the sky. Hardly able to believe my senses, I picked up a stone and threw it in. It made a satisfying 'plop'. Overnight, water had seeped through the sandstone to a depth of three or four feet. It was not an abundance and never would be but it was enough." The water diviner had been right after all.

The history of dowsing is far from clear, though we know that a rod or wand has been used in magical ceremonies for thousands of years. We read in the Bible that Aaron threw down before Pharaoh a rod that turned into a serpent (Exodus VII : 10). Later, Moses used a rod to strike water from a rock when the Israelites were dying of thirst during the flight from Egypt (Exodus XVII : 6). Wands or rods are a suit of the tarot pack of cards and even today a rod is the symbol of many eminent offices. In Britain's House of Lords, order is maintained by an official called "Black Rod," which is short for "Gentleman Usher of the Black Rod." He takes the name from his official staff, a black wand with a gold lion.

Dowsing as we know it may have been practised in ancient Mesopotamia, Greece and Rome. Certainly, Marco Polo, the celebrated Venetian traveller, came across it in China in the late thirteenth century. In 1556, the German writer known as Georgius Agricola published what is probably the earliest known account of divining techniques in his *De Ra Mettallica*. Like most of the early dowsers, he was interested primarily in finding metals with a divining rod and by the end of the century, his methods were being used in Cornish tin mines. We know too that in 1602 Jean du Chastelet, Baron de Beau Soleil and d'Auffenbach, successfully divined metal ores in the Guyenne area of France.

Jacques Aymar of Lyons, France, is said to have discovered the art of divining for water later in the seventeeth century. He was a protégé of the Prince de Condé and had many successes but he was said to have confessed in later life that he was an impostor and did it only for the money. He had numerous imitators, many of them genuine, but dowsing also attracted rogues. They could extract a fee for their services and be many miles away before a well was sunk and found to be dry. However, there must have been genuine finds because divining was accepted all over Europe and, later, America. Numerous books were written on the subject, especially in France where some of the best-known diviners were priests.

A. E. Waite gives a good idea of the status of divining in nineteenth-century England in *The Occult Sciences* (Kegan Paul, U.K., 1891). He quotes two cases from contemporary journals. In one of them, a dowser found two sources yielding "an apparently inexhaustible" quantity of water needed for the Flelton Wagon Works of the Midland Railway Company. In the other, the owner of a Yorkshire estate with "a large colliery population" had found his reservoirs drained by neighbouring coal pits and following the advice of "Members of Parliament, magistrates and others" sent for John Mullins, Waterspring Discoverer, of Colerne, Chippenham, Wiltshire.

Mullins arrived in Yorkshire at ten p.m., "a plain, working mason, who has been employed most of his life on the same gentleman's estate. There was no pretence of quackery or jugglery about him in any sense. He comes for a moderate fee and his expenses, and he undertakes to 'find' water if it be in the ground. The best guarantee for his integrity is that he contracts to sink and build the wells himself on the spot where he says the water exists." Mullins was an immediate success. He convinced local sceptics, including the Vicar, by uncovering an old well and tracing the exact course of every underground pipe and drain with water flowing through it. He also found several unsuspected springs. Within two days, his work was done and he was on his way back to Wiltshire.

Though most of us associate "divining" with "water," most practitioners would regard Mullins' talents as somewhat limited. From Aymar on, they have used their rods to forecast the presence of many other substances beneath the earth. "If we can sniff out water," they reasoned, "why not oil? Why not gold, silver and other metals? Why not diamonds?"

One of the most famous modern diviners is Miss Evelyn Penrose whose career as a dowser took her all over the world. She gave up using a hazel twig early on, since she found that a pendulum gave better results. It consisted of a plain wooden ball suspended by twine from a small stick which she held in her hand. Later still, she preferred a "motorscope," a piece of thick, twisted wire with a pointer. These however were merely technical refinements. They did not affect the basic principles of divining and often, she was able to work with her hands only.

As she explains in her autobiography, *Adventure Unlimited* (Spearman, U.K., 1958), she inherited the gift from her father, a Cornishman whose grounds had veins of tin and copper running beneath them, as well as several streams. All his lunch guests, even bishops and M.P.s, were expected to try their hand at divining with a freshly cut willow or hazel twig. When they went indoors again, he handed it to his daughter. "I never had to learn how to divine," she wrote, "and I looked on it as a natural thing like riding a pony and, when I was older, finding the north with a compass." After school in Belgium and beekeeping in the Channel Islands, where she lived with her widowed mother, she sold up the home on her mother's death and embarked on a life of travel.

First stop was Sacramento, California, where she had a widowed aunt. It happened to be an election year and she joined her aunt's brother, a leading politician, in a tour of his constituency, which included the oilfields of Signal Hill. While he gathered votes, she tried her hand at oil divining. After getting a reaction from a group of producing wells, she was asked to pick out the most prolific. She did so and also identified one that was dry, even though she had been led to believe it was a producer. Over undrilled land, she was almost thrown to the ground by her wildly jerking rod and was then told that she was over a known gas source.

During a visit to Hawaii she found numerous water springs for a sugar planter. She then crossed to Canada, where the apple-growers faced ruin because of drought. They asked her to help but she realized that they would need money from the government if they were to drill wells in the underlying granite. She got an interview with the Finance Minister and was appointed Water-Diviner to the Government of British Columbia. She travelled all over Western Canada, bumping along primitive roads to remote farmsteads, being taken for a witch by the Indians and coming face to face with a black bear in the forest. She says that she nearly always found water where it was needed and in the Peace River Block confirmed the government geologists' findings as to the whereabouts of oil and gas.

The rest of Miss Penrose's globe-trotting career makes equally fascinating reading. She was called in by the British Army to find water on Salisbury Plain. She traced tin and wolfram lodes in Cornish mines. She hunted for the huge brass body belonging to the detached brass head of the goddess Minerva at Bath but found only her spear and shield under a main road, which could not be dug up. She discovered useful springs on Chilean farms and some too deep to work in the Kruger National Park in South Africa. She located previously unknown passages in the ruins at Zimbabwe, Rhodesia, and found water on drought-stricken sheep stations in Australia.

One of the few offers she turned down was a suggestion by the pre-war Italian Embassy in London that she should work for the Italian army in Abyssinia. The troops were suffering from lack of water. The idea was that she should be flown into enemy territory thirty miles ahead of the advancing Italians and, working entirely on her own, mark out sites for them to drill when, and if, they caught up with her. She was so terrified that she booked a passage for Jamaica before Mussolini could confirm her appointment. She did not leave a forwarding address.

Miss Penrose does not claim that she was always successful. Searching for gold in Australia, she found some "fairly promising spots" but "on the whole, the results were disappointing." When she pinpointed what she hoped would be a major strike in the Snowy Plains, the government declared the area a national park and stopped issuing mining leases.

Diamonds are always difficult. During one expedition in South Africa, she never found a single stone, "although I got every reaction which I expected and in likely places." She mentions a geologist who was also a diviner. After helping one prospector by marking eighteen spots, each of which produced a diamond, he picked out another twenty-eight spots next day but only fourteen of them were successful. "Although he marked many more claims on the same flat, under similar conditions, and with the same reactions, he never found another diamond."

Most of us can accept, at least provisionally, the idea that water and minerals can be found by divining, even though we do not understand how. The fact that diviners admit occasional failures makes us all the more ready to believe them when they claim success. It is harder to credit some of their wider claims. Some say that they can check whether seed is fertile, whether a given sample of food will suit a dyspeptic and whether the subject of a photograph is alive or dead. Others say they can diagnose disease by dangling a pendulum over the patient or even over a drop of his blood. They distinguish between different diseases by the number and manner of the pendulum's swings. Some of the "radiosthetists" are qualified doctors and go on to treat the diseases they find, often with homeopathic remedies.

Many, perhaps most, diviners also claim that they can detect "harmful radiations" arising from the earth, possibly at points where underground water passes through strata of poisonous minerals. People, or animals, living immediately over these spots may become unaccountably ill. Some dowsers believe that they can eliminate these radiations by burying coils around the house or by diverting underground streams. Often, they say, it is only necessary to move a bed or armchair to the other side of the room where the occupant will be out of range of the radiations.

More to our present purpose is the dowser's claim that he can predict the presence of water or minerals without even visiting the site. He simply holds his pendulum over a map. "After 'tuning-in' my map and making it alive, I ask 'It'—whatever 'It' may be— questions and instruct 'It' to tell me where the watersheds are," wrote Miss Penrose (*op. cit.*). "I only use a survey-plan and not a topographical map but, if there are any hills from which the streams are coming, a strong draught comes up off the map and lifts my hand on to the high land, after which my hands float gently over the map, showing me the direction of the streams from the watershed. The little pendulum then outlines the course of the underground streams with the most minute accuracy and I draw them in. Before the map is finished, the depth must be added to each stream and a test made for the potability of the water."

Both she and other diviners claim many successes by this method. In *Practical Dowsing: A Symposium* (ed. A. H. Bell, Bell, U.K., 1965; Irwin Clarke, U.S.A.), the Reverend H. W. Lea-Wilson, M.A., admits that he "started out as a complete sceptic" but after finding that he could divine water under a tennis court by working on a rough plan of it, he used the method regularly. A woman doctor wrote from India to ask if he could find water in her village compound. It was only 50 feet square. Mr. Lea-Wilson asked her to send him a plan. "When we got it, I found streams within the compound actually intersecting, though at different levels. A bore was made and very good water was struck at 30 feet. If water ever failed at that level, there is a deeper and stronger stream at 52 feet. We have recently had a letter from her from which I quote 'The whole of Kasner marvels at your power of finding water by post. . . . Our water supply has enabled us to grow a nice little garden within our mud walls. . . . We grow quite the biggest holly-hocks I have ever seen and sweet corn that melts in the mouth. Our next venture is to be a grape vine.' "

Equally puzzling to most people is the claim that missing persons can be traced by diviners. They work with an object belonging to the missing person (a "sample") or sometimes a photograph. The late John Clarke of Ab Kettleby in Leicestershire, England, is said to have located the bodies of a dozen or more drowned people, six of them between March and May of 1933. In *Practical Dowsing* (*op. cit.*), Mr. W. H. Burgoyne of Torcross, Devon, mentions four occasions between 1945 and 1959 on which he successfully found bodies. A pair of braces helped him solve one mystery. They belonged to one of two boys missing from Slapton village. Using the braces as a sample, Mr. Burgoyne followed their trail to a bridge leading from South Grounds Farm to Ireland Farm. "Then, from the bridge, I followed them to the edge of the Ley, where the boys had gone on a small skiff. I thought I could do no more but at the father's request, I agreed to try. A fisherman was engaged and on criss-crossing a line where they entered the Ley to where the punt was found, I felt a strong pull, and realised that the bodies were there. The police marked the spot from the shore, engaged a fisherman and found the bodies tangled in a tree at the bottom. It was my first experience, but a comfort to the parents."

Water, oil, metals, diseases, missing persons : there seems to be no limit to the claims made for divining. But are those claims justified? If they are, how does divining work? If they are not, how is it that so many of us are willing to give diviners the benefit of the doubt?

It must be said straightaway that few scientists take dowsing seriously. It does not fit in with any generally accepted scientific theory and has never proved itself under experimental conditions. One wonders, however, if the scientists are being fair. Dowsers have never claimed infallibility and the fact that they cannot produce results with the same certainty that a glowing splint bursts into flame when plunged into oxygen is irrelevant. Geologists and geophysicists are not infallible either. They can say with a fair degree of certainty that at such-and-such a point the underlying strata are of a kind known to be capable of bearing water or oil. They cannot say whether water or oil is, in fact, present. The only way to find out is to drill a well. When exploring new territories, oil companies reckon to drill at least five dry holes for every one that produces oil. Why should we condemn dowsers simply because they are not always successful?

The late Abbé Mermet, a French priest who enjoyed an international reputation as "King of the Dowsers" and was consulted by clients ranging from the pope to the Suchard chocolate firm, put the point forcibly in his *Principles and Practice of Radiesthesia* (translated by Mark Clement, Stuart, U.K., 1959; Nelson, U.S.A., 1959): "Let us imagine the case of a surgeon who has discovered a new method of operating for cancer. In performing 100 operations, he achieved success in 80, leaving 20 failures. The president of a society of surgeons suggests that he should perform two controlled operations. Result: two failures. It would be fair to conclude: 102 operations, 80 successes and 22 failures. But the reckoning in this case is different: two operations, two failures. All the facts involved, confirmed by the cured patients themselves as well as by the professional staff, are ignored so that the final impression is falsified."

It is hard to see what sort of controlled experiment would satisfy both scientists and diviners. It would not be enough to extend the period of trial from a single day to one year or even ten years. We should also have to be sure that the diviner was using only his craft. How could we exclude the possibility that he had secretly studied geology and consciously, or unconsciously, was using this knowledge to help him? And what about chance? If we dropped a thousand markers at random from a helicopter and dug a well at each of the spots on which they landed, we might well find that some produced whatever we happened to be seeking. The odds on doing so would clearly be much higher in some places than in others. How could we possibly work out with any degree of accuracy the chance expectation for each? Near misses pose another problem. An error of one foot can make the difference between success and failure. Yet we could not allow for them because we should never know whether the well was almost scraping a source or whether it was ten miles away. Unless we did allow for them, we could not fairly decide whether or not there was some unknown principle at work which had clearly guided the diviner, even though he made a slight error in applying it.

So we are driven back on experience. Have men found that by and large dowsing works?

It is hard to ignore the testimony of history. Though not infallible, it gives strong grounds for thinking there might be "something in" divining. The art has persisted for hundreds, possibly thousands of years. It has no esoteric appeal like astrology or the *I Ching*. It does not offer a comforting view of life in general. It is strictly practical. It is also precise. The diviner does not say, "This tract or territory is broadly favourable to the presence of water, but of course any manner of influences may prevent your finding it." He bangs a peg in the ground. "Dig here," he says, "and you *will* find water." Could dowsing have survived if it did not produce results?

Apart from the cases we have already mentioned, there are numerous other examples of success. Alois Wiesinger, O.C.S.O., lists some of them in his *Occult Phenomena* (translated by Brian Battershaw, Burns, London, 1957): "Professor Bert Reese discovered Rockefeller's petroleum deposits; M. Boulenger discovered water for Brugmann Hospital in Jetter St. Pierre; while Emil Jausé discovered petrol on the property of Princess Radziwill and the coal deposits of Count Potocki in Poland. M. Moineau discovered large sources of water with which it was possible to supply the city of Toulon."

Yet the fact remains that major oil companies do not normally employ diviners. They say that trials have been made and they consistently get better results by using orthodox, geophysical methods. There is a long tradition of water divining in the British Army and as recently as 1952, when a new £14 million headquarters town was built for the British and Allied Forces in Europe between Mönchen Gladbach, Germany, and the Dutch border, Colonel H. Grattan, C.B.E., the Chief Engineer, personally found abundant water with his divining-rod. Even so, diviners came out badly in official trials and are no longer officially recognized by the British Army.

On the one hand, then, we have a large number of individuals who believe in divining because it worked for them. On the other, firms and large institutions say that it compares unfavourably with other forms of prospecting. Is there any way out of the impasse?

It may help if we draw a parallel with psychoanalysis. While thousands of former neurotics are convinced that analysis has transformed their lives, no one has ever been able to produce statistics showing that neurotics who underwent analysis are any better off than those who were treated with drugs or had no treatment at all. Some people totally reject psychoanalysis because of this. Most prefer the explanation that the success or otherwise of the treatment depends on the individual personalities of the analyst and his patient and the way in which they relate to each other. Could there be a personal element in dowsing?

Most dowsers agree that they have a special gift which they share with perhaps one person in five. The rest are either completely without it or have it to only a negligible degree.

Some dowsers say that this gift is mainly physical. Abbé Mermet (*op. cit.*) describes the process like this:

A. All bodies without exception are constantly emitting undulations or radiations.

B. The human body enters these fields of influence and becomes the seat of nervous reactions, of some kind of current, which flows through the hands.

C. If an appropriate object, such as a rod or a pendulum, is held in the hand, the invisible flux is made manifest in the movements given to this object, which acts as a kind of indicator.

He also says: "In the action produced on the radiesthetist [dowser] and his pendulum, by bodies, distant and invisible, but represented by a photo, map, plan or drawing, distance is of no account; whether such bodies are 10 miles away, 1,000 or 10,000 miles away, they act in the same way." Dowsers can distinguish between various minerals and states of health by the way in which the pendulum swings. This view is admittedly extreme and many dowsers, while believing that they can pick up radiations from water and minerals, flatly reject distant dowsing, the diagnosis of illness, the finding of missing persons and so on.

Other dowsers take a completely different view. The postscript to *Practical Dowsing* (*op. cit.*), states flatly that "the whole practice of dowsing is dominated by the subconscious mental factor. . . . Nowadays, nearly every experienced dowser examines the area in which a location is required on maps of varying scale before dowsing on the actual site, whilst all the various methods of medical treatment depend entirely on the subconscious mental power of appreciation." It ends: "There is not yet any justification for the glib talk of radiations, vibrations, horizontal, vertical and carrier waves, used by many dowsers, the existence of which has not been verified by instrumental methods and must be regarded as largely notional."

There is still another school of dowsers who distinguish between "physical" dowsing, which finds nearby water and minerals by picking up their radiations or vibrations, and "psychical" dowsing which works at a distance by means of a faculty indistinguishable from clairvoyance. It should be added that no dowser believes that his rod or pendulum has magic powers. It is agreed, even by total sceptics, that the swings or jerking movements are caused by involuntary movements of certain arm muscles.

Though not proved, the idea that some people can act as radio receivers for radiations given off by minerals is far from absurd. Geophysicists themselves use similar methods. They measure variations in the earth's magnetic field to give them clues about the underlying strata. They detonate charges and work out from returning shock waves the pattern of the underlying strata. They use instruments for this. But since we already have eyes and ears which convert different forms of vibrations into sights and sounds, it is not inconceivable that some, perhaps all of us, might be capable of picking up vibrations or radiations of a kind not yet known to science. It would then follow that by finding the point at which they affected the tell-tale rod or pendulum most strongly, we could locate their source. Nor can the possibility of clairvoyance or precognition be dismissed. As we saw in Chapters 5 and 7, there are good grounds for thinking that either can operate in favourable circumstances.

The supporters of both physical and psychical theories can also give good reasons for dowsing's admitted failures. If the basis is physical, it could easily be upset (as radio reception is upset) by many kinds of interference. Abbé Mermet lists thirty-three causes of errors ranging from a failure to hold the pendulum properly to the chattering or scoffing of bystanders. If the basis is psychic, we should not expect complete reliability. The one thing (perhaps the only thing!) on which all psychical researchers agree is that feats of precognition, clairvoyance and such cannot always be performed to order.

These, then, are additional reasons why dowsing may not show up well in trials. Coupled with the fact that it cannot yet be explained in a way acceptable to orthodox scientists, they are bound to damn it in the eyes of major companies and institutions. If geologists and geophysicists fail to find oil after spending £300 million, shareholders and tax-payers will happily write it off because they were acting in the best traditions of science. If diviners fail to find oil after spending only £300 shareholders and taxpayers will give management hell for wasting their money on superstition and magic.

Why then are diviners called in at all? Well, many people believe in them. In country districts, it is far simpler and far cheaper to call in the local dowser who has a long standing reputation for finding water than to hire geologists and hydraulic engineers who may have to come from many miles away. Where water is scarce and elusive,

the man with local knowledge and a lifetime of experience might
even be able to pick out a site for a well when the geologists are
baffled. This would apply, of course, whether or not he had the
"gift" of divining.

But perhaps there is a gift after all. Miss Penrose (*op. cit.*) says
that she was once approached by an American oil tycoon who had
read an account of her work in a book about another diviner. On one
of his leases, only a single well was productive. His scientific experts
had chosen the sites for eight others but every one was dry. He
enclosed a plan indicating the positions of all nine wells and that was
all. There were no other details. Would Miss Penrose tell him what
had gone wrong? She set to work with a pendulum and found that
the oil lay in a series of "pools" linked by a band. The producing
well hit one of the pools; the dry wells did not. Later, the oilman
sent her more plans to work on and as a result drilled ten wells. Nine
of them were producers. The tenth, which was dry, was later found
to have been drilled outside the area marked. On further advice from
Miss Penrose, the oilman drilled nine more wells and his neighbour
three. All produced oil.

Was it chance, clairvoyance or a genuine gift of divination? Could
Miss Penrose really locate oil in America by studying plans thousands
of miles away in Australia? I simply do not know.

10   Heads, Hands and Colours

The future of every human being is deeply affected by politics, economics, wars, "acts of God" and other outside influences. But it is his own personality that decides how he will cope with them. If we can accurately assess personality, therefore, we can go a long way to predicting future performance.

Unconsciously, we try to do this all the time. When we first meet someone, we automatically note his stance, gestures, speech habits, mental attitudes and quirks of behaviour. Almost intuitively, we decide what kind of person he is, what kind of relationship is possible between us and how it might develop.

Some psychologists, mainly American, have tried to turn the study of body movements into a science. They call it kinesics. The nearer someone stands to us, they say, the more intimate he wishes to be. Average distance for casual acquaintances is between two and five feet. Anyone who speaks to us from a greater distance is putting the relationship on a more formal basis; anyone who comes closer implies that he is on more intimate terms. If he stands squarely face to face, he is probably friendly; if at an angle and looking away or over our head, he is probably indifferent or even hostile. A hunched stance with crossed arms speaks of a closed mind, but crossed arms with an upright stance and feet wide apart means "Keep your distance." Head held high implies dominance, head bowed—submission. A finger to the nose may indicate fear, to the mouth—shame. Eyes are especially revealing. A steady gaze suggests honesty and reliability but if it is held too long, it could be a sign of a calculating liar. A woman is said to show her interest in a man by smoothing her hair or checking her make-up. A man will indicate his interest in a woman by pulling up his socks or adjusting his tie.

Whether or not we agree with these interpretations in detail, few of us would deny that bodily mannerisms are often a reliable guide to what we can expect of a person's character and possibly also of his health. (If we are sufficiently detached, they may even give us an

Prediction and Prophecy

insight into ourselves.) Sometimes these habits become so ingrained that they leave permanent marks on our bodies: a stoop, frown lines, a tight mouth. Health too can permanently affect our appearance. Hardened mental attitudes can result in stereotyped responses to almost every kind of situation.

For thousands of years, men have worked out elaborate systems of predicting a person's future from these persisting marks and attitudes. Some of them are widely used by business firms when hiring staff. Candidates may be asked to "apply in own handwriting" or "send recent photograph." They may be given psychological or aptitude tests. Fashions change and the fact that some method of personality prediction is currently out of fashion, does not necessarily mean it is unreliable. It may well come back in a slightly different form. Similarly, many systems now claimed to be scientific will themselves be discredited, perhaps to be rehabilitated when the wheel of fashion turns once again. In this chapter, we shall examine a number of these systems and try to find out how reliable they are, and why.

Physiognomy

Is a man's face his fortune? Innumerable authors have suggested that a man's future can be foreseen, at least partly, in his features. "The physiognomy of Alcibiades indicated that he was destined to raise himself to the highest rank in the republic," wrote the Greek historian Plutarch (50–120). Shakespeare's Cassius worried Caesar with his "lean and hungry look" and according to Thomas Dekker (c. 1570– c. 1632), "honest labour bears a lovely face." George Crabbe (1754– 1832) considered "the face the index of a feeling mind" and Joseph Addison (1672–1719) quoted with approval the saying that "a good face is a letter of introduction."

When the poet and artist William Blake (1757–1827) was thirteen, his father took him to see an engraver called Ryland. "I don't like that man," said William. His father asked, "why not?" "His face," said the boy. "looks as if he will yet be hanged." Twelve years later, Ryland was hanged for forging banknotes.

Most of us think facial expression is important in judging character potential. We know that a blush reveals embarrassment and pallor fear. We believe that a person's face can tell us whether he is happy, sad, tired, ill, worried, relaxed or drunk. It seems reasonable to think that the permanent creases worn by a person's habitual range of expressions show persisting character trends. It is even tempting

156

to believe that the shape of a man's features and the underlying bone structure are linked genetically with personality traits.

How far is it possible to make a science of these rather vague impressions and conjectures? Can we analyse a man's features and say with certainty that a particular type of ear, eye, mouth or pattern of lines across the forehead tells us something about his future?

It is true that the appearance of a patient's face sometimes helps a doctor diagnose illness. Lepers often have a lion-like appearance. Puffy features may be a sign of kidney disease. Sufferers from the rare rheumatic disease known as "S.L.E." (systemic lupus erythmatosus) may have a "butterfly" flush with the wings spread out across their cheeks and the body on their nose. But when we try to forecast character, we are on less certain ground.

In the seventeenth century, numerous enquirers tried to work out a science of physiognomy. In 1610, Jerome Cortes of Valencia, Spain wrote a book in which he stated, "Physiognomy is nothing but an ingenious and subtle science of human nature, thanks to which one may know the good or bad complexion, the virtues and vices, of the man considered as an animal." Some linked physiognomy with astrology and claimed they could distinguish seven lines across the forehead corresponding to Saturn, Jupiter, Mars, the sun, Venus, Mercury and the moon. They could tell a person's future from the direction of the lines and from various breaks and crossings. But others were doubtful. "The head is indubitably the epitome of the whole heavens," said one writer. "Like these, it has its constellations and its signs. But if we note the stars, their situation and their movements, without knowing their nature, nor why they are thus disposed, we may say as much of all parts of the face."

The next generation of physiognomists rejected both astrology and caution, but they did at least try to work from observation. In 1672, the Italian, Ghirsdelli, published a book of a hundred faces with interpretations. "The nose," he said, "helps to manifest passion and contempt. For instance, when we want to make fun of and mock another we make a certain movement of the nose. And when we wish to express contempt we make a certain sign with the nose. And when we see anything unpleasant done to another, we twitch back the nostrils. When we get into a passion, the nostrils are dilated and the tip of the nose red." Too often, however, physiognomists fell back on prejudice. At the beginning of the seventeenth century, Giovanni Ingegneri, bishop of Capo d'Istria, published a list of aphorisms:

Prediction and Prophecy

A beard on a woman is a sign of little honesty.
Excessive size of the brow is a sign of idleness.
The smallness of the forehead indicates a choleric man.
Very red eyes are the sign of a bad nature, inclined to cruelty.
Bright eyes are the sign of wantonness.
Those who are flat-nosed are very wanton.
Men with curved noses are magnanimous.

The most famous of all physiognomists was Johann Lavater (1741–1801), a Zurich clergyman with mystical tendencies. He seems to have been a most lovable man who painted, wrote poetry and composed songs, sermons and plays with equal facility. He became a physiognomist almost by accident. Every time he came across a face he particularly liked or disliked, he drew it and added a character sketch. In 1772, he published his collection in *The Physiognomical Bible,* subtitled *Essay on Physiognomy, destined to make a man known and loved,* with between five and six hundred plates. He worked entirely by intuition, which was not always reliable. When he was shown a death mask, he correctly identified it as that of the revolutionary, Mirabeau (1749–91). "One recognises at once," he said, "the man of terrible energy, unconquerable in his audacity, inexhaustible in his resources, resolute, haughty." But when a friend sent him an anonymous profile, he believed it to be that of Johann Herder (1744–1803), the German philosopher, and rhapsodized over the distinction of its features. It was, in fact, the profile of an assassin who had recently been executed.

After Lavater, the true scientists. Peter Camper (1722–89), the Dutch anatomist, sought to measure intelligence by the facial angles. Sir Charles Bell (1774–1842), the Scottish anatomist, studied expression. Other landmarks were the work of Burgess on blushing, Duchenne on the muscular mechanisms of the face and Darwin on the expression of emotions. These and other discoveries are summed up by Paolo Mantegazza, president of the Italian Society of Anthropology, in his *Physiognomy and Expression* (Scott, U.K., 1894), a work on which I have drawn for the foregoing.

Mantegazza starts by clearing away much of the nonsense previously written. He points out that the essential features of a face which distinguish it from other faces are the eyes, the nose and the upper lip, but it is not enough to take two or three characteristics "as a shorthand portrait of all faces." All parts must be observed and in particular, anatomy must be distinguished from expression. Anatomy enables us to decide whether or not a face is beautiful and also gives us clues about the subject's racial inheritance. But we can make moral, intellectual and physiological judgements only from the expression. He lists dozens of possible expressions both passing and permanent. They cover the senses, the passion, the intellect, health and occupation. He is sometimes astute in his observations: "In the expression of hatred the eye is not only closed or concealed; it also frequently becomes vividly coloured; this is the sign of strong congestion tending to the head. In the gravest cases, the eye starts from the orbit. . . . The nose dilates, the wings of the nose are raised. . . . The mouth sometimes remains spasmodically closed to indicate the general tension of the muscles preparing for the struggle; more frequently it opens, shows all the teeth, or at least the front teeth, or only the canines."

Too often, however, he shades off into the subjective. Good humour, which comes from perfect health and serenity "is expressed by an expansive smile; by a permanent tonicity of the muscles of the face and slight brightness of the eyes. It is the face of children in good health; it is the joyous expression of a brave man who is well. Before such beautiful representations of life we cry—What a laughing face! What a picture of contentment! It is a pleasure to look upon it!"

Mantegazza, one feels, pushes the "science" of physiognomy as far as it will go. In fact, he shows it covers not one subject but several. These have now been dismissed by serious thinkers or assigned to other sciences. Today, we accept that the shape of our ears or the colour of our hair is decided by our genes and has no known connection with personality or intellectual ability. Nor is it possible to link creases or bulges with character potential. Frown lines may equally well mean that the person is a worrier or that he needs a new pair of glasses. It is, of course, true that our features are changed by emotion and this has become the concern of the physiologist, who is interested in the mechanism involved, and also of the ethologist, who studies behaviour. Medicine has taken over the diagnosis of illness by facial appearance.

So where does physiognomy stand? On an intuitive level, most of us believe that we can form a reasonable judgment of what we can expect from a person by his facial appearance. Yet often we are unwittingly taking into account speech, dress, posture and other clues as well. We can easily prove this by cutting out a selection of faces from newspaper photographs. Unless we know the individuals personally, it is impossible to distinguish between a stockbroker, a condemned criminal, a university professor or a road-sweeper. Again, many actors and actresses are typecast for life because their faces suggest cunning, cruelty, stupidity, kindliness, intelligence, tartiness or rage. When we meet them off stage, we discover that our pre-conceptions are totally unfounded. Apart from medical conditions and passing expressions, a person's face tells us far less than we like to think.

Phrenology

When Johann Lavater began drawing his collection of faces, Franz Joseph Gall (1758–1828) was a nine-years-old schoolboy at Tiefen-bronn on the borders of Baden and Würtemberg. He took an unusually keen interest in his fellow pupils. He noticed that each was unique with his own special talents and personality traits. These never changed. Gall used to think for himself but he soon found that boys who learned their lessons off by heart often got better grades. When the family moved, he changed schools but again he found himself at a disadvantage to the rote-learners. He then made a surprising discovery. They all had prominent eyes, just like the boys who had a similar knack at his first school.

He now felt he was on the track of an important discovery. When he went up to university to read medicine, he studied his fellow undergraduates and again found a link between prominent eyes and an ability to learn lessons off by heart. Could other peculiarities of the head indicate particular skills and talents? Soon he found features common to students with a gift for painting, music or the mechanical arts. Perseverance also went with a particular development of the skull. He did not believe that mere bone predetermined a man's talents. He was convinced that both came from the brain inside the skull. At the time, many leading psysiologists and philosophers thought otherwise; they were also convinced that men were born with equal mental ability and that differences were caused only by environment. Gall recalled his own schooldays. "Often," he said, "we were accused of want of will or deficiency of zeal; but many of us could not, even with the most ardent desire, followed out by the most obstinate efforts, attain, in some pursuits, even to mediocrity; while in some other points, some of us surpassed our schoolfellows without effort."

After graduating, Gall spent years studying heads. He visited lunatic asylums, prisons and schools. Whenever he came across someone who was in any way unusual, he studied the shape of his skull. He proved, at least to his own satisfaction, that particular characteristics always went with particular features of the skull. But did the brain follow the shape? Whenever one of his subjects died, Gall asked permission to do a post-mortem. He found, again to his own satisfaction, that the shape of the brain was always similar to the shape of the skull.

Gall was now convinced that a man's whole character could be read from his skull. When the prison doctor of the House of Correction at Graetz in Stiria sent him a box of skulls, he immediately picked out one which was extremely wide in the temples. "Mon Dieu," he exclaimed, "quel crâne de voleur!" Only then did he open the covering letter and read that the skull was that of an incorrigible thief.

With his colleague Dr. Johann Gaspar Spurzheim (1776–1832), he worked out a comprehensive theory of the functions of the various parts of the brain. If the shape of the skull suggested that one of these was large, the faculty which it controlled was well developed; if small or absent, the corresponding faculty was feeble or absent too. By measuring a head with calipers and running his hands over it, Gall claimed that he could assess such qualities as amativeness, philoprogenitiveness, concentrativeness, adhesiveness, destructiveness, alimentiveness, wit, ideality and a host of other characteristics. The belief implied that all these qualities were given at birth. One man was good because he had a well-developed organ of benevolence. Another was a robber because his organ of theft was prominent. The system was a scientific form of predestination.

Nor surprisingly, other doctors did not take kindly to his system. When he gave his first lectures in Vienna in 1796, he was ridiculed. Priests and moralists joined in the attack. After lecturing throughout Europe, Gall settled in Paris. In 1813 Spurzheim left him to lecture in England and finally sailed for Boston, Massachusetts, where he died. In both Europe and America, the number of doubters steadily grew. Later research showed that Gall's theory was totally false. The brain, a much more complicated organ than he had imagined, simply did not function in the way he described. Psychologists still do not agree why men behave as they do but few, if any would deny that inheritance is only part of the story. Environment is even more important. The new "science" slipped down the social scale. The doctrine that was to revolutionise the study of human nature petered out in fairground booths where charlatans read the "bumps" of giggling girls.

Prediction and Prophecy

Palmistry

In both Britain and America, palmistry is still one of the most flourishing forms of prophecy. Leading practitioners command fees of five guineas for a straightforward hand analysis, seven guineas for a life sketch with future indications, ten guineas for a more detailed treatment and twenty guineas for an exhaustive analysis. They offer to solve problems, assess aptitudes and give us guidance for the future. They claim that actors, businessmen and leading politicians are amongst their clients. Rightly, they do not disclose names but we know that William Gladstone, Lord Kitchener, Oscar Wilde and numerous Hollywood stars had their hands read by the world-famous "Cheiro" (1866–1936), and there is good reason for thinking that their present-day successors may also consult palmists. Surveys of university students on both sides of the Atlantic have shown a surprising proportion who believed that the lines on our hands can foretell our futures—as many as 20 per cent of male adult students about to study psychology at Columbia University in 1950.

It is easy to understand why palmistry is popular. Every hand is different. Creases, fingerprints and overall shape are unique. Our hands are the most familiar parts of our bodies. They are usually uncovered and we notice them dozens of times a day. They are used in most every human activity from worship to bomb-aiming, from love-making to computer-programming. How could they fail to reflect the experience of a lifetime? How could they fail to reveal the underlying character that will influence our future behaviour?

Palmistry has its roots deep in the past. The ancient Chinese, Chaldeans, Greeks and Romans were among the peoples who practised it. Like astrology, it fell into disrepute during the Middle Ages because it seemed to take away free will and smacked of paganism. According to Cheiro (*You and Your Hand*, revised by Louise Owen, Jarrold, U.K., 1969), Job xxxvii:7 was deliberately mistranslated in the Authorized Version of the Bible because it gave credence to palmistry. Cheiro says that the original Hebrew means, "God placed signs and marks in the hands of all the sons of men that all men might know their works." The English translation reads, "He sealeth up the hand of every man; that all men may know his work." Under James 1, palmists were lumped with astrologers, witches and "all who traffic with the Devil" and were made liable to prosecution. Even to-day, their legal position is unclear.

For centuries, the tradition lingered on among gypsies and other travelling fortune-tellers. Popular education gave it a further boost. In the 1870s, it reached a twelve-year-old boy living in Dublin, Ireland, and inspired him to write a book on palmistry. He was Count Louis Hamon, who for the next fifty-two years was known equally well in Europe, the Americas and the Far East as "Cheiro." A man of many parts, Cheiro was a story writer, a film writer and a war correspondent in the Japanese War with China in 1894 and in the Russo-Japanese War of 1904–5. He travelled widely and helped found the Pacific-Geographic Society, as well as becoming a Fellow of the Royal Geographic Society. Though he also studied astrology, palmistry always took first place in his life.

His rise to fame was rapid. He visited India in his early twenties to learn the secrets of Brahmin priests, and on his return set up in London as a palmist. He was lionized by hostesses. Tall and handsome, with thick wavy hair and a ravishing Irish brogue, he was widely in demand for personal consultations. The cream of London society thronged to his rooms or begged him to attend their parties. He was in demand not just for his elegance and charm. He had a devastating knack of summing up character and of making prophecies that were to prove startlingly accurate. "During my first season in London," he wrote (*op. cit.*) "I read Oscar Wilde's hands from behind curtains at a large reception. He was then at the very height of his fame. I told him his Lines of Fate and Success were broken just seven years further on. Instead of taking the warning, he turned and announced gravely to the assembled guests: 'Cheiro may be right. As fate keeps no road-menders on her highways—*Che Sara Sara*—what is to be, will be.'" Wilde's trial and downfall came at the exact time Cheiro predicted.

For Cheiro himself, only success lay ahead. In 1897, he was summoned to Hawarden the house of William Gladstone. He took a palm print and noted signs of "exceptional mentality and brain power . . . the mental ability to dictate to others . . . eloquence and the gift of expression . . . strong individuality . . . success in public life . . . unusual vitality and a robust constitution . . . the promise not only of length of life but excellent health to the end." (Gladstone was then a vigorous eighty-eight and had been prime minister four times!) In 1900, Cheiro found in the hand of Mata Hari, the Dutch dancer, indications of the double life that she was to lead as a German spy during the First World War. An intersection of her Life Line foreshadowed her execution in 1917. He had happier news for King Edward VII, who in 1902 was thought to be dying. He predicted, rightly, that the King would live for another eight years. He compared the palms of the politician Joseph Chamberlain and his son

163

Austen, and was able to say, again rightly, that Austen would also be successful in politics, reaching the high point of his career in 1925. This was the year when Austen was knighted for his work at the International Peace Conference.

Perhaps the most famous of Cheiro's predictions was that of Lord Kitchener's death. The palmist called on the 44-year-old soldier at the War Office on July 21st, 1894, and found not just indications of the dour, practical temperament so familiar to the public but also of an artistic streak. It appeared that Kitchener was also an amateur pianist, a student of literature and a fancier of Chinese porcelain. Even more surprising, Cheiro noticed "a cross at the end of the travel line," a feature which he interpreted as meaning that Kitchener would die after a longish life while on a journey. He narrowed this down to death at sea when Kitchener was sixty-six. It was a daring prediction. After all, a soldier would not normally be expected to die at sea, especially so late in life. Yet it proved exactly right. On June 5th, 1916, the cruiser H.M.S. *Hampshire* struck a mine while taking Kitchener to Russia. His body was never found.

Cheiro himself lived on to the age of seventy, attracting to the very end a distinguished stream of clients who included the Irish tenor Count John MacCormack and the film stars Mary Pickford and Lillian Gish. He died in Hollywood where he ran a school of metaphysics.

No other palmist of recent years has been as successful as Cheiro but hundreds still benefit from the boost he gave to the craft. Some are charlatans, making claims they do not believe in themselves. The majority are sincere. Like Cheiro, they may combine palmistry with astrology, clairvoyance and numerology when making predictions. Some also consult the tarot.

Today, study of the hand falls into three distinct categories. In *cheirognomy,* the shape of the fingers, nails and hands are considered, as well as unconscious habits involving the hands. In *cheiromancy,* the lines of the palm are interpreted. In *dermatoglyphics,* the fingerprints and similar fine lines on the palm are studied. Some palmists also claim that they can diagnose physical and mental illness, and even identify mineral deficiences by markings on the hand. This, however, is a specialized field and we shall examine only the three main categories in broad outline. Details can be found in Cheiro's book (*op. cit.*) or in many others, such as Beryl B. Hutchinson's *Your Life in Your Hands* (Spearman, U.K., 1967; Paperback library, U.S.A., 1968).

Cheirognomy. Palms are usually square (practical, well-balanced), spatulate, *i.e.* splaying out from a narrow wrist (nervous, unconventional, creative), long and thin (studious, philosophic, spiritual), conic, *i.e* a broad base narrowing towards the finger tips (artistic, extrovert but may lack persistence) and psychic, *i.e.* long, slender, willowy (idealistic, "feeling," perhaps over-sensitive). If the types are mixed, the possessor may be versatile but also changeable. Similar deductions are made from the shape of the fingers, nails, moons and knuckles, from the relative lengths of the fingers and from the angles between them. Distortions are reckoned a bad sign. Palmists say that flexible joints mean flexible minds, rigid joints a strait-laced attitude. If a man tucks in his thumbs when he folds his hands, he is said to be immature.

Cheiromancy. In right-handed people, the right palm is usually thought to be more important than the left because it is more affected by experience. In left-handed people, the left is thought more significant. Ideally, lines should be strong and undistorted, though in practice very few are. The main ones are the upper line across the palm (heart line), the lower line across the palm (head line) and the line which curves up from the centre of the wrist to a point between thumb and forefinger (life line). There are various other lines which may or may not be present. They relate to marriage, money, career, family relationship and so on. Interpretation depends on their length, strength and wholeness; the presence or absense of dots, "islands," squares, crosses and other modifications; and especially in the way they are related to each other and the lines on the other hand. Palmists do not always agree on the precise meaning of each variation and rely on experience to help them. They work out the time at which a future event will occur by measuring the point at which a line is marked, crossed or broken.

Dermatoglyphics. All over the world police use fingerprints for identification. The system works because no two have ever been found to be identical. (The Chinese realized that fingerprints were unique some thirteen hundred years ago.) The main types are arches, loops, whorls and composites, to which some palmists add "tented arches." According to Beryl Hutchinson (*op. cit.*) their basic meanings are:

Loops, show a graceful, adaptable outlook on life. Best for team work. Sometimes symbolized as a reed.
Whorls ("fixed") the sign of the individualist. A whorled hand wants to perform or organize any task himself.

Arches ("fixed") are essentially practical people. Reliable.

Composite this pattern is composed of entwined loops and may be summed up as a warning of a dual approach to life.

Tented arches, this pattern looks like a loop that has been frozen upright in the middle of the phalange (finger section). So have the owner's ideas. This is the sign of the enthusiast, the reformer but he is inclined to say "Why don't *they*?" rather than get on with the task himself.

Again, precise interpretation varies with the finger, the hand, and the individual experience of the palmist. So does the interpretation of similar marks on palms.

How reliable is palmistry as a method of prediction? Clearly, it is not a science. Otherwise, anyone could learn it from a text-book. As it is, we know that truly successful palmists are very rare indeed. At the same time, there is more scientific support for some of its claims than many of us perhaps realize. In *The Body* (Allen and Unwin, U.K., 1968; Walker, U.S.A., 1968), Anthony Smith says that by 1965, links had been discovered between abnormal palm prints and some forty diseases.

As palm-prints are indelibly engraved five or six months before birth the disorders are congenital and predominantly decided at the moment of conception; but in 1966 abnormal palm-prints were linked for the first time with a virus infection. The catching of German measles by mothers early on in their pregnancies had been known for a quarter of a century to cause large numbers of congenital malformations; but its infection was suddenly linked with abnormal prints. Three New York paediatricians, having first devised a better system for recording the prints of new, tight-fisted wriggling babies than the policeman's inky pad, found that about half of the babies affected by their mother's infection also had abnormal prints. Normally, and in babies without noticeable malformations, the proportion of strange prints is 14 per cent. A typical palm abnormality is the presence of a simian crease, namely one fold traversing the palm from the area at the base of the forefinger instead of the conventional two. The mere existence of a palm abnormality is certainly not diagnosis of a larger congenital abnormality elsewhere, but it is a striking hint that one is more likely to exist than in a baby whose podgy palm is normal.

There may also be some scientific basis for cheirognomy. As long ago as 1940, Dr. William Sheldon examined the photographs of some

4,000 American college students and found that they could be divided into three basic physical types: endomorphs—heavy and round; mesomorphs—big-boned, well-muscled with broad shoulders and narrow hips; and ectomorphs—tall and skinny. All of us are mixtures of the three types, though we range from *almost* pure specimens to those in whom all three are equally balanced. Dr. Sheldon typed individuals by giving them a score on a scale ranging from 1 to 7 for each of the three basic types. An extreme ectomorph would be 1–1–7, an extreme endomorph 7–1–1 and an extreme mesomorph 1–7–1. A perfectly balanced specimen would be 4–4–4 and so on.

Research by Dr. Tanner of Oxford University into the physiques of athletes at the Rome Olympics showed that competitors for the various events were surprisingly similar in their physical types. Runners tended to be 2–4–4 types, shot-putters 4–6–2. There were no extreme endomorphs or extreme ectomorphs. Physical type not only decides which sports we shall be good at. Other medical research has shown that our temperaments and even illnesses are at least partly decided by our shape.

Clearly, the shape of our hands is largely decided by our body type. It is doubtful whether any palmist says to himself, "This is a 2–4–2 man or a 1–1–1 woman." Even so, the cumulative experience of countless practitioners over many centuries may well have contributed to an empirical knowledge of these tendencies. I say "may" because no one has yet identified the shapes of hand relating to the various body types, let alone compared the known tendencies of those body-types to the traditional interpretations of palmistry. But once again, we may eventually find scientific support for what has so far been regarded by scientists as a mere superstition.

Finally, cheiromancy. Despite the discovery of simian creases and other abnormalities in men and women who suffer from congenital diseases, there is little reason as yet to think that we can analyse character or predict the future by studying minute variations in the various lines that cross our hands. Many of the features studied are given names that have links with astrology: line of sun, girdle of Venus, mount of Jupiter and so on. It is hard for the outsider to accept that they can be linked directly with physical or psychological qualities, still less with future tendencies or the exact prediction of future events. Yet many clients think that such links do exist and back their belief with substantial sums of money, not once but repeatedly. Why?

Leaving aside the palmist's role as confidant, adviser and shoulder to cry on, I suggest that two factors may be at work.

Prediction and Prophecy

First, commonsense and intuition. When a client consults a palmist, there must be some sort of communication between them. Consciously or unconsciously, perhaps both, the practitioner with the least trace of sensitivity is bound to form an impression of the general personality of his client before even glancing at his palm. If the client visits the palmist in person, his dress, speech and bearing shriek out information about his background, way of life and psychological make-up. We saw this when we were discussing the tarot consultant in Chapter 4.

Many palmists ask clients to send in a palm print, together with their date and place of birth and sometimes even a recent photograph. All these bristle with clues. The paper may be clean or dirty, cheap or expensive. A client born before 1939 is likely to have a different set of values, different life expectations and different psychological hang-ups from a client born in the Pop Era. Regional influences also come in. So do differences between a town and country upbringing.

Then again, we may suppose that most clients send a covering letter. Anyone who regularly receives letters from total strangers knows how strong a picture they give of the writer's make-up. One does not have to be a graphologist to pick out the old, the young, the cranks and the sick from the handwriting. The text is even more revealing. The writer may not say a word about himself, but usually, his "tone of voice" comes through strongly: brusque, clinging, businesslike, whining, kindly, detached, ingratiating, even flirtatious. A brief, typed letter can be just as revealing as a long, hand-written one. An electric machine suggests a businessman writing through his secretary or a secretary using the office typewriter for her personal correspondence because she wishes to make a good impression. A portable typewriter used with tinted, private paper suggests that the writer is businesslike but "superior" to the humdrum world of an office. A portable used with white quarto probably means a businessman or woman working at home—and so on. Even the absence of a covering letter is itself revealing.

Suppose the palmist works behind curtains at a fête or reception. This time, he sees only a pair of hands. But again, extraneous clues abound. Apart from the fact that he may also catch a glimpse of dress, shirt or jacket cuffs, which may be clean or dirty, rumpled or ironed, new or frayed, he may well notice a wristlet watch or other jewellery. Is it quiet or flashy? Well maintained or neglected? Cheap or valuable? The superficial appearance of the hands is even more revealing. You do not have to be a psychiatrist to know that chewed nails or broken cuticles are commonly associated with nervous tension. The woman with the beautifully manicured lily-white hand is more likely to be self-regarding than the woman whose hands are rough from housework. A fragment of paint may reveal a home decorator, an embedded thorn a gardening enthusiast, an overlooked speck of grease a motoring enthusiast. Colour and condition of the skin and nails may show the client's age and state of health.

I am not suggesting that palmists necessarily base their interpretations wholly or partly on such things. I do say that having the sensitivity essential to their work, they cannot help but be influenced by them.

Secondly, the palmist's claim that he can foretell a client's future, even when it is affected by events completely outside himself. Most palmists do, in fact, hedge their bets by saying that they deal only in tendencies and probabilities and that even when they foresee disaster, the client can still avoid it by heeding their warning and taking evasive action. Cheiro (*op. cit.*) uses the simile of an engine-driver who has been told of a broken bridge ahead. "If he is a sensible man he will accept the warning—wait for the bridge to be repaired—and so save his life and the lives of others. If, on the contrary, he is too stupid or headstrong to be guided by the knowledge he has gained he will dash on to destruction."

But how does the palmist know about the broken bridge in the first place? Cheiro expresses his belief in a pre-existing fate which broadly determines man's future. The palmist may have access to it by what he calls "the 'subconscious' brain—the mystery by which science explains the inexplicable without being able to solve it." His meaning is by no means clear but if we do accept that some palmists have an insight into the future (and there is no evidence, other than anecdotal, that they do), it seems that we must once again credit them with the power of precognition discussed in Chapter 5. A *prima facie* case for its existence has been established under laboratory conditions and until the evidence is challenged in a more convincing manner than it has so far been, we must accept at least the *possibility* of its existence. Thus far, and no further, can we accept the claims of palmists that they can see into the future.

Graphology

Graphology, or the study of handwriting, claims to be a science. It has always been used informally by business firms when choosing staff ("apply in own handwriting") and many now call in professional graphologists to help decide whether a candidate is likely to prove suitable for a job. It is the only formal method of prediction of which I have had personal experience. An old friend introduced me to a graphologist over a sandwich in a pub and suggested I collaborate with him on a book. (In fact, it was never written.) I must have appeared sceptical, for the graphologist, an elderly Viennese, pushed a notepad towards me and asked me to write a few words. I quickly scribbled "The quick brown fox jumps over the lazy dog" and handed it back. He studied it for a few moments and then delivered a shatteringly accurate analysis of my character which I do not propose to reveal here. I had only met him some twenty minutes before. The friend who introduced me was little more than an acquaintance and did not know me well enough to have briefed the graphologist in advance. At first, I suspected that he was working by intuition alone. He had been watching me carefully and had seen me eating, drinking and giving our order to the barmaid. The manner in which I did these things, not to mention my dress, speech and bearing, must have given him numerous clues. After much thought, however, I decided that these could never have given him so accurate an insight and I had to admit, at least tentatively, that these came mainly from his analysis of my handwriting.

It has always been accepted that our writing is peculiarly our own. A cheque, a property conveyance or a formal deposition is not normally valid unless we sign it personally. We are even required to inscribe our signatures in our passports. We speak of an artist's "handwriting," meaning the details of brushwork which distinguish him from other painters.

It has also been accepted that a man's general character can be deduced from his handwriting. The Roman historian Suetonius (c.75–160) has left us a detailed description of Augustus's script and the eleventh-century Chinese philosopher and painter, Kuo Jo-hsu, said that a man's hand infallibly revealed whether he was noble or plebeian. In the seventeenth century, works on handwriting analysis appeared in Italy and a century later, in Switzerland and Germany. In her *Handwriting Analysis* (Bell, U.S.A., 1967), Dorothy Sara mentions that the artist, Thomas Gainsborough kept on his easel a letter written by the person whose portrait he was painting. She quotes from a letter written by Goethe in 1820 : "There can be no doubt that the handwriting of a person has some relation to his mind and character; that from it one may conceive at least some idea of his manner of being and acting, just as one must recognize not only appearance and features, but also bearing, voice, even bodily movements as being significant and congruent with the total individuality." She also notes a passage in Sir Walter Scott's novel, *Chronicles of Canongate,* written in 1827 : "I could not help thinking . . . that something of a man's character may be conjectured from his handwriting. That neat but crowded and constrained small hand argued a man of good conscience, well-regulated passions, and, to use his own phrase, an upright walk in life; but it also indicated narrowness of spirit, inveterate prejudice, and hinted at some degree of intolerance, which, though not natural to the disposition, had arisen out of a limited education."

Modern graphology goes back to a group of French clergymen who met to study the relationship between character and handwriting in the middle of the nineteenth century. They included Cardinal Regnier, Archbishop of Cambrai, but perhaps the best known is Abbé Flandrin. It was he who taught the man generally looked on as "the father of modern graphology," Abbé Jean Hippolyte Michon (1806–81). Michon invented the word "graphology" and after studying thousands of scripts over thirty years wrote up his findings in two books published in the 1870s. He concentrated on individual letters, finding indications of character in the way they were formed—the shape of hooks and loops, the crossing of t's and the dotting of i's. He interpreted these rigidly and was unwilling to admit exceptions.

Michon's pupil, Jules Crépieu-Jamin, carried on his work but took a wider view than his master. Besides examining the individual letters, he considered the writing as a whole. He looked for psychological patterns and managed to enlist the support of Alfred Binet (1857–1911), deviser of the well-known Binet intelligence test for children.

By the end of the nineteenth century, the lead had passed to a group of German academics: the psychiatrist Dr. Georg Meyer, the professor of physiology Dr. William Preyer and above all the philosopher Dr. Ludwig Klages, who worked out an all-embracing system of interpretation which allowed for wide variations depending on underlying character trends. Other workers have studied the links between handwriting and the psychology of the unconscious, the influence of national "copybook" traditions, the use of handwriting in medical diagnosis, the identification of scripts for legal purposes and graphology as a tool in personnel selection.

Today, graphology is at the crossroads. Few people would claim that it is a science in the sense that chemistry, physics and even psychology are sciences. Even so, doctors, psychiatrists and social workers are said to consult graphologists about the character potential of their patients. I say "potential" because graphologists seek out trends revealed by handwriting. Unless they also use other techniques or faculties, such as astrology or clairvoyance, they do not claim to predict exact future events. They cannot even be sure of a client's age or sex and ask for these to be stated before the analysis. They are especially cautious when dealing with the handwriting of young children, the very old and the sick or disturbed.

In *A Manual of Graphology* (Duckworth, U.K., 1969), the late Eric Singer, a Doctor of Law of Vienna University, deals with the three standard arguments used against graphology.

Argument 1 runs, "There is no real difference between handwritings as they are all formed according to text-book patterns learnt in school." He easily disposes of this by showing how numerous variations creep in, not just in the shapes of individual letters but in their size, spacing, linking and direction across the page.

Argument 2 is more plausible : "Everybody changes his handwriting even during a single day just according to his varying mood and disposition. How can his basic character be revealed by such a changing barometer?" Mr. Singer shows, however, that the changes affect only a small part of the total script. Unless the character of the writer changes, the basic features of his writing do not. These basic features include size, layout, spacing, shading, direction of lines, degree and form of connection, regularity, rhythm, speed and angle of writing, and the form of letters.

Argument 3 attacks from a completely different angle. "Handwriting is produced by the movement of the hand only," it says. "Therefore, differences in handwriting can only reveal skill, routine or deficiencies of the hand, but can tell nothing of the writer's character." Why then, adds Mr. Singer, does handwriting change completely when the subject is hypnotized and told he has taken on the character of a king or a child? Why do the basic features remain the same even when a person writes with a stick held in his mouth? In Germany, a farmer was accused of libelling his neighbour by sowing seeds which grew into plants forming a pattern of rude words. The court held the case proved—because the "handwriting" was identical with that of the farmer. Apart from unconscious slips, omissions and emphases in the text, says Mr. Singer, the manner and layout of the script shows how the writer tackles a job of work. It may indicate intelligence, perseverance, skill, education, vitality, discipline —or the reverse of these qualities. It may reveal inner conflicts or a well-integrated personality.

Max Pulver, the Swiss graphologist, stressed the symbolic aspect of handwriting. Expounding Pulver's view, Singer writes (*op. cit.*) :

Every problem of form and space becomes symbolic in the individual's mind of his own position in the different spheres of space and time, that is to say, his spiritual, social and material world. And so the point along a line of writing at which the moving pen of a writer arrives becomes a symbol of his own position in the world around him; to the left of this point lies the past, origin, mother and childhood, to the right lies the work to be done, the future, the writer's fellow men and the social world. Movement upwards above the extension of the short letters (*m, n, u,* etc.) symbolizes gravitation towards spiritual and intellectual spheres; movement below symbolizes a dive into the material, sub-human and subconscious world. Thus the manuscript becomes a symbol of the writer's attitude to the past and the future, to himself and to others, to the spiritual, social and material world, to airy dreams and to subconscious impulses.

These are large claims. How are they substantiated in practice? Clearly, we cannot examine the detailed interpretation of every characteristic and in any case, graphologists claim that their science calls for experience and intuition, as does medicine and psychiatry. But it is worth taking a look at some of the more general features.

The slope, they say is significant. If to the left, the writer is backward looking and introverted; if to the right, forward looking and extroverted. An upright script suggests independence. Large handwriting goes with an expansive attitude to life, which could, of course, be linked with a wide range of characteristics from generosity to megalomania. Small handwriting, too, may be interpreted positively or negatively. It can be a sign of modesty and realism or of meanness and inferiority. If the letters at the end of a word are smaller than those at the beginning, the writer is mature; if larger, infantile or blunt. Regularity in a copy-book style suggests lack of imagination but in an individual style, it could mean balance, even stubbornness.

Layout is also significant. Evenness, clarity and regularity usually indicate intelligence but lines that crash into each other may be a sign of absentmindedness that could go with genius. Lines that climb across the page often mean that the writer is ambitious. This is especially true of a climbing signature. Falling lines are a sign of depression or lack of energy. The person who continues his letter on every available margin is probably garrulous but if he tries to cram in more and more words as he gets to the bottom of a page, he may be a ditherer who even has difficulty in deciding when to turn over. Pressure, speed, spacing, width of margin and connections between letters and parts of letters are all considered.

This summary grossly over-simplifies the graphologist's technique. A skilled practitioner goes into the finest details and interprets these not literally, as if they were a code, but in relation to each other and to the script as a whole. All I have tried to do is indicate the sort of things he looks for.

To sum up. Almost any of us can make broad generalizations about a writer's personality and background from his handwriting but to achieve the degree of precision attempted by the expert graphologist clearly needs training and a special kind of talent. Whether we yet know enough (or indeed *can* know enough) about the relationship between personality and handwriting to make an accurate prediction of a person's potentialities has not yet been proved. Many people think that such predictions are possible and judging from my own, admittedly limited, personal experience, I am inclined to agree with them.

Colour Tests

Many attempts have been made to predict character by various forms of colour test. In some, the subject is asked to say which colours he most likes and most dislikes. In others, he is asked to list a number of colours in order of preference. The devisers of the tests claim that the results have proved useful in personnel selection, marriage guidance, vocational guidance and even as an early warning system in medical diagnosis. Is this really possible?

Our experience of colour is highly subjective. An object that appears red to a normally sighted person looks yellow to someone with a particular kind of colour-defective vision. Someone who is colour-blind would see no colour in it at all. Nor can we be sure that even normally sighed people experience similar sensations when they look at a "red," "blue" or "yellow" object. What you see as yellow, I may see as blue, even though we both agree to call it "red."

In practice, we assume that colours are the same for everybody with normal vision. We share, too, numerous emotional experiences linked with colour. Red suggests blood and fire, and hence warm, positive, even aggressive attitudes. We "see red" when angry and know it's "red for danger" at the traffic lights. Before computers, our bank manager used to warn us of a debit by putting our account literally "in the red". Symbolically, red has always been the colour of martyrdom, fortitude, magnanimity.

Blue is the colour of clear skies and of such "heavenly" qualities as hope, spirituality, serenity. We seek the "blue bird of happiness" somewhere "beyond the blue horizon." Green, which we associate with spring and new life, expresses joy and even immortality in art. It can suggest immaturity, as in "greenhorn" and "green bacon" but it can also imply sympathy with nature, as in "green fingers." "Green Man," a common name for a public-house in England, probably harks back to an early wood spirit. Yellow is ambiguous. Associated with gold and sunlight, it suggests faith, glory and insight, but it is also the colour of bile, which reminds us of sickness. So we have the yellow flag of quarantine, the yellow (or green-yellow) of envy and "yellow-belly" cowards.

Colour associations affect us profoundly. At a North of England mill complaints of stuffiness ceased abruptly when the warm, brown walls were repainted in cool greens and greys. An airline traced its above-average airsickness rate to the yellow decor of the cabin. A change to grey-blue cut the proportion of air-sick passengers by a half. It has also been shown that we can be deeply disturbed by unexpected colours. In America, dinner guests sat down at a table under trick lighting. The steaks looked grey, the salads blue, the milk blood red and the coffee yellow. Most of the guests could not eat. Those who did became ill.

Marketing men are well aware of our colour preferences and tint their products accordingly. Orange juice, which is naturally an insipid yellow, sells better when artificial colouring matter turns it a brilliant orange. Tinned rhubarb, naturally a muddy brown, pleases most when coloured pink. In supermarkets, fresh foods are often kept away from the white, fluorescent lighting in the centre, which makes them look dark. Instead, they are displayed around the walls under separate tinted lighting—pink to give meat a healthy glow, yellow to flatter fruit and vegetables. Popular colour preferences also influence packaging. Greens and blues, known to be associated with hygiene, help sell shampoos. Yellows, greens and blues, suggesting sunshine, butter, fields and blue skies, are "right" for dairy products.

These preferences are general. But sometimes, age, income and even personality affect colour choice. A major U.K. paint manufacturer found that over-55s bought almost twice as much cream and beige paint as under-35s in the year 1970. The under-35s bought almost three times as much orange or tangerine. The lowest income group (DE) plumped for both red and green almost three times as

175

often as the highest (AB). In white, the positions were reversed. A British car manufacturer found that buyers of G.T. models preferred strong, bright colours. Greys and "metallics" appealed to the more affluent.

Clearly, there is a link between colour choice and one's position in life. Is it possible to go a stage further and by assessing character on the basis of colour preferences predict likely behaviour in the future?

On an everyday level, most of us form different expectations of people who tend to wear brightly coloured clothes from those we form of people who stick to greys, blacks and browns. Some years ago, Dr. Faber Birren, the American colour consultant, worked out a personality test based on both the colour we most like and that we most dislike. For the many people who like two colours equally well, the test is said to be equally valid. If a woman is attracted to one colour but tends to buy clothes of another, it means that she is overlaying her true personality with a façade. Here, very broadly, are some of Dr. Birren's findings for those who like or dislike the various colours.

RED

Like. Extrovert, eager, generous, impulsive, optimistic, partisan, a gambler. Attracts friends. Doesn't suffer fools gladly.
Dislike. A tendency to turn away from life, perhaps through a disappointment in love, career or social ambitions.

YELLOW

Like. A dreamer, impractical, seemingly cool to friends, but loyal. Interested in ideas rather than people. Possibly attracted to Eastern religions.
Dislike. Practical, realistic, distrustful of high-flown theories and ideals.

BROWN

Like. Shrewd, sensible, dependable, rather stubborn. Understands the value of money. May become self-centred.
Dislike. Extrovert, impulsive, volatile, distrustful of over-careful people.

ORANGE

Like. Equable, care-free, mostly in high spirits, popular. Likes people.
Dislike. Distrustful of fun, gaiety, friendship. Seeks deeper values.

BLUE

Like. Reliable, controlled, confident, cautious, perhaps intolerant of the stupid and over-clever.
Dislike. A rebel, perhaps from self-disappointment or a feeling that success is a result of luck or superior birth.

PINK

Like. Sheltered, cosseted. Likes others, provided they do not bring disturbing thoughts.
Dislike. Tough, intolerant of those who apparently attain an easy life without effort.

GREEN

Like. Tolerant, relaxed, well-adjusted, mature, appreciates the good things of life. The backbone of society.
Dislike. Immature, lacking self-confidence, probably unsociable. Emotionally withdrawn.

LAVENDER

Like. Refined, fastidious, aloof, witty, self-professed lover of the arts. Can be superficial.
Dislike. Down-to-earth. Dislikes pretence. Perhaps has unrealized cultural ambitions.

BLACK

Likes. Sophisticated, up-to-date, in touch. A pace-maker. Mysterious and therefore attractive to the opposite sex. Possibly insecure.
Dislike. Possibly a fear of death. Alternatively, immature or resentful of others "showing off."

Prediction and Prophecy

BLUE-GREEN

Like. Discriminating, cultivated, sensitive. Well-organized but can be self-centred.
Dislike. Shows a tendency to withdraw from life.

PURPLE

Like. Artistic, moody, profoundly aware of our special qualities. Tolerant but may be affected.
Dislike. Discriminating, far-sighted, suspicious of affectation. Prefers life to be simple, friendships straghtforward.

WHITE

Like. Uncomplicated, unpretentious but possibly immature or naive.
Dislike. If white suggests lilies, a fear of death. Alternatively, a dislike of simple solutions to complicated problems.

Dr. Birren's system sketches out broad personality types. We can check its accuracy by trying it on ourselves and our friends. The Lüscher colour test, devised by Dr. Max Lüscher, professor of psychology at Basle University, is more ambitious. As he explains in *The Lüscher Colour Test* (translated and edited by Ian Scott, Cape, U.K., 1970; Random House, U.S.A., 1969), a full test, in which the subject makes 43 separate choices from 73 patches of 25 different colours and shades, can be interpreted only by someone with both training and insight. It "affords a wealth of information concerning the conscious and unconscious psychological structure of the individual, areas of psychic stress, the state of glandular balance or imbalance, and much physiological information of great value either to the physician or to the psychotherapist."

The shortened form of the test, based on only eight colours, also shows up personality traits, as well as areas of physiological and psychological stress. "Physicians in Europe use this short version of the test as a useful aid to diagnosis, since it has been found that such stresses show up in the Lüscher Test often long before their physiological results make themselves evident; in this, the test provides them with an incomparable 'early warning system' of stress ailments in their early stages—ailments such as cardiac malfunction, cerebral attack or disorders of the gastro-intestinal tract." He also claims that the test has been successfully used in education, marriage guidance, personnel selection and even by a correspondence school to guide prospective students in their choice of courses.

Lüscher starts from the assumption that different colours have different effects on us. Experiments have shown that heart-rate, blood pressure and speed of breathing all increase if we concentrate on red. (This is widely agreed.) So red can be said to be exciting or stimulating. It represents "force of will" and is "ex-centric, active, offensive-aggressve, autonomous, locomotor, competitive, operative." It indicates desire, excitability, domination, sexuality.

Dark blue produces an opposite effect, with heart rate, blood pressure and speed of breathing all falling. Dark blue is therefore a calming colour. It represents "Death of feeling" and is concentric, passive, sensitive and perceptive (I use only a selection of Lüscher's adjectives), indicating tranquillity, contentment and tenderness. Lüscher gives appropriate descriptions and indications of his other two primary colours—blue-green ("elasticity of will") and bright yellow ("spontaneity"). He also has four auxiliary colours—violet ("a mixture of red and blue"), brown ("a mixture of yellow-red and black"), neutral grey ("psychologically and physiologically neutral") and black ("a denial of colour altogether").

In the shortened test, the candidate is asked to arrange in order of preference eight cards, each showing one of the eight colours. He must choose spontaneously, avoiding associations with dress fabrics, curtains, cars, furnishings and so on. His choices are then arranged in pairs, starting with the first two.

The idea behind the test is that our attitude to individual colours and therefore to the qualities they represent is shown by the position in which we place them. Our first choice, says Lüscher, shows our "essential method" or "modus operandi," the second what we are aiming at. Those in the third and fourth positions show the subject " 'the actual state of affairs', the situation in which he actually feels himself to be or the manner in which his existing circumstances require him to act." The next pair indicate qualities or functions that we are not currently using but are keeping in reserve. The last pair relate to inhibitions and repressions.

Lüscher gives interpretations for all these combinations. Red and blue as the first pair show that the subject "strives for a life rich in activity and experience, and for a close bond offering sexual and emotional fulfilment." Grey and green as the second pair shows that he "feels he is receiving less than his share, but that he will have to conform and make the best of his situation." And so on.

But there is more to the test than that. Lüscher claims that his four primary colours represent basic emotional needs—"the need for contentment and affection, the need to assert oneself, the need to act and succeed and the need to look forward and aspire." In a well-adjusted individual, all these should show up in the first four or five places. If one (or more) occurs in the last three places, it (or they) have been rejected. This rejection could lead to stress and anxiety, and ultimately to psychosomatic illness. It almost certainly means that some other function will come to the fore as "compensation." In the test, this is indicated by the colour of first choice. If grey, black or brown appear in any of the first three places, the "compensation" will be exaggerated. It may take the form of an obsession, over-conscientiousness, argumentativeness or excessive busy-ness.

Lüscher claims that his test will also throw light on the "actual problem," ambivalence, the suppressed characteristic, "emotional" personalities, conflicts between our objectives and our behaviour, instabilities of the autonomic nervous system and our capacity for work. Some of the more subtle interpretations are only possible if the shortened test is taken a second time a few minutes after the first and the results of both tests compared. But how valid is the test?

Many psychologists refuse to believe that colour tests are a reliable way of assessing personality or predicting future behaviour. They agree that, generally speaking, a person who chooses red as his favourite colour will probably be a different type from someone who chooses brown. But they do not believe that enough experiments have yet been done to pinpoint the basic indications, let alone justify the subtleties introduced by Lüscher.

Some think that his claim " 'colour blindness' makes no difference" invalidates the whole test. "If a subject cannot even distinguish the different colours," they argue, "how can he put them in a meaningful order?" Lüscher contends, "If an organism is psychically or physically in need of emotional peace, physical regeneration and release from tension or stress, then the instinctive response will be to choose the darker colours. If the organism needs to dissipate energy by outgoing activity or in mental creativeness, then the instinctive response will be for the brighter colours." He quotes a German paper by L. Steinke, published in *Confinia Psychiatrica,* vol. 3, no. 2 (1960). This describes experiments comparing the results of normal people with those suffering from either total or partial red-green colour blindness. Steinke concluded, "colour vision need not be considered in the Lüscher Test at all."

Another objection is that our choice may be influenced by neigh-bouring colours when the cards are first shuffled and laid out. If violet happens to fall between grey and black, for instance, it looks much more attractive than it does between brown and almost any other colour. Red between violet and brown loses much of its glow. Blue and green both look better apart, than they do when next to each other, and so on. If two choices are made instead of one, this objection is partly, not wholly overcome.

Again, one finds that one tends to make different choices on different days. This may well reflect passing changes of mood but it does not instil confidence in the claim that the Lüscher Test is "a 'deep' psychological test." On the other hand, it must be admitted the first and last choice usually remain the same, as does the fact that the four primary colours occur in the first four places, even though in varying orders. To this extent, the result is stable.

To sum up. The Lüscher Test clearly deserves serious consideration. At the moment, too little work has been reported for us to form a balanced judgment. Most of the papers quoted by Lüscher are in German and are published in either Germany or Switzerland. Only one paper is quoted from America and only two from England, both by the translator of Lüscher's book. Personally, I have found the Test surprisingly accurate. But this is a sample of one. The verdict to date must be "not proven."

11   The Anxious Society

Why is enthusiasm for so many forms of divination strong and growing? In earlier civilizations, such practices were an integral part of the general culture. They still are in many primitive societies of our own times. In the words of Konrad Lorenz (see Chapter 3), they have a "species-preserving function."

Advanced societies of the twentieth century have put their faith in technology. They do not need the support of beliefs that are derided by most scientists and frowned on by official religion. If all our astrologers, palmists and clairvoyants shut up shop tomorrow, there would be no revolution. State, industry, business, trades unions and the church would continue exactly as before. Interest in prediction is almost wholly private. Why then is the individual so keen to know about the future?

One reason is curiosity. We hate to live in ignorance. When new neighbours move in next door, we want to know what kind of people they are, how many children they have, what the husband does for a living. According to our individual interests, we are curious about almost everything that happens, not just in our own street, town or even country, but in the world beyond and now, too in outer space. We read newspapers by the million and listen to radio and television news bulletins dozens of times a day. We are curious by nature. It is inevitable that we should wish to find out about one of the few unexplored areas left—the future.

Man, too, is a pattern-making animal. Numerous experiments have shown that we cannot bear to see things, people and events in isolation. We need to relate them to each other. The scientist delights in a new theory that explains observations which were not previously understood. All of us take pleasure in a well-plotted story, an elegantly-designed building, a skilful manoeuvre on the sports field. We do so because we see the pattern behind them. It is the same with life as a whole. Most of us can make some sort of pattern out of what we have done so far. But we are like a man sitting in a cinema in the middle of a film. We want to know what happens next. We want to see how the pattern will continue to develop.

There is a still more compelling reason for our interest in the future. We live in an anxious society. We worry about jobs, money and health; pollution, over-population and the Bomb. Sports fans worry about their teams, investors about their shares, housewives about the cost of living. If we have nothing to worry about, we invent something. We gamble. We play tense games. For many of us, a game of Monopoly is as nerve-racking as a gun-battle fought with live ammunition. We do not know why man should have this almost universal anxiety. Apart from individual psychological problems it may be because we have lost faith in traditional values without finding new ones.

Anxiety implies uncertainty. We worry about calamity only in advance. Once it happens, we stop worrying about the calamity itself and worry instead about the possible consequences. When these are determined, we look round for something else to worry about. The one thing that all of us can worry about continuously is the future. None of us knows what will happen to us tomorrow or the day after. We could live happily for years or be crippled a second from now by some totally unforeseeable accident. The only certainty is death, and even that is uncertain in the time and manner of its coming.

To resolve our anxiety, we need to know the future. Will my husband still love me twenty years from now? Shall I keep my job after the takeover? Is that speck of blood I coughed up the result of an inflamed throat or the first sign of lung cancer? We want to know the answers. Or do we? Suppose the answer we get is the wrong one. Suppose my husband will not love me twenty years hence. Suppose I am already earmarked for dismissal. Suppose I really do have lung cancer. Do I still want to know? The answer, usually, is "No." We would prefer to remain in ignorance for as long as possible. Any doctor will tell you that many a patient who clearly knows that he is dying does not want to be told so. Mostly, he does not even ask, for fear of getting the wrong answer.

That is why we can turn so confidently to astrology, palmistry and other techniques of prediction. We can rely on the professionals not to give us bad news. Prophets of doom rarely stay in business long. Successful practitioners avoid pessimism. If some omens are bad, and others good, they concentrate on the good. If the whole tendency is bad, they tell us that it is only a tendency and that, forewarned, we can influence it in our favour. They are *reassuring*.

They offer double indemnity. Even assuming that it is sometimes possible to foretell the future, we know that no technique yet discovered is wholly reliable. Sometimes it works, sometimes it does not. So we can apply two separate standards. If a prophecy is favourable, we can believe it. If it is unfavourable, we can laugh and say, "Who believes in prediction, anyway?" The attitude of clients to diviners is "Heads I win, tails you lose." Even if the prophet does predict disaster, the client can fall back on his second line of defence, which is impregnable. Astrology, palmistry and other techniques of prediction, as we now know them, are custom-made for the relief of anxiety. The anxious—and that includes most of us—find them irresistible.

But what of the truth of prophecy and prediction? Apart from their anxiety-relieving function, do they work?.

We have traced the history of prophecy and prediction over some eight thousand years. We have assessed dozens of techniques for which success has been claimed and have found everything from the crudest frauds to the most conscientious scientific experiments. Millions have been duped, and still are being duped, by rogues, by self-deceiving cranks and by honest, sensible men who do not know as much as they think they know. Yet some well-documented glimpses into the future cannot be explained away as tricks or delusions. Nor can they be fitted into the generally accepted scheme of things.

Three points must be made.

The first is that many, perhaps most, men have believed that it is possible to see into the future by some means that we do not yet understand. They have never thought that this can always be done everywhere by everybody, but they have sensed that it can probably be done more often and by more people than many of us in the twentieth century care to admit. Many, perhaps most, of the best minds of the past believed this. Are we not a little naive in thinking that just because we have lived *after* them, we necessarily know better than they about everything? Could we not be, as they sometimes were, the victims of ignorance, prejudice and intellectual fashion?

The second point is linked closely with the first. No-one has ever denied that it is possible to foretell the future by methods acceptable to modern science. These must be verifiable, repeatable and consistent with existing knowledge. In the last two hundred years, this approach has helped bring about technological progress faster and further than our ancestors could conceive of. It has enriched billions of lives. (It has also given man the means of his own destruction. But that is another story.) Because of its undoubted success, far too many of us have jumped to the conclusion that the scientific approach is the only one worth following. Yet why should this be so? Just because one approach works in some circumstances, it does not follow that other approaches are not valid when the circumstances are different.

The third point is that literal-minded scientists (and this does not include all scientists by any means), together with many non-scientists, have closed minds. They are so prejudiced against any other approach that they do not even bother to study the evidence. They write it off as nonsense without even looking at it. Yet as we have seen, there is a vast body of experience that merits further investigation. Some of our best scientists now realize this. So do many young people. They are seeking other paths by way of religion, mysticism, meditation and drugs.

There is always the chance that the experiences we have described are delusions. There is also the possibility that further scientific progress may enable us to fit them into the orthodox scheme of cause and effect. If so, well and good. But at the moment, there is a strong *prima facie* case for thinking that at least some of us can sometimes see into the future, by means of an unexplained sense. It seems to show itself spontaneously in dreams and at times of deep emotion. It can sometimes be stimulated by such devices as the *I Ching,* the Tarot, a glass crystal or a study of the heavens. On the whole, it has not yet been satisfactorily pinned down under laboratory conditions. It may be an atrophied form of some faculty that was stronger in an earlier stage of our evolution. It may be a new faculty, which we are only now developing.

We clearly need more scientific research. But that in itself is not enough. An open mind is the key. What we have seen so far suggests that this faculty, if it exists, does not fit neatly into any accepted categories. We need to get rid of all pre-judgements not only about its nature but also about the best way of investigating it.

Most important, we must rise above our simplistic view of passing time. It is useful in everyday life but it does not explain so many other things which we know to be true.

An old man lies dying. Few of us believe that he is only a machine that is running down, will shortly stop and then decompose. We know that he has had thoughts, ideas, desires, feelings and aspirations. He has been a baby, a schoolboy, a soldier, a workman, a husband, a father, a grandfather and much else. He will still have been these even when he is completely forgotten by everyone living on earth. Conversely, the baby sucking at the breast is also, and always will be, the dying old man, and whatever lies in between, before and beyond.

I am not suggesting that there is a conventional life after death or before birth, but that ultimately, time is all one. This has been a commonplace of idealist philosophy and mystical religion for thousands of years. Johann Scheffler, the nineteenth-century German mystic who was also known as the "Silesian Angel", crystallized it in a couplet which Henry Bett translated as:

> The rose that with your earthly eyes you see
> Has flowered in God from all eternity.

Scientists have already spoken of time as a fourth dimension. If we can look back along it, is there any reason why we should not be able to look forward along it too? It seems at least possible that the history of prophecy and prediction to date is not the end of a chapter. It may well be the first, stumbling sentence of a new volume.

Books for Further Reading

Practical Dowsing, ed. A. H. Bell, Bell, U.K., 1965; Irwin Clarke, U.S.A.

Chance, Skill and Luck, John Cohen, Penguin, U.K. & U.S.A., 1960.

The Pursuit of the Millennium, Norman Cohn, Temple Smith, U.K., 1970; Oxford, U.S.A., 1970.

The Story of Fulfilled Prophecy, Justine Glass, Cassell, U.K., 1969.

The Origin of the Zodiac, Rupert Gleadow, Cape, U.K., 1968.

A Complete Guide to the Tarot, Eden Gray, Studio Vista, U.K., 1970; Crown, U.S.A., 1970.

You and Your Hand, Count Louis Hamon ("Cheiro"), Revised by Louise Owen, Jarrold, U.K., 1969.

E.S.P.—A Scientific Evaluation, C. E. M. Hansel, MacGibbon and Kee, U.K., 1966; Scribner, U.S.A., 1966.

Your Life in Your Hands, Beryl B. Hutchinson, Spearman, U.K., 1967.

I Ching, translated from Richard Wilhelm's German version by Cary F. Baynes, Routledge, U.K., 1951; Pantheon Books, U.S.A., 1950.

The Psychology of Superstition, Gustav Jahoda, Penguin, U.K. and U.S.A., 1969.

The Lüscher Colour Test, Translated and edited by Ian Scott from Dr. Max Lüscher's German, Cape, U.K., 1970; Random House, U.S.A., 1969.

Dreams and Dreaming, Norman Mackenzie, Aldus, London, 1965; Vanguard, 1965.

The Astrologers and their Creed, Christopher McIntosh, Hutchinson, U.K., 1969, Praeger, U.S.A.

Living Time, Maurice Nicoll, Stuart, U.K., 1952; Hermitage, U.S.A., 1953.

Astrology in the Modern World, Derek Parker, Taplinger, U.S.A., 1970.

Adventure Unlimited, Evelyn Penrose, Spearman, U.K., 1958.

Man and Time, J. B. Priestley, Aldus, U.K., 1964; Doubleday, U.S.A., 1964.

The Reach of the Mind, J. B. Rhine, Faber, U.K., 1948; Sloane, U.S.A., 1947.

Handwriting Analysis for the Millions, Dorothy Sara, Bell, U.S.A., 1967.

A Manual of Graphology, Eric Singer, Duckworth, U.K., 1969.

Modern Experiments in Telepathy, S. G. Soal and F. Bateman, Faber, U.K., 1954; Yale U.P., U.S.A., 1954.

Occult Phenomena, Alois Wiesinger, O.C.S.O., Burns and Oates, U.K., 1957; Newman Press, U.S.A., 1959

Index

Index

Prediction and Prophecy